ULTIMATE

X-MEN™

UPDATED EDITION

PETER SANDERSON

MARVEL

DK

A DORLING KINDERSLEY BOOK

CONTENTS

FOREWORD

WHY 'THE X-MEN'? LET ME TRY TO EXPLAIN....

It was the year 1963. Marvel Comics had already bestowed 'The Fantastic Four', 'The Incredible Hulk', and 'Spider-Man' upon an unsuspecting though grateful world. But the comic-book-reading public's appetite proved to be insatiable. They demanded more, still more Super Heroes – and we were determined to rise to the challenge.

Staring at my typewriter (alas, the personal computer had not yet been invented), I endeavoured to create a team of Super Heroes with unique powers. But even before dreaming up those powers, I knew I'd have to explain where they came from.

You may recall that the Fantastic Four had been inundated by cosmic rays, the Hulk had been the victim of a massive gamma-ray explosion, and Spider-Man had been bitten by a radioactive spider. That accounted for cosmic rays, gamma rays, and radioactive spider bites. But I knew I couldn't keep hitting the public with a constant barrage of rays and radiation.

Suddenly, an idea hit me; an idea that was simplicity itself and which guaranteed I'd never have to worry about explaining the origin of a superpower again!

It hit me when I thought of the word 'mutant'. We all know that mutations occur in nature. For no apparent reason a frog will be born with three legs, or a banana will be the size of a watermelon, or a child prodigy will have the ability to play Mozart at the age of three. And the beautiful thing about such mutations is, they don't require any explanation. They can happen to anyone. Once I decided that our little cast of characters would have mutant powers, the rest was simplicity itself. I merely had to decide who our team would be and who would lead it.

For their leader, I thought it would be interesting to have a man who was seemingly the weakest of all, a man in a wheelchair. But, that man, Professor Charles Xavier, would have incredible mental powers and would be able to mould the others into a formidable fighting team. For sheer strength, I created the Beast, but once again, to go against the usual cliché, I made him the most literate and eloquent of all the team. Then, having always liked the Fantastic Four's Human Torch, I thought it would be fun for our new group to include his exact opposite, Iceman. Add the winged, flying Angel, the telekinetically powered Marvel Girl, and the somewhat tragic Cyclops, who always had to wear special eyeglasses to shield his deadly eye beams, and you had the original X-Men – a far cry from the countless new and fantastic members that have been constantly added to the world's most colourful cast of characters ever since those early days.

Another character I was always extremely fond of was the villain Magneto. I felt that his mastery of magnetism was one of the most interesting powers of all. And I'll admit to having a soft spot in my heart for the Blob, Juggernaut, and the Toad as well.

Today, of course, there are so many X-Men heroes and villains that hardly anyone can name them all without referring to a reference book. Over the years, Wolverine has definitely become the star of the series although everyone has his or her own particular favourites.

Now, before I turn you loose, you may have wondered how the title 'X-Man' was chosen. Here's the inside scoop…

I originally wanted to call the book 'The Mutants' but my publisher rejected the title because he doubted that most comic-book readers would know what the word 'mutant' meant. After thinking about it for a while, it occurred to me that all our characters had an extra power and their leader's name was Professor Xavier – so I suggested the name 'X-Men'. My publisher okayed it, but I laughed to myself as I left his office, thinking 'If people wouldn't know what a "mutant" is, how on earth would they know what an "X-Man" is?' However, happy that we had a title at last, I never posed that little question to him.

And now, having paid your literary dues, it's time for you to enjoy the wonderment on the pages ahead. But it isn't goodbye because I'll be with you in spirit.

Excelsior!

Stan Lee

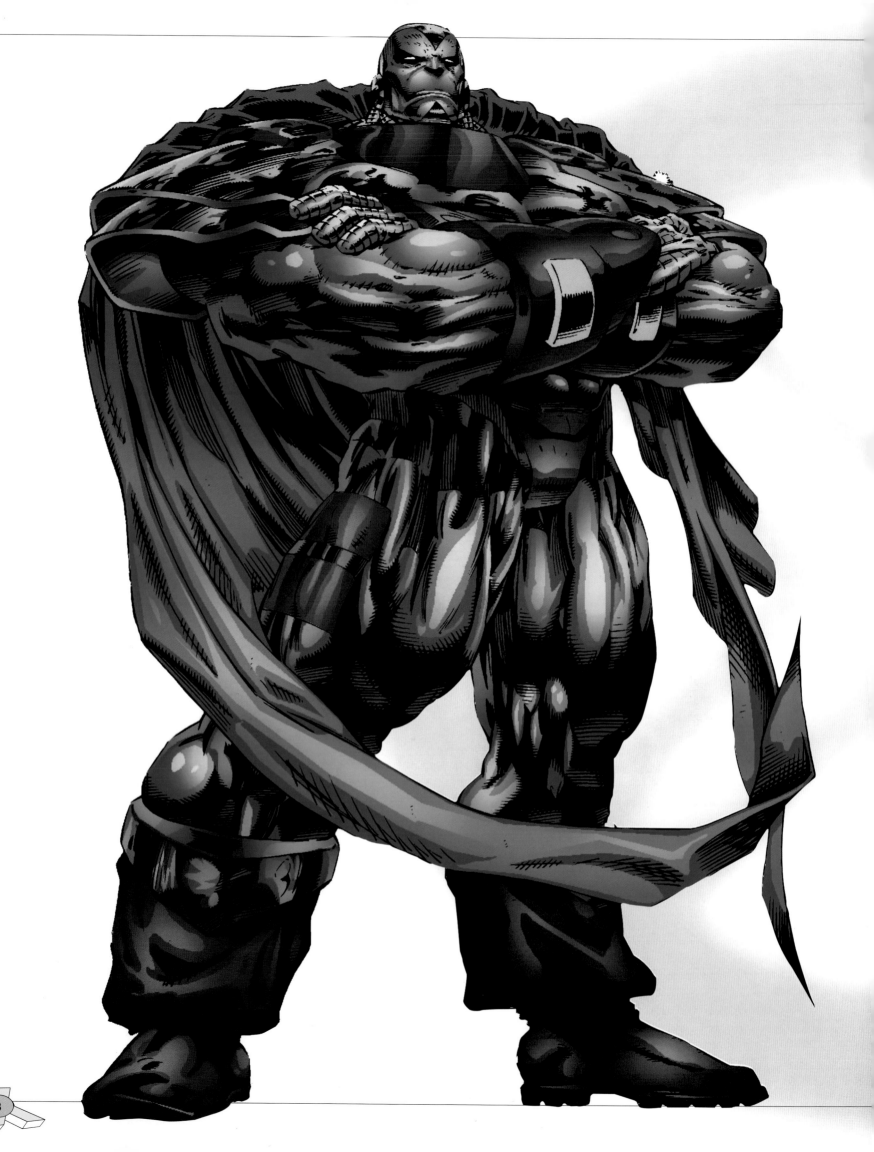

INTRODUCTION

THE LAST HUNDRED YEARS have brought extraordinary social and technological changes. In the world of the X-Men, they have also brought the evolution of the human race to a crossroads. Throughout the world, individuals were born who developed unusual, superhuman abilities as they grew into adolescence. They were mutants: people born genetically different from the rest of humankind. Some people saw the rise of these superhuman mutants as the next step in human evolution. Many, however, regarded mutants as dangerous freaks, threatening the existence of the 'normal' human race.

The growing numbers of mutants needed a champion, and they found one in a visionary named Charles Xavier. A mutant himself, Xavier had a dream of a future in which 'normal' humans and mutants would live together in peace and harmony. It was to make his dream a reality that Xavier created his organization of young mutants, the X-Men.

He turned his home, a mansion close to New York City, into a school for young mutants. Xavier realized that these adolescents might be as frightened of their new powers as the humans around them were; he showed them how to master their mutant abilities and to take pride in them. Xavier's mansion was also a haven for his young students. In the outside world these young mutants would be outcasts; within Xavier's mansion they found others like themselves. Xavier's school became the centre of a growing community of mutants, an alternative to the hostile society that lay outside its doors.

Xavier had another motive in founding the X-Men. He knew that there were other mutants who were indeed the threats that humanity imagined all mutants to be. Among them was another mutant with a vision opposed to his, Magneto. A victim of the Holocaust in his childhood, Magneto knew the horrors humanity was capable of perpetrating on those who differed in some way from the majority. Magneto vowed that he would use any means he considered necessary to prevent the evolving race of mutants from suffering a similar fate. Ironically, the Nazis' victim had developed his own master race philosophy: he contended that mutants, with their superhuman powers, deserved to supplant bigoted humanity as rulers of the planet. Xavier saw it as his responsibility to stop Magneto and other mutants who sought to exploit, conquer, or even destroy humanity. Utilizing their mutant powers, Xavier and his X-Men would fight to defend the very humans who regarded them with fear and distrust.

Xavier began with only five mutant pupils, but far more have joined his cause since then. Not only have the ranks of the X-Men swelled, but other mutant groups have formed: the New Mutants, X-Factor, Excalibur, X-Force, and Generation X. Yet as the years have passed, Xavier's efforts to bring about what he has called 'a golden age' for mutants and humans have grown more difficult. Human fear and hatred of mutants has manifested itself in increasingly violent actions organized by mobs, politicians, and paramilitary forces. Yet Xavier and the X-Men struggle onward, searching for tolerance amid an increasingly contentious world.

THE X-MEN IN THE 1960s

X-MEN is currently the best-selling American comic, but this was not always the case. In its first decade, far from being a fan favourite, the series was a commercial failure.

Making its debut in 1963, *X-Men* was the creation of writer/editor Stan Lee and penciller/co-plotter Jack Kirby, the two men most responsible for building the Marvel universe. Together, Lee and Kirby had already created the Fantastic Four, the Hulk, Thor, and Iron Man, among many others. Within the initial 17 bi-monthly issues of this new comic book series, Lee and Kirby not only created the original X-Men, Magneto, Juggernaut, and the Sentinels, but firmly established the theme of humanity's persecution of the mutants. For the last five of those issues Werner Roth (under his alias Jay Gavin) had been doing the finished pencil artwork over Kirby's layouts, and Roth took over fully with issue 18. Two issues later, new talent Roy Thomas started writing *X-Men*, the first major Super Hero assignment

X-Men #12 (July 1965)
First appearance of Juggernaut
(Cover art by Jack Kirby)

in what has become a long and impressive career. Though still underrated, the Thomas-Roth team won the admiration of many for their appealing and sensitive characterizations of the original X-Men.

Nevertheless, compared to the creative fireworks in other Marvel series of the time, *X-Men* seemed only a secondary title. Marvel began a series of experiments to attract new readers, giving the X-Men colourful, individualized costumes in issue 39, and, most shockingly, killing off Professor X in issue 42. Shortly thereafter, the team broke up, and the book instead featured stories about different pairings of X-Men. This did not work, and the team quickly regrouped in issue 49. Jim Steranko, one of the most exciting and innovative comics artists of the decade, started drawing the book but left after two issues.

X-Men #42 (April 1968)
'The Death of Professor X'
(Cover art by John Buscema)

Sales had fallen dangerously low, but now Roy Thomas returned to the title in collaboration with artist Neal Adams. Adams combined the visual dynamism of Kirby with his own background in illustration into a style blending heightened realism, idealized beauty, and epic grandeur. At the decade's end *X-Men* had at last become the equal of the best Super Hero comics of its time.

1963

X-Men #1 (Sept. 1963)
First appearance of the
X-Men and Magneto
(Cover art by Jack Kirby)

1965

X-Men #14
(Nov. 1965)
First appearance
of the Sentinels
(Cover art by
Jack Kirby)

1966

X-Men #19 (April 1966)
First appearance of
Mimic
(Cover art by Jack Kirby
and Werner Roth)

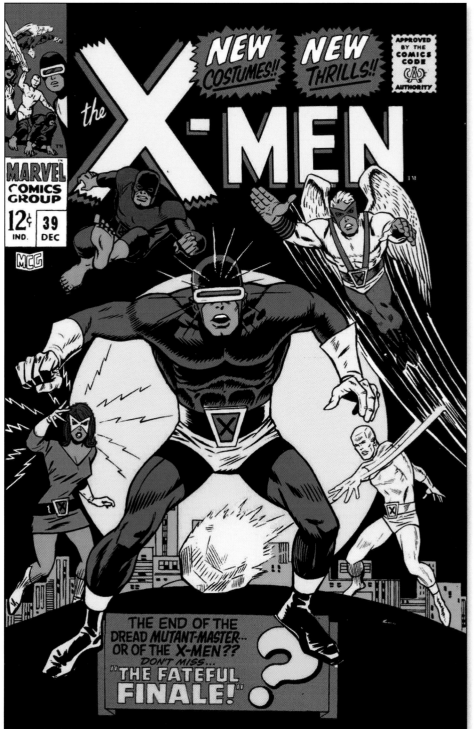

X-Men #56 (May 1969)
First cover appearance of the Living Monolith
First cover by Neal Adams

X-Men #39 (December 1967)
First appearance of the X-Men's new costumes
(Cover art by George Tuska)

1967

X-Men #28 (Jan. 1967)
First appearance of
Banshee
(Cover art by Jack Kirby
and Werner Roth)

1968

X-Men #49
(Oct. 1968)
First cover art by
Jim Steranko

1969

X-Men #61
(Oct. 1969)
Sauron against
Angel
(Cover art by
Neal Adams)

Making an entrance

The panel to the left is from the first page of the first issue of the original *X-Men* series, from 1963. This remarkable issue introduced Charles Xavier, his 'School for Gifted Mutants', and his original mutant students. Xavier explained that their mission was to protect humanity from 'evil mutants' and then sent his X-Men into their first battle against their greatest mutant nemesis, Magneto.

MARVEL GIRL
1960s Marvel heroines tended to have powers that did not require them to grapple physically with their enemies. Nonetheless, even then Marvel Girl proved to be a surprisingly formidable adversary. In later decades, X-Men would become known for strong female characters who were the equals of their male colleagues.

Before joining the X-Men, Angel was a vigilante.

The 'Avenging Angel'

The Iceman cometh

Flashback stories recounted the origins of the male X-Men. For example, Iceman first publicly used his powers to rescue his girlfriend from an assailant. Rather than honouring Iceman's heroism, frightened townspeople tried to kill him.

CHANGING FACES – 1960s

GRADUATION
The original X-Men 'graduated' in issue 7; though they continued training at the school, they could now operate without Xavier's supervision.

PROFESSOR X
Charles Xavier was a physically challenged Super Hero. Though confined to a wheelchair, his mental abilities made him the mightiest X-Man.

PROFESSOR X
IN HIS
ORIGINAL
WHEELCHAIR

WHEN CHARLES XAVIER'S original students – Cyclops, Marvel Girl, Angel, Beast, and Iceman – first appeared, they were teenagers attending school, much like their potential readers. But they were also the X-Men, young mutants capable of shouldering adult responsibilities. In the series' first issue Xavier sent them into what he called their 'baptism of fire': their first battle against the man who was to become their archenemy, Magneto. The X-Men thwarted his attempted takeover of the Cape Citadel missile base, and over the coming months they clashed repeatedly with Magneto's Brotherhood of Evil Mutants.

It was soon clear that the introverted Cyclops – Scott Summers – was deeply in love with Marvel Girl – Jean Grey – but felt his dangerous mutant power made it impossible for him to become close to anyone. Jean was equally attracted to Scott but likewise shy. Several years passed before they admitted their feelings to each other. In their true identities Iceman, Beast, and Angel found their own girlfriends: Zelda the waitress, Vera the librarian, and heiress Candy Southern, respectively. They regularly congregated at the Coffee A-Go-Go in Manhattan's Greenwich Village and listened to its beatnik bard, Bernard the Poet.

Though Xavier warned of humanity's fear and distrust of mutants in issue 1, the X-Men were treated as heroes by humans in their first two issues. But in issue 5, the X-Men rescued a mutant from an enraged mob, and three issues later another anti-mutant crowd attacked Beast and Iceman. Then in issue 14 scientist Bolivar Trask set off a frenzy in the media by proclaiming that, unless stopped, mutants would conquer humanity. Trask introduced his inventions, the mutant-hunting Sentinel robots, and the X-Men have been treated as outcasts ever since.

The 1960s saw the X-Men's first clash with the Juggernaut, their earliest journeys to the Savage Land, and the introduction of their next member, the Mimic. The X-Men first met the Banshee when he unwillingly served the Factor Three conspiracy. With its defeat, Xavier rewarded his students with new, individualized costumes. The X-Men were shocked when Xavier died (or so it seemed) in their final battle against Grotesk. The team split apart, but soon reunited. They also gained new mutant allies: Lorna Dane and Cyclops' brother Havok. As the decade closed, the X-Men first battled the Living Monolith, Larry Trask's new Sentinels, and Sauron, before vying against Magneto once again.

PROFESSOR X

THE PUBLIC KNOWS Professor Charles Xavier as one of the world's leading authorities on genetics and mutation. But they do not know that Xavier himself is a mutant who is the most powerful telepath alive, able both to read minds and to communicate mentally with others. Nor is it generally known that Xavier is the founder and leader of the mysterious group of mutants called the X-Men. What is most important about Xavier, however, is the dream to which he has dedicated his life and work: that some day mutants and the rest of humanity will live together in peace.

TRAVELLING MAN

Charles' mental powers began emerging when he was a boy. While attending graduate school he fell in love with his fellow student Moira MacTaggert, but when she broke their engagement he began travelling around the world. In Egypt he first met and battled a criminal mutant, Amahl Farouk. As a result of this encounter, Charles decided to dedicate himself to protecting mutants and humans from harming one another. Xavier went to Israel, where he met and became friends with the young Eric Lehnsherr, who later became Magneto. Finally, in Tibet, Xavier led a successful rebellion against an extraterrestrial conqueror, Lucifer, who took revenge by crippling Xavier's legs. Returning to America, Xavier eventually conceived the idea of his school for teaching young mutants how to master their superhuman abilities. Although he was confined to a wheelchair, his students, the X-Men, would battle criminal mutants in his stead. Xavier continues to head the X-Men today and has founded two other mutant teams, the New Mutants and Generation X.

Charles Xavier's telepathic powers began to emerge while he was in his early teens. As a side effect, by the time he graduated high school he was completely bald. A genius, he entered college at 16, graduated in two years, and went on to do postgraduate work at Oxford University.

ASTRAL PROJECTION
Xavier's astral form can leave his body to travel in physical reality or on astral planes of existence. Sometimes, when he communicates telepathically with the X-Men, they mentally 'see' an astral image of his head.

Hoverchair
Originally Xavier used a non-motorized wheelchair (see top-left illustration). But after he fell in love with the alien Princess Lilandra he accompanied her back to the Shi'ar galaxy, where he acquired his first hoverchair. Employing Shi'ar technology, Xavier's hoverchair floats just above the ground and is more manoeuvrable than any wheelchair.

Xavier crippled

Travelling around the world as a young man, Xavier arrived in Tibet, where he discovered that the inhabitants of a walled city had been enslaved by a mysterious outsider. Xavier led a revolt against the masked tyrant, who called himself Lucifer, and who was the advance agent for an alien invasion. Defeated, Lucifer took vengeance by dropping a massive stone block on Xavier, crippling his legs. This tragedy motivated Xavier to create the X-Men: if he could not go into action, then he would train others to combat evil mutants instead.

ON SCREEN

Professor Xavier is one of the characters in the *X-Men* movie who is the least different from his forebear in the comics. In both media Xavier is a wise visionary striving to create harmony between mutants and 'normal' humans. As in the comics, Xavier is a powerful telepath, and he uses this power to read the minds of others, including Senator Kelly, through whom he learns of Magneto's plans.

Bank of cybernetic frequency antenna exciters

Signal digitizer and spectrum analyzer

Super-cooled cybernetic frequency amplifier network

Cerebro phased array simulator

Cerebro

Cerebro is a system of machines invented by Charles Xavier to locate superhuman mutants by detecting certain psionic energies emitted by their brains. Wearing a special headset, Xavier can use his own powers to boost Cerebro's ability to pinpoint these psionic waves. The X-Men use portable Cerebro devices to locate mutants at short range. These are linked electronically to the main Cerebro computer.

Cerebro housekeeping computer

Status display

Primary psion detector and waveguide pedestal

Liquid helium conduit

Professor X also uses his psychic powers to influence people's minds, guiding the confused Wolverine around the mansion by making him 'hear' approaching footsteps. One other power he exhibits is an ability to take control of others, as he does so with Sabretooth in an attempt to stop Magneto from killing the helpless policemen outside the Westchester train station. As in the comics, Xavier's Mansion in New York State is the site of a school for mutants. When we first see this school in the film, it is already populated by a number of different mutants of different ages. Although little is revealed of his own past in the movie, we learn that, as in the comics, Charles Xavier is the former friend of the man who has now become his archenemy, Magneto.

TO WALK AGAIN
After the alien Brood implanted an embryo in Xavier's body, Moira MacTaggert and the Starjammers saved him by using Shi'ar technology to transfer Xavier's mind into a new body cloned from his own. But his spine was broken in battle against the Shadow King, and he is crippled once more.

XAVIER AND MAGNETO
When they first met, Charles Xavier and Magneto became friends. But they became bitter enemies, for while Xavier chose the path of peace, Magneto chose to wage war with humanity. Enraged, Xavier once used his powers to wipe Magneto's mind blank. However, Magneto eventually regained his memories and continued the feud.

CYCLOPS

Scott Summers must wear glasses with ruby quartz lenses to diffuse his eye-beams harmlessly.

THE FIRST YOUNG MUTANT to be recruited into the X-Men, Scott Summers, alias Cyclops, has always been the team member who is the most dedicated to Xavier's ideals. Cyclops has long borne the responsibility of leading the other X-Men in combat. But an even greater burden is the nature of his own mutant power. He continually emits force beams from his eyes; only the ruby quartz lenses of his visor and glasses can safely disperse this energy. Scott lives with the knowledge that he could kill a man merely by glancing at him. The son of Air Force pilot Major Christopher Summers, Scott was forced to leap from his father's burning plane when he was a boy and was placed in an orphanage. When Scott first unintentionally unleashed a power blast, terrified onlookers turned into a mob and pursued him. Eventually, he was found by Xavier, who made him the first member of the X-Men. Scott proved to be Xavier's prize pupil, and the Professor made him the X-Men's deputy leader. At one point Cyclops helped found a new team, X-Factor, but he always returns to the X-Men.

SCOTT AND JEAN

For years, the emotionally reserved Scott secretly loved his fellow X-Man, Jean Grey. However, he believed that his powers made it too dangerous for him to become close to anyone. During a period when he thought Jean was dead, Scott married Madelyne Pryor, and they had a son, Nathan. But since then, Scott and Jean were reunited and are now husband and wife.

Deadly gaze
When Scott parachuted from his father's plane, he suffered brain damage on landing. As a result, when his mutant power emerged, he was unable to shut off his optic blasts at will. As long as his eyes are open, enough energy shoots from them to kill a human being.

The first X-Man
When Scott first publicly used his powers, he was forced to flee from a mob. A criminal mutant with diamond-hard hands named Jack O'Diamonds found Scott and forced him to become his accomplice. Xavier rescued Scott and invited him to become the nucleus of the new team he was forming. Thus, Cyclops became the first X-Man.

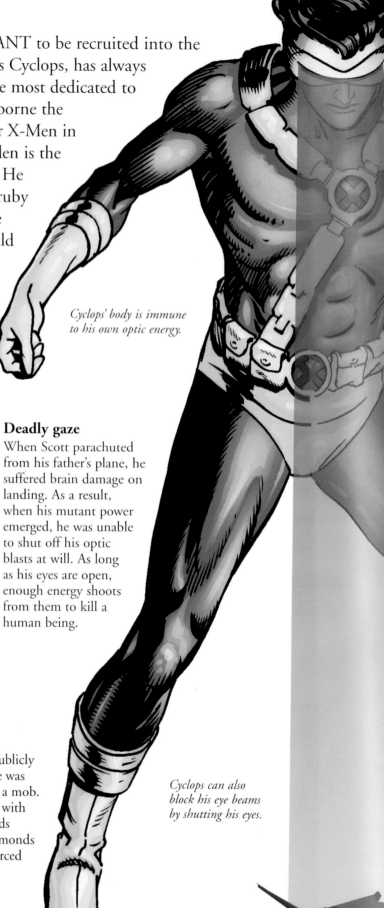

Cyclops' body is immune to his own optic energy.

Cyclops can also block his eye beams by shutting his eyes.

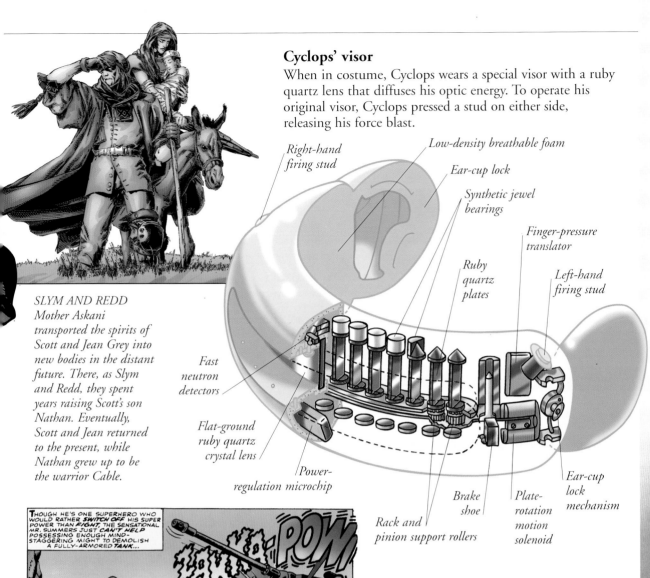

Cyclops' visor

When in costume, Cyclops wears a special visor with a ruby quartz lens that diffuses his optic energy. To operate his original visor, Cyclops pressed a stud on either side, releasing his force blast.

Right-hand firing stud

Low-density breathable foam

Ear-cup lock

Synthetic jewel bearings

Finger-pressure translator

Ruby quartz plates

Left-hand firing stud

Fast neutron detectors

Flat-ground ruby quartz crystal lens

Power-regulation microchip

Brake shoe

Plate-rotation motion solenoid

Ear-cup lock mechanism

Rack and pinion support rollers

SLYM AND REDD
Mother Askani transported the spirits of Scott and Jean Grey into new bodies in the distant future. There, as Slym and Redd, they spent years raising Scott's son Nathan. Eventually, Scott and Jean returned to the present, while Nathan grew up to be the warrior Cable.

THOUGH HE'S ONE SUPERHERO WHO WOULD RATHER *SWITCH OFF* HIS SUPER POWER THAN *FIGHT*, THE SENSATIONAL MR. SUMMERS JUST *CAN'T HELP* POSSESSING ENOUGH MIND-STAGGERING MIGHT TO DEMOLISH A FULLY-ARMORED *TANK*...

POW!

The power of Cyclops

Cyclops' body absorbs solar energy and converts it into the ruby-red concussive force that shoots from his eyes. Cyclops' power beam can puncture a 2cm carbon-steel plate at a distance of less than a metre. He and his younger brother Alex, alias Havok, are immune to each other's power blasts.

XAVIER'S SECOND-IN-COMMAND
Xavier named Cyclops as the X-Men's 'deputy leader', the one who led them in combat. Others have served in this capacity since, but the X-Men still defer to Scott's long experience and wisdom.

ORIGINAL X-MEN UNIFORM

X-MEN UNIFORM DESIGNED BY JEAN GREY

X-FACTOR UNIFORM

ON SCREEN

As in the comics, the *X-Men* movie version of Scott Summers was the first mutant to be recruited into the X-Men. And, as in the comics, Cyclops fires force beams from his eyes. These beam are controlled by a visor or special glasses. During the film, Scott shows the power of these force beams when he nearly demolishes Westchester train station. He also shows his ability to finely control them using his visor, when he shatters the Toad's hardened slime which is suffocating Jean Grey.

Since he discovered his powers at his High School Prom, Scott has been aware that he must continually guard against accidentally harming people with his optic blasts. Over the years, this has given him a rigid and introverted personality. This is in stark contrast to the more relaxed attitude of the newly arrived Wolverine, who challenges Cyclops' ability as the X-Men's leader in battle. The clash of personalities between the two leads to some friction, which is made worse by the attraction of both men to their beautiful team-mate, Jean Grey.

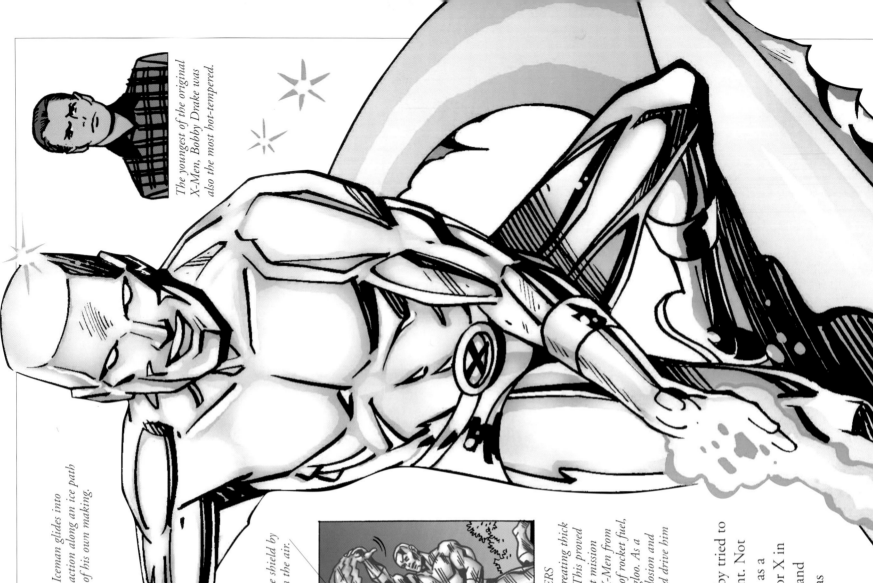

The youngest of the original X-Men, Bobby Drake was also the most hot-tempered.

Iceman glides into action along an ice path of his own making.

Iceman forms a defensive shield by freezing water vapour in the air.

ICEMAN

THE YOUNGEST of the original X-Men, Robert Drake has the mutant ability to lower temperatures both inside and outside his own body to sub-zero levels without harming himself. As a result, Bobby can transform his entire body into ice, making it hardly surprising that he is called Iceman. Bobby can also freeze the moisture in the air around him to create any kind of object he wishes, from bats, to shields, to slides. His powers have continued to evolve over the years, and he recently learned how to transform his body into an ice-like substance and then back to human form at will. Although he secretly discovered his powers in his teens, Bobby preferred to lead a mundane existence in a small town on Long Island, New York. But one night he had to use his powers to save his girlfriend from being assaulted. The community panicked, and soon Bobby became the target of a lynch mob. It was Professor Xavier and Cyclops who rescued him, and invited him to become the second member of the X-Men.

AFTER XAVIER'S SCHOOL

After some time with the X-Men, Bobby quit the team and joined Angel's new group, the Champions. When that group failed, Bobby tried to follow his parents' wishes to lead an ordinary life, studying to become an accountant. Not surprisingly, though, Bobby could not resist rejoining his friends, Beast and Angel, as a member of the Defenders, and later reuniting with the original students of Professor X in X-Factor. He remained with X-Factor until he and his partners dissolved the team and returned to the X-Men. Anti-mutant bigotry still haunts Bobby's life. His father was nearly killed by thugs working for the anti-mutant presidential candidate Graydon Creed, for speaking out against the politician.

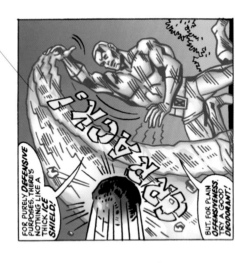

FOR PURELY *DEFENSIVE* PURPOSES, THERE'S NOTHING LIKE A *THICK ICE SHIELD!*

BUT, FOR PLAIN *OFFENSIVENESS* TRY A GOOD *DEODORANT!*

ICEMAN'S DEFENSIVE POWERS

Iceman can use ice for defence, creating thick walls and shields in an instant. This proved invaluable in the team's very first mission against Magneto. To shield the X-Men from the blast of an exploding tanker of rocket fuel, Iceman created a protective ice igloo. As a result, the team survived the explosion and was able to surprise Magneto and drive him away from the military base.

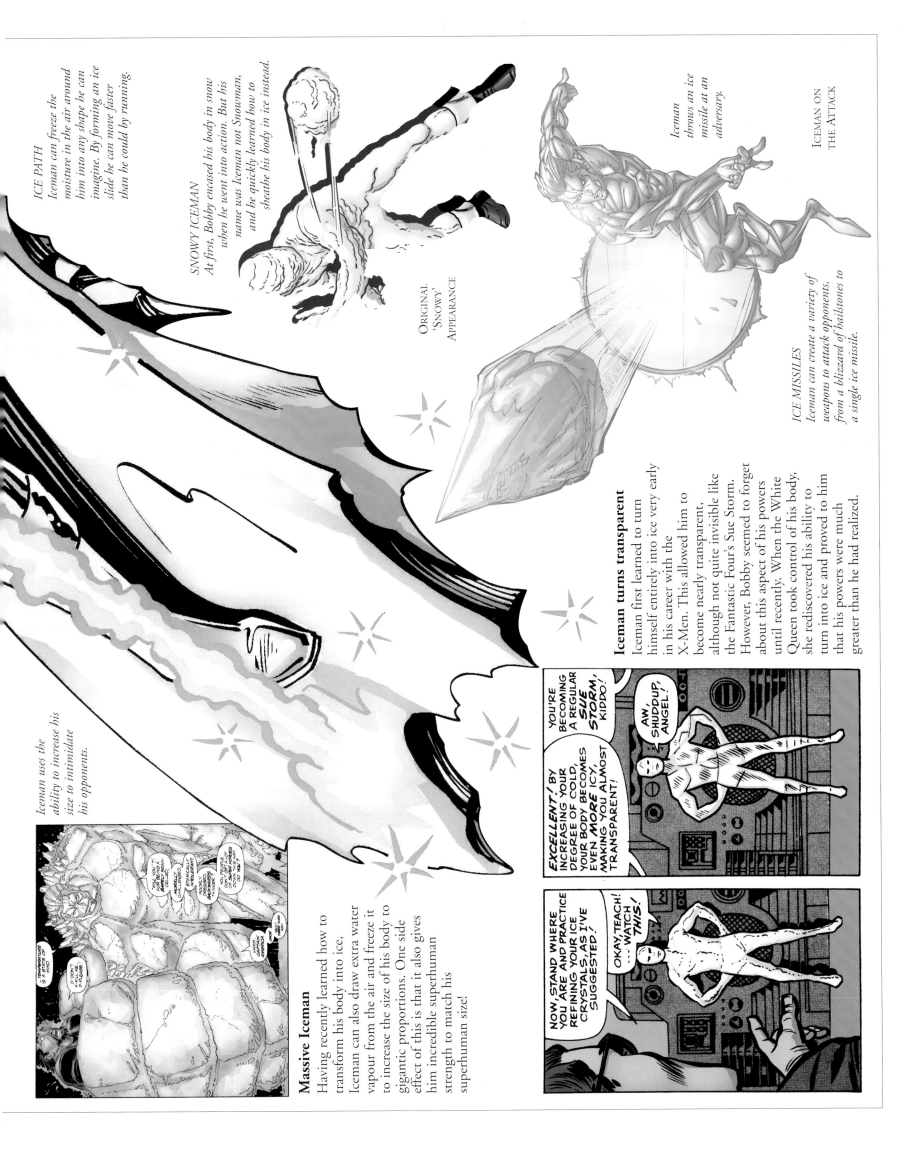

ICE PATH
Iceman can freeze the moisture in the air around him into any shape he can imagine. By forming an ice slide he can move faster than he could by running.

SNOWY ICEMAN
At first, Bobby encased his body in snow when he went into action. But his name was Iceman not Snowman, and he quickly learned how to sheathe his body in ice instead.

ORIGINAL 'SNOWY' APPEARANCE

Iceman throws an ice missile at an adversary.

ICEMAN ON THE ATTACK

ICE MISSILES
Iceman can create a variety of weapons to attack opponents, from a blizzard of hailstones to a single ice missile.

Iceman turns transparent

Iceman first learned to turn himself entirely into ice very early in his career with the X-Men. This allowed him to become nearly transparent, although not quite invisible like the Fantastic Four's Sue Storm. However, Bobby seemed to forget about this aspect of his powers until recently. When the White Queen took control of his body, she rediscovered his ability to turn into ice and proved to him that his powers were much greater than he had realized.

Iceman uses the ability to increase his size to intimidate his opponents.

Massive Iceman

Having recently learned how to transform his body into ice, Iceman can also draw extra water vapour from the air and freeze it to increase the size of his body to gigantic proportions. One side effect of this is that it also gives him incredible superhuman strength to match his superhuman size!

ARCHANGEL

THE AVENGING
ANGEL

During his early career as a Super Hero, Warren kept his dual identity a secret.

HANDSOME AND BORN into vast wealth, Warren Worthington III was a member of society's elite. But when wings began sprouting from his shoulders, Warren thought he was turning into a freak. As his wings grew to full size, though, he discovered that, thanks to his amazing mutant anatomy, he could fly like a bird! Thrilled by this new-found ability, Warren went to New York City and became a masked crime fighter, dubbing himself the Avenging Angel. Soon afterwards, the X-Men contacted him, and he became the third member to join the original team, after Cyclops and Iceman. Some years later, Warren publicly revealed his dual identity and used the fortune he had inherited to establish his own Super Hero team, called the Champions, based in Los Angeles. When that team broke up, Angel joined another team, the Defenders, who were based in the Colorado mountain estate jointly owned by Warren and his longtime girlfriend, Candy Southern. Inevitably, though, Angel was reunited with the other original X-Men in founding the New York City-based organization known as X-Factor.

THE AVENGING
ANGEL

ORIGINAL
X-MEN
COSTUME

> THESE RESTRAINING BELTS OF MINE KEEP MY WINGS FROM BULGING UNDER MY SUIT, BUT AFTER A WHILE THEY FEEL LIKE I'M WEARING A *STRAIT-JACKET!*

WING HARNESS
Back when Warren Worthington III kept his dual identity a secret, he used a special harness to strap his flexible wings behind his back. He then concealed them under his clothes. In later years, he used a Stark Industries image inducer to create the illusion of a normal appearance in public.

CHANGING ANGEL

It was during his time with X-Factor that Angel was seriously wounded in combat by the Marauder Harpoon; this led to the amputation of his original wings. He was then approached by the sinister mutant Apocalypse, who genetically altered Warren, causing his wings to grow back in a strange, metallic form and his skin to turn blue. In exchange for giving him back his wings, Warren served Apocalypse as one of the Four Horsemen, Death. However, he finally came to his senses, left Apocalypse's service and returned to X-Factor, under the new name of Archangel. Since then, not only has Warren returned to the X-Men after X-Factor disbanded, but his wings have regained their original feathered appearance – they had been regenerating beneath the metallic ones all along. His skin, however, remains the blue colour it turned after Apocalypse's genetic tampering.

ANGEL'S
SECOND
COSTUME

ANGEL'S
X-FACTOR
COSTUME

Different costumes

Over the years, Angel has worn a number of different costumes. Even before he met Charles Xavier, Warren had decided to become a Super Hero, fighting crime under the name of the Avenging Angel. His first X-Men costume was black and yellow like those of his fellow classmates. His next outfit was designed by Jean Grey and was a much more colourful affair. After he revealed his identity as a Super Hero, Warren no longer needed to hide his face when going into action as the Angel. As a result, the costumes he's worn since his days with X-Factor have done away with any mask whatsoever. When Warren served Apocalypse as one of his four horsemen, his wings were of an organic metal and they could shoot feathers that were as sharp as daggers.

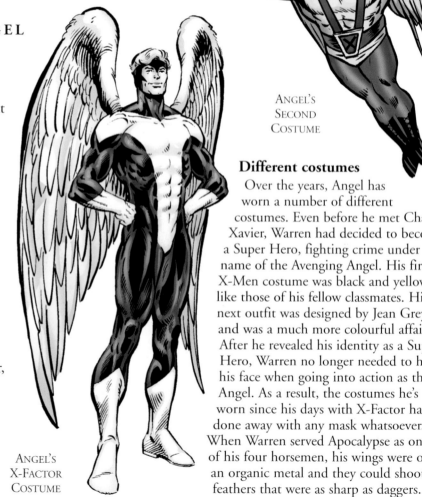

Archangel as he appears today, with blue skin and feathered wings.

Blockbuster   *Harpoon*

Clipped wings

When the team of evil mutant mercenaries called the Marauders massacred the Morlocks, who lived in tunnels beneath Manhattan, Angel and the other members of X-Factor came to the Morlocks' aid. During the fight, one of the assassins, Blockbuster, captured Angel, while another, Harpoon, impaled Angel's wings with two of his trademark weapons. Angel was eventually rescued by the thunder god, Thor, but his wings had been so severely damaged that surgeons had to amputate them.

Apocalyptic change

Warren became depressed and suicidal after he lost his wings. He was so desperate that he agreed to accept the help of one of the X-Men's greatest enemies, Apocalypse. Using his knowledge of genetic science, Apocalypse made Warren undergo extremely painful genetic engineering that turned his skin blue and regrew his wings in a strange metallic form. Under the stress of these events, Warren even agreed to work for his new benefactor in return, as one of his Four Horsemen – Death!

ARCHANGEL WITH METAL WINGS

WINGSPAN
When fully extended, Angel's wings span a total of 5 metres! Despite their great size, they are extremely flexible, which is why they could be concealed under his clothing so well during his early days with the X-Men.

Angel's wings are just like those of a bird, complete with different types of wing feathers.

23

BEAST

Despite appearances, Beast is a brilliant scientist and an expert in the field of genetics.

THE BEAST is a paradox. He looks like a friendly, hyperactive, blue-furred ape, literally bouncing off walls or hanging upside down by his feet. But he is really a mutant human named Henry McCoy, a scientist whose extraordinary intellect and expertise in genetics rival those of Charles Xavier. A serious campaigner for mutant rights, Hank has known the pain of being an outcast from normal humanity. Yet he has not only learned to accept his furry appearance, he has also become an inveterate prankster and wit, who delights in showing off his voluminous vocabulary. When he was born, Hank McCoy looked entirely human except for his enormous hands and feet. In college he became a football star, nicknamed 'the Beast' for his amazing ape-like agility. Hank's growing fame brought him to the attention of Charles Xavier, who made him his fourth recruit into the X-Men. The oldest member of Xavier's original class of students, Hank was also the first to leave.

BEFORE THE X-MEN
In college Hank learned how people would try to exploit mutants when the self-styled Conquistador forced him to steal a portable nuclear device.
Luckily, Hank was rescued by the X-Men and inducted into the team.

In his animal form, the Beast has large canine teeth resembling fangs and large pointed ears.

FURRY BEAST

Hank drank a serum that activated his latent mutations, changing him into his fur-covered form. He joined a Super Hero team, the Avengers, and publicly revealed his true identity. Since then, he has reorganized another team, the Defenders, before rejoining his old classmates from Xavier's school to found X-Factor. He finally returned to the X-Men and the Xavier Institute, where he remains its resident scientist.

FREEING THE BEAST WITHIN
While working as a genetic researcher, Henry McCoy learned that one of his discoveries, a chemical that induced mutations, was about to be stolen. Rather foolishly, Henry drank the chemical, only to be metamorphosed into his now familiar simian form.

Beast's athletic powers

Even in human form, Hank possessed superhuman agility. His enormous hands and feet helped him to perform breathtaking jumps and somersaults. His later transformation increased his speed, agility, and reflexes even further, while making him strong enough to lift ten-tonne weights. He can perform athletic feats that no Olympic athlete could hope to equal.

It's just a normal workout in the Danger Room for the Beast, as he nimbly evades traps and literally bounces off walls with astonishing speed.

Hank can outperform any trapeze artist.

The Beast is equally capable of performing acrobatics on his feet and his hands!

"I WASN'T EXACTLY PREPARED FOR THE PROFESSOR'S SUDDEN AND UN-EXPECTED DEPARTURE AFTER GRADUATION.

"NOW THAT OUR MENTOR HAS TAKEN OFF ON A MYSTERIOUS ERRAND TO PARTS UNKNOWN--

"--I CAN'T HELP FEELING SOMEWHAT... ABANDONED.

CHANGING FACE
Even in human form, the Beast could walk with an ape-like gait. For a short period when he was in X-Factor he regained his human form, but he has since returned to his fur-covered state.

Other teams

After leaving the X-Men, the Beast found a new home with the mighty Avengers, one of Earth's foremost Super Hero teams, whose members included Captain America and Iron Man. The public idolized the Avengers, and as one of them, the Beast shared in the acclaim and acceptance – something the mistrusted X-Men never received. Trying his hand at leading a team of his own, the Beast organized the Defenders. Angel and Iceman served alongside the Beast, and the experience helped prepare them for their subsequent role in co-founding X-Factor with the other original members of the X-Men.

Massive ape-like hands

Originally grey, Hank's fur became blue-black

Massive ape-like feet

The Beast was one of the original members of X-Factor.

The Beast in his original Xavier's school uniform.

Later, Jean Grey designed this costume for Hank.

The Beast in his original furry appearance.

The Beast in his X-Factor uniform.

25

PHOENIX

A LTHOUGH JEAN GREY was the fifth of Xavier's recruits into the X-Men, she was actually the first of his mutant students. Originally code-named Marvel Girl and now known as Phoenix, Jean possesses both telepathic powers, enabling her to read minds and communicate mentally, and telekinetic powers, allowing her to levitate and manipulate objects by mental force. Jean's story is inseparable from that of her team-mate Scott Summers, alias Cyclops, who is now her husband: the love between these two spans the entire history of the X-Men. When Jean was ten years old, her best friend Annie Richardson was struck by an automobile. It was then that Jean's mutant powers first awoke, and she psychically felt Annie's own emotions as she died. The experience left Jean deeply depressed, and the following year her parents sought out Charles Xavier for help. Xavier tutored her for years and finally inducted her into the newly formed X-Men, giving her the code name Marvel Girl.

Born in Annandale-on-Hudson, New York, Jean is the daughter of Professor John Grey and his wife Elaine. Jean also has a niece, Gailyn, and a nephew, Joey.

IN THE BEGINNING
When eleven-year-old Jean began training with Xavier, she was too young to control her telepathic powers. Hence Xavier psychically blocked her ability to use them until she grew more mature, teaching her to use her powers of telekinesis instead.

'DEATH' AND REBIRTH

Jean and Scott quickly fell in love with each other, although years passed before the two shy teenagers admitted their feelings. Later, Jean encountered a cosmic entity of pure energy called the Phoenix Force, which gave itself a human form identical to hers, even incorporating a portion of her consciousness. This being, calling herself Phoenix, then took Jean's place in the X-Men, while Jean's original body lay in suspended animation. When Phoenix went insane, Jean's personality reasserted itself long enough to make Phoenix commit suicide. The other X-Men, including the anguished Scott, believed Jean to be dead. But the part of Jean's consciousness that Phoenix had taken returned to Jean's original body, which awoke from its coma-like state. Thus Jean was reunited with Scott, first in X-Factor and then back in the X-Men. She has since adopted the name of Phoenix. Best of all, Jean and Scott are at long last married. Now, as at the beginning, their relationship is at the very heart of the X-Men.

JEAN'S FIRST MARVEL GIRL COSTUME

JEAN'S SECOND MARVEL GIRL COSTUME

At first Jean wore the standard X-Men school uniform, but she designed her Marvel Girl minidress ensemble herself, and has worn a variety of costumes since then.

Sensing the dying Jean's telepathic cries for help, the Phoenix Force manifested itself to her in Jean's own likeness. It offered Jean her 'heart's desire': to save the lives of herself and the X-Men.

The birth of Phoenix

Following a battle in space, Jean was piloting the space shuttle transporting the X-Men back to Earth when she was exposed to lethal radiation from a solar storm. The Phoenix Force saved her life by casting her into suspended animation in a pod at the bottom of a bay off New York City. In this pod she slowly recovered from the ravages of the radiation. Having taken on part of her psyche, an energy being then rose from the bay in a physical form identical to Jean's, proclaiming herself to be Phoenix.

X-FACTOR COSTUME

LATER X-MEN COSTUME

Jean in action

When she first joined the X-Men, Jean primarily used her telekinetic powers to lift small objects. But over time her powers have greatly strengthened, making her one of the mightiest of the X-Men. Recently, she has sacrificed her telekinesis, at least temporarily, to concentrate on her telepathic abilities.

Married at last

From almost their first days in the X-Men, Scott Summers and Jean Grey were in love, although each was too shy to admit it. Their love seemed doomed when the Phoenix Force took Jean's place and died before Scott's eyes. But finally, Scott and Jean were united in marriage on the most festive day in the X-Men's history.

ON SCREEN

Although the *X-Men* movie Jean has reddish hair, alluding to the comics' version, she wears a functional black uniform instead of the colourful comic-book costumes. Moreover, the film's Jean does not use a code name, such as 'Marvel Girl' or 'Phoenix'. In the movie, Jean is a scientist who is an authority on genetic mutation. The public knows that she teaches mutants at Xavier's school, but does not know that she is a mutant herself who learned to use her telekinetic and telepathic powers there.

In the *X-Men* movie, she has yet to tap into the huge psychic potential which her comic-book counterpart achieved as Phoenix. Her telepathic skills are still developing. She shows an ability to read Logan's mind, but she struggles to control Cerebro as it tracks down Magneto's whereabouts. However, she can use her telekinetic ability with some skill, as she proves by guiding Wolverine from the Statue of Liberty's crown to its torch in the film's climax. As in the comics, she is deeply in love with Scott Summers; she also has to contend with romantic advances from Logan.

XAVIER'S ESTATE

THE X-MEN'S BASE of operations is the Xavier Mansion located at 1407 Graymalkin Lane in Salem Center, in Westchester County, New York State. The great house was originally built by a Dutch ancestor of Xavier, using stone from the edge of nearby Breakstone Lake. The entire Xavier estate covers a considerable area, from Graymalkin Lane to Breakstone Lake, which is also known as the Neversink Reservoir. There is an Olympic-size swimming pool directly behind the mansion, and the grounds include stables, a boathouse and docks, and even Japanese gardens. There are also underground hangars and a take-off pad for the X-Men's Blackbird jets.

HISTORIC HOUSE
Xavier Mansion has been in Professor X's family for ten generations, since 1698. During that time the house has been destroyed and rebuilt a number of times.

Graymalkin Lane

Communications tower

The communications tower provides monitoring and equipment logs. The structure is explosion-proof and has seismic alarms below ground and motion detectors above.

Gardens

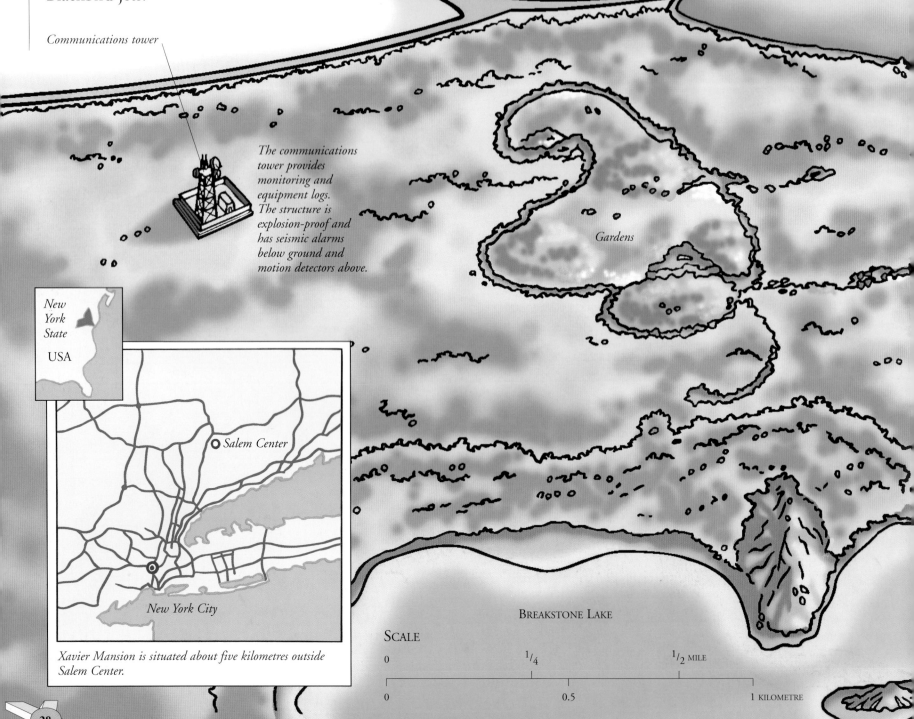

New York State

USA

Salem Center

New York City

Xavier Mansion is situated about five kilometres outside Salem Center.

BREAKSTONE LAKE

SCALE

0   ¼   ½ MILE

0   0.5   1 KILOMETRE

Alien upgrade

One recent destruction of the mansion led to the incorporation of Shi'ar technology, especially in the underground facilities. This includes inherent self-improving aspects that rebuild and replace malfunctioning or worn components.

Mansion security

Security is paramount at Xavier Mansion. The front gate is equipped with a voice and vision intercom which links directly to mansion security. There are also Stark International anti-acceleration field generators to prevent the gates from being rammed.

Stark International anti-acceleration field generators

Voice and vision intercom

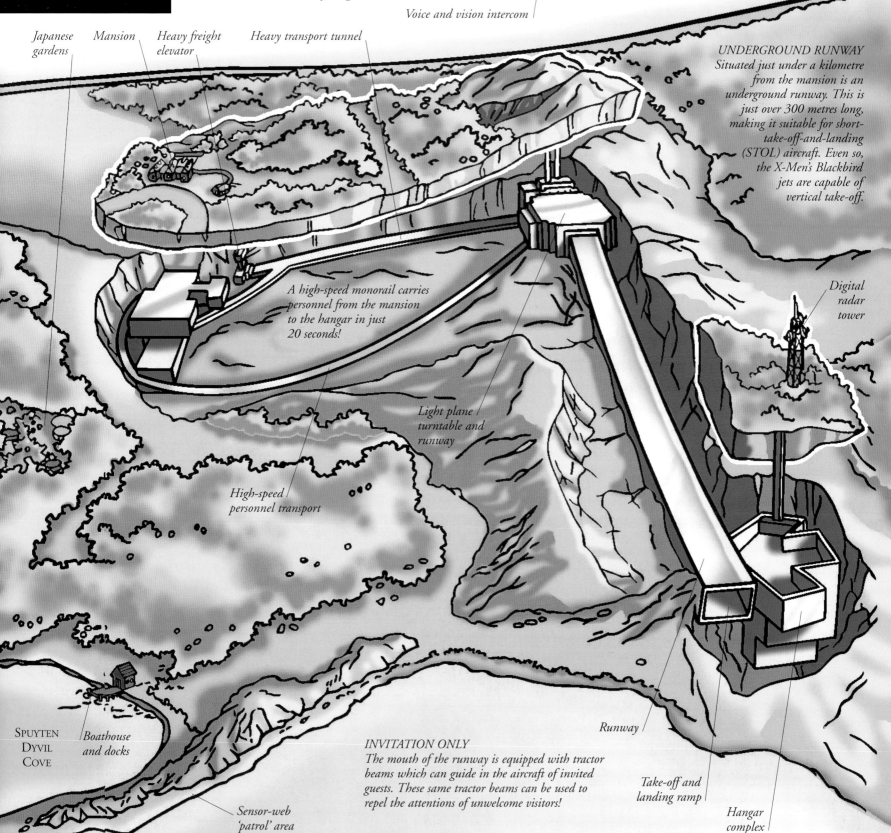

Japanese gardens

Mansion

Heavy freight elevator

Heavy transport tunnel

UNDERGROUND RUNWAY
Situated just under a kilometre from the mansion is an underground runway. This is just over 300 metres long, making it suitable for short-take-off-and-landing (STOL) aircraft. Even so, the X-Men's Blackbird jets are capable of vertical take-off.

A high-speed monorail carries personnel from the mansion to the hangar in just 20 seconds!

Digital radar tower

Light plane turntable and runway

High-speed personnel transport

SPUYTEN DYVIL COVE

Boathouse and docks

Runway

INVITATION ONLY
The mouth of the runway is equipped with tractor beams which can guide in the aircraft of invited guests. These same tractor beams can be used to repel the attentions of unwelcome visitors!

Sensor-web 'patrol' area

Take-off and landing ramp

Hangar complex

XAVIER'S MANSION

THE XAVIER MANSION originally consisted of two main floors, an attic and a basement. In recent years, two sub-basement levels have been constructed as well. Most classes are held in Xavier's vast library. He conducts school business from his first-floor office, and he also has a study, where the main terminal of the Cerebro computer system is installed. The main computer room is also on the first floor, as is the kitchen. The second floor is almost entirely devoted to the X-Men's living quarters.

MAINTAINING HISTORY
Despite the fact that the mansion has been demolished on several occasions, every effort has been made to rebuild it while maintaining the architectural and historical integrity of the structure.

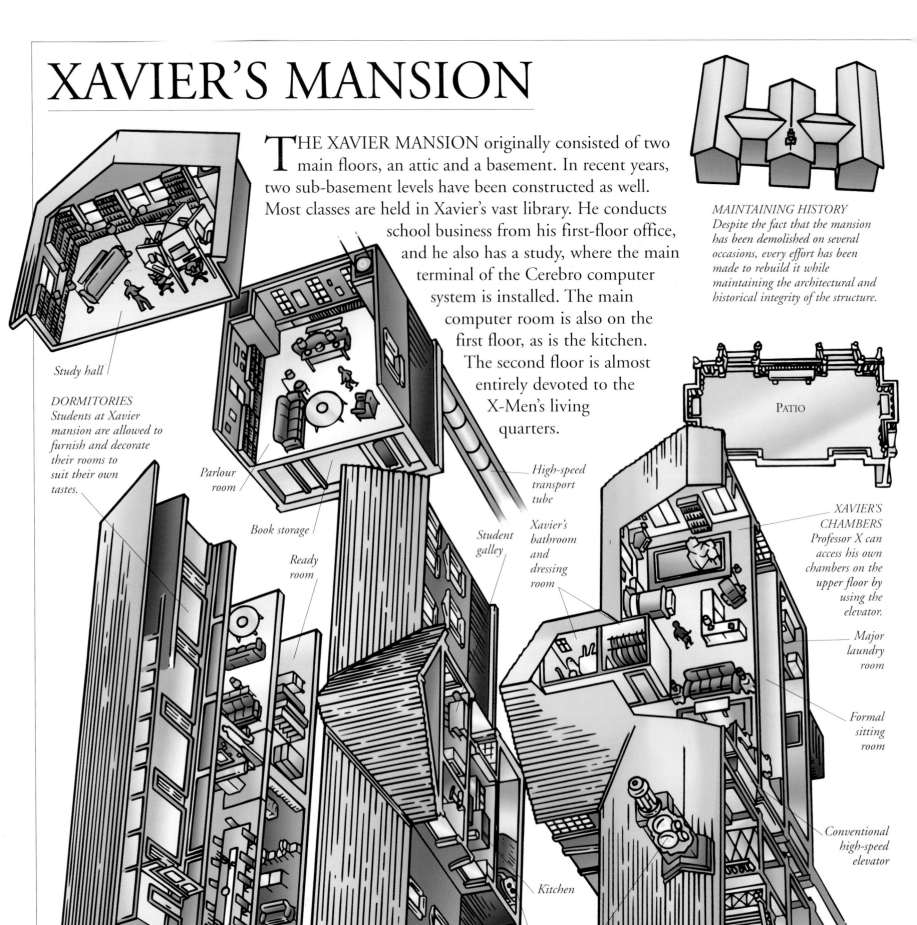

Study hall

DORMITORIES
Students at Xavier mansion are allowed to furnish and decorate their rooms to suit their own tastes.

Parlour room

Book storage

Ready room

Student galley

High-speed transport tube

Xavier's bathroom and dressing room

PATIO

XAVIER'S CHAMBERS
Professor X can access his own chambers on the upper floor by using the elevator.

Major laundry room

Formal sitting room

Conventional high-speed elevator

Kitchen

Oil heater

RADAR
The mansion's radar relays data to and from the communications tower situated in the grounds of the mansion.

Furniture storage

Wine cellar

Formal dining room

Workshop

Front entrance

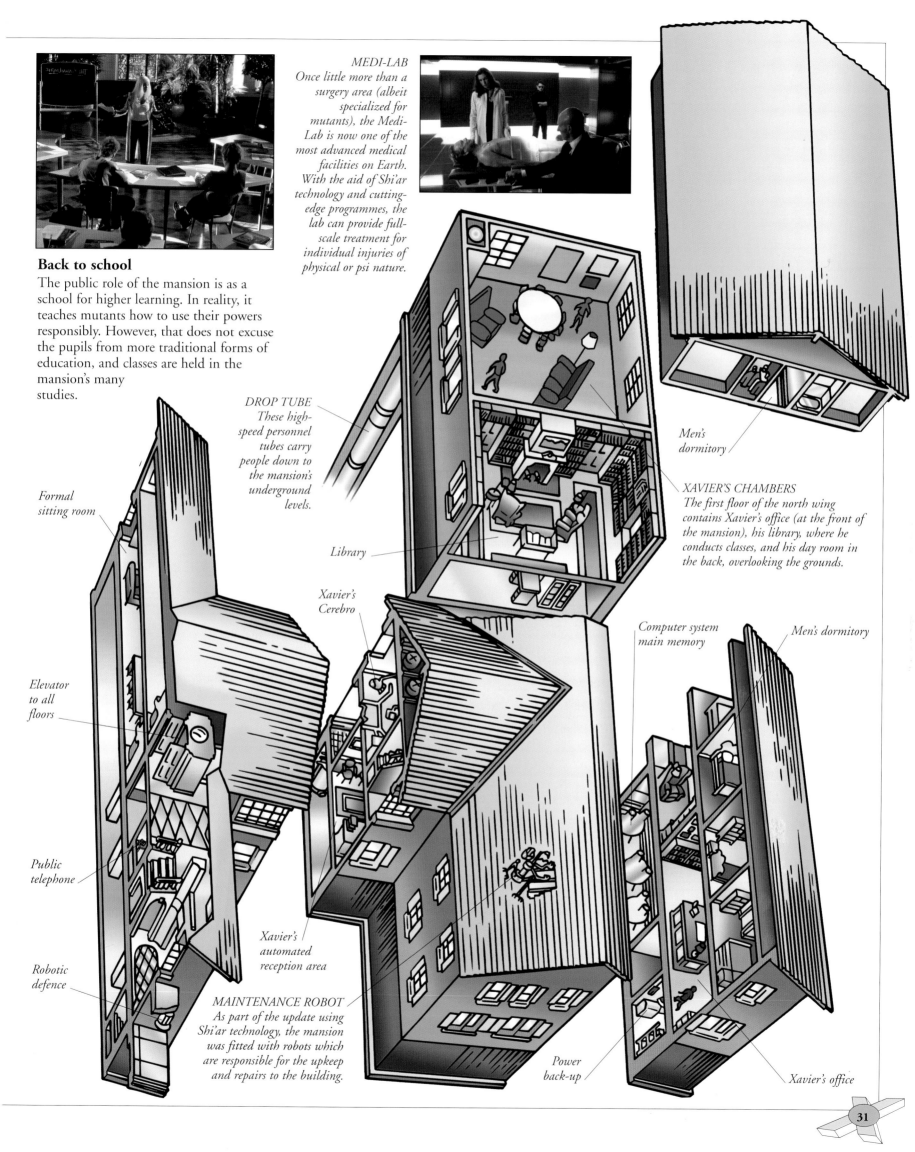

MEDI-LAB
Once little more than a surgery area (albeit specialized for mutants), the Medi-Lab is now one of the most advanced medical facilities on Earth. With the aid of Shi'ar technology and cutting-edge programmes, the lab can provide full-scale treatment for individual injuries of physical or psi nature.

Back to school

The public role of the mansion is as a school for higher learning. In reality, it teaches mutants how to use their powers responsibly. However, that does not excuse the pupils from more traditional forms of education, and classes are held in the mansion's many studies.

Formal sitting room

DROP TUBE
These high-speed personnel tubes carry people down to the mansion's underground levels.

Library

Xavier's Cerebro

Elevator to all floors

Public telephone

Robotic defence

MAINTENANCE ROBOT
As part of the update using Shi'ar technology, the mansion was fitted with robots which are responsible for the upkeep and repairs to the building.

Xavier's automated reception area

Power back-up

Men's dormitory

XAVIER'S CHAMBERS
The first floor of the north wing contains Xavier's office (at the front of the mansion), his library, where he conducts classes, and his day room in the back, overlooking the grounds.

Computer system main memory

Men's dormitory

Xavier's office

THE DANGER ROOM

THE CENTRE OF XAVIER'S training programme for mutants is the Danger Room, where the X-Men hone their athletics and combat skills. The original Danger Room was located on the first floor of Xavier's mansion. Within the room the X-Men would in effect run a hi-tech obstacle course, contending against anything and everything from metal tentacles, to jets of flame, to robots. Xavier's relationship with Lilandra, ruler of the alien Shi'ar Empire, led to his creation of a radical new version of the Danger Room concept. The current Danger Room is located on Sub-Basement Level Two of the mansion and employs Shi'ar technology. Through the use of solid holograms (images created with lasers), the Danger Room can now simulate any environment. Moreover, Shi'ar technology can create a whole range of formidable adversaries for the X-Men to test themselves against.

Danger Room doors and walls are made of nickel-titanium alloy. In these walls are localized force fields triggered by Master Control Intruder Detection Systems. Electromechanical security devices also regulate entry to the Ready Room Elevator and Control Room.

MUTANT GYM
Originally, the Danger Room was a gymnasium for mutants, specially equipped to challenge the X-Men's unusual abilities. Here, the Danger Room's automatic systems have Beast literally jumping through hoops and bouncing off the walls!

TRAPS GALORE
Aside from normal athletic equipment, the original Danger Room was replete with specially designed traps, ranging from laser beams, to steel mesh nets, to a pile-driver – and even a huge metal vice!

Holographic Danger Room

Utilizing the futuristic technology of the Shi'ar Empire, Professor Xavier redesigned the Danger Room to create effects far beyond the capabilities of Earth science. Now he can test the X-Men's battle prowess by using holograms to mimic any potentially dangerous setting or adversary he or they can imagine. For instance, the Danger Room can create a solid hologram of Wolverine's archenemy, Sabretooth, for him to battle and perfect his fighting skills.

Redesigned Danger Room

The Danger Room underwent its first renovation when Xavier organized his second-generation of X-Men. Xavier could monitor and control its operations from the safety of an observation booth. By now he was pitting his students against sophisticated robots in combat training. With so many things happening in such a small space, the odd near miss happens frequently. Here, a barrage of missiles causes Angel to swerve violently, putting him on a collision course with Nightcrawler.

The holographic generators can create anything – even an 'alien world'!

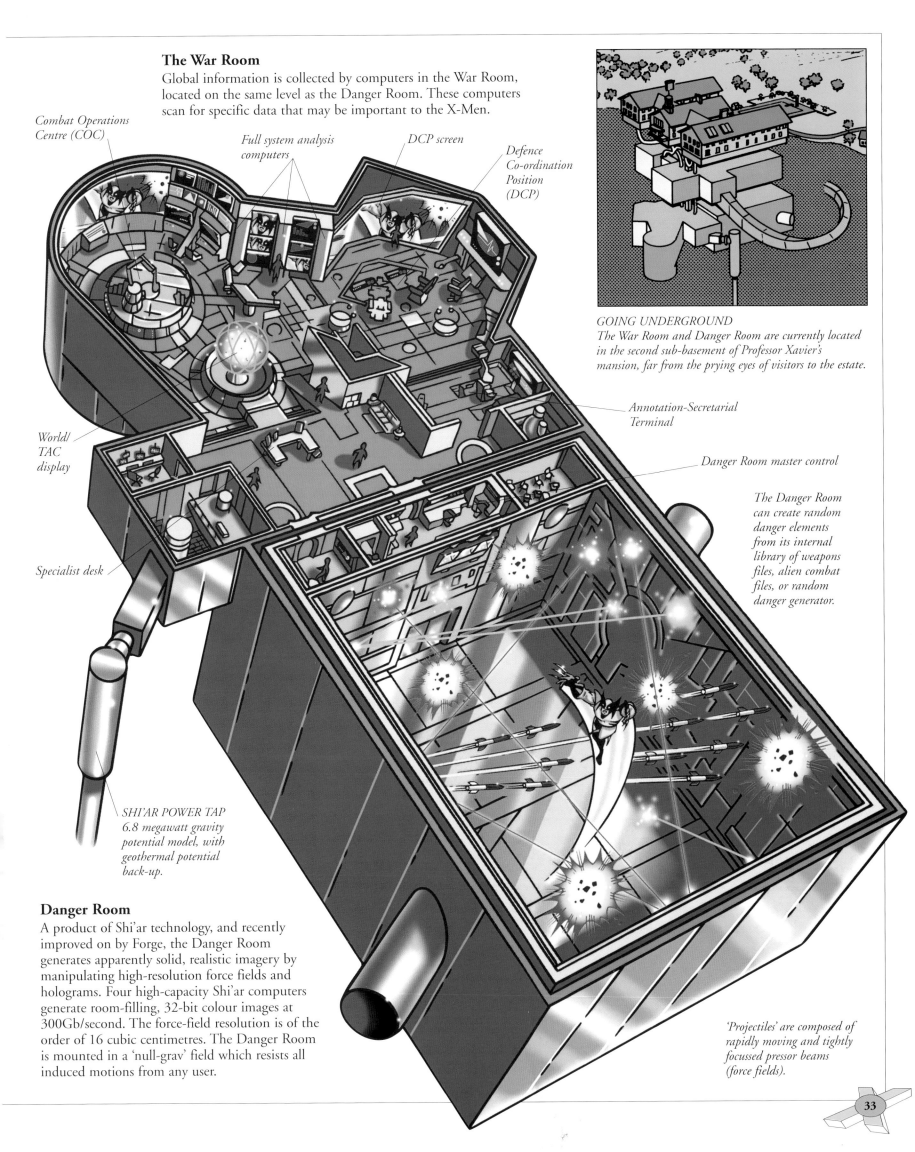

The War Room

Global information is collected by computers in the War Room, located on the same level as the Danger Room. These computers scan for specific data that may be important to the X-Men.

Combat Operations Centre (COC)

Full system analysis computers

DCP screen

Defence Co-ordination Position (DCP)

World/ TAC display

Specialist desk

SHI'AR POWER TAP 6.8 megawatt gravity potential model, with geothermal potential back-up.

Annotation-Secretarial Terminal

Danger Room master control

GOING UNDERGROUND
The War Room and Danger Room are currently located in the second sub-basement of Professor Xavier's mansion, far from the prying eyes of visitors to the estate.

The Danger Room can create random danger elements from its internal library of weapons files, alien combat files, or random danger generator.

'Projectiles' are composed of rapidly moving and tightly focused pressor beams (force fields).

Danger Room

A product of Shi'ar technology, and recently improved on by Forge, the Danger Room generates apparently solid, realistic imagery by manipulating high-resolution force fields and holograms. Four high-capacity Shi'ar computers generate room-filling, 32-bit colour images at 300Gb/second. The force-field resolution is of the order of 16 cubic centimetres. The Danger Room is mounted in a 'null-grav' field which resists all induced motions from any user.

MAGNETO

FROM THE VERY BEGINNING, Magneto, the master of magnetism, has been the X-Men's foremost adversary. Although he and Charles Xavier were once friends, Magneto now stands in direct opposition to Xavier's dream of peaceful coexistence between humans and mutants. A lifelong victim of bigotry himself, Magneto believes that mutants can only be free if they enslave the rest of the human race. In times past, Magneto used the alias Erik Magnus Lehnsherr, but his true name is a mystery. Little is known about his earliest years, but he is thought to have been born into a gypsy family in 1928. During World War II, he was imprisoned in the Nazi concentration camp at Auschwitz, where his family was slaughtered. After the war, he married a woman named Magda and had a daughter, Anya. When a mob prevented him from rescuing Anya from dying in a fire, Magneto lashed out and killed them all with his emerging mutant power to manipulate the planet's magnetic forces. Over the years, Magneto has developed this ability, making him one of the most powerful mutants alive.

Magneto's helmet gives him protection from psionic attack.

NOTHING CAN RESIST MY MATCHLESS *MAGNETIC POWER!* BY HARNESSING ONLY A *FRACTION* OF THE NATURAL MAGNETISM THAT IS MINE, I CAN RAISE THEIR ENTIRE *SCHOOL BUILDING,* ONLY TO SEND IT CRASHING DOWN IN *RUINS!*

Magneto has the mutant ability to control magnetism and other related electromagnetic forces. As such, he can lift and move enormous objects, control ferrous particles in the atmosphere, and has even attempted to alter the magnetic field of the Earth!

THE WAR WITH XAVIER

Terrified by Magneto's powers, Magda deserted him, without divulging that she was pregnant with twins (now known as the Super Heroes Quicksilver and the Scarlet Witch). Devastated by the loss of his wife and child, Magneto made his way to Israel, where he befriended Charles Xavier. But it was there, embittered by his tragic experiences in Europe, that Magneto became convinced that mutants could only survive if they took control of the planet. Decades later, he launched a terrorist war against the human race, only to be repeatedly thwarted by Xavier and his X-Men. Through a strange series of events, Magneto was rejuvenated, and instead of possessing the body of an elderly man, he appears to be in his physical prime. Recently, he won his first great victory, when the United Nations awarded him sovereignty over the island nation of Genosha. Magneto sees this as a stepping stone to world domination.

MAGNETO'S X-MEN COSTUME

Magneto in Auschwitz

Where Magneto was born remains a mystery, but he spent his childhood in the concentration camp at Auschwitz, Poland. Though his family perished there, Magneto managed to survive. The horrors he endured left him determined to use any means, however violent, to ensure that mutants never suffered a similar fate.

HE HAD BEEN HERE FROM THE START...

Magneto in shackles before the World Court.

Magneto transformed into an infant

REJUVENATION
Alpha, a mutant Magneto had genetically engineered, rebelled and used his massive psionic powers to revert Magneto into infancy. Eric the Red, an agent of the Shi'ar, later restored Magneto to the prime of adulthood. For this reason, though Magneto was alive during World War II, he now seems to be a much younger man.

The trial of Magneto

The nations of the world have long sought to capture and punish Magneto for his acts of mass murder and continual efforts at world conquest. When he was finally put on trial before the World Court, he used his powers to manipulate the mind of the chief judge into setting him free.

DON'T BE ABSURD. IT'S OUT OF OUR HANDS.

PROMISE ME, MAGNETO-- YOU'LL CARRY ON IN MY PLACE.

TAKE OVER... MY SCHOOL. LOOK AFTER MY X-MEN. TEACH THE NEW MUTANTS.

JOINING THE X-MEN
When Magneto had turned into a baby, Moira MacTaggert altered his mind so that, after returning to adulthood, he would abandon his war on humanity. Hence, when Xavier was in danger of dying, he was able to ask the reformed Magneto to take over the running of his school.

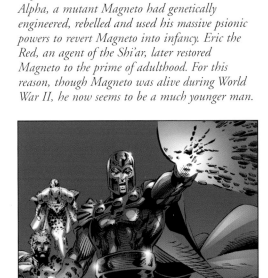

Magneto's Acolytes

In recent times, Magneto has gathered a new band of mutants, the Acolytes. They revere Magneto as the prophet of a new age in which mutants will ruthlessly use force against the human race to ensure their freedom. For a time, Magneto sheltered his Acolytes in an orbiting space station called Avalon.

ON SCREEN

As with the comic books, the *X-Men* movie version of Magneto has control over magnetic forces. He can lift cars with ease, snatch weapons out of policemen's hands and turn them back on their owners, and even halt the progress of an entire train! He is also a former friend and colleague of Charles Xavier. The two, however, have formed very different ideas about the future of humans and mutants.

Based on his experiences of the Nazi concentration camps, Magneto is determined to stop the same persecution happening to mutants. To achieve this, he has built a device which will turn humans into mutants. What he does not seem to realize is that this transformation will have fatal consequences. However, Magneto cannot power the device himself, as such an exertion would kill him. Instead, he must find another mutant to do it for him.

MINUTES LATER, THE SILENT SHIP REACHES A JAGGED ASTEROID, CIRCLING THE EARTH! BUT, UPON DRAWING NEAR, WE SEE THAT IT IS MORE THAN JUST A SIMPLE ASTEROID... MUCH, MUCH MORE!

QUICKSILVER TO ASTEROID M! REQUEST PERMISSION TO LAND! OVER!

ASTEROID M TO QUICKSILVER! PERMISSION GRANTED! FOLLOW LANDING PLAN B!

Asteroid base

The original X-Men first learned about Asteroid M when Magneto held the Angel prisoner there. Angel's team-mates reached the base by stowing away on the Toad's spaceship. In the ensuing battle with Magneto's Brotherhood, the asteroid's self-destruct system was activated. The X-Men escaped as it exploded. Magneto survived, and later rebuilt Asteroid M.

...SHOULD ALSO BE WHEN I AM MOST *VULNERABLE* TO ATTACK.

THIS SUDDEN MALFUNCTION-- COULD IT HAVE BEEN CAUSED BY THE *X-MEN?!*

IMPOSSIBLE! THERE ARE A *SCORE* OF ALARM SYSTEMS IN THE COMPLEX--ALL SET TO *GO OFF* IF THOSE CURSED MUTANTS BROKE *FREE.*

By building his Antarctic headquarters beneath a volcano, Magneto made sure that he would not receive unwanted visitors. When entering or leaving, Magneto protected himself from the heat of the lava with a bubble of magnetic force.

Fire and lava

When the X-Men fought their way out of imprisonment in Magneto's Antarctic base, the controls for the base's protective dome were destroyed in a spectacular battle. The X-Men and Magneto managed to get to safety just before the volcano exploded and flooded the complex with molten lava.

MAGNETO'S BASES

MAGNETO HAS WAGED war against the human race from secret bases in outer space and around the world. The evil mastermind has made sure that each base's location is inaccessible to non-mutants. Two of them are on islands he raised from the floor of the Atlantic Ocean. On one of them, he built a base armed with a vast magnet powerful enough to lift a ship into the air. On the other, he housed his base inside a mysterious lost city. Magneto built yet another base beneath an active volcano in Antarctica, and many of his operations were co-ordinated from a laboratory in the Savage Land itself and a mansion outside New York City. His primary base, however, was always Asteroid M, a massive rock that orbits the Earth. He regarded this location, high above the planet, as symbolic of his superiority over non-mutant humans. Magneto recently renamed his asteroid base 'Avalon', after the legendary isle on which King Arthur is said to dwell, awaiting the time when he will again return to rule his people.

FROM AVALON TO GENOSHA

Magneto saw Avalon as a haven in which mutants could live free from persecution. The asteroid base became a refuge for his Acolytes, a band of mutants who worshipped him as a saviour. But despite its remote location, Avalon was attacked and destroyed several times. Recently, after staging an attack on the Earth, Magneto won the largest and what may become the most formidable of his many bases. In a bid to make peace with Magneto, the UN granted him sovereignty over Genosha, an island nation lying off the coast of East Africa. Could this be the foundation of a new terrestrial empire for Magneto?

A kilometre beneath the crater of an active volcano, Magneto's Antarctic complex spanned five square kilometres. A ceramic-steel dome protected the complex from the intensely hot lava in the volcano above.

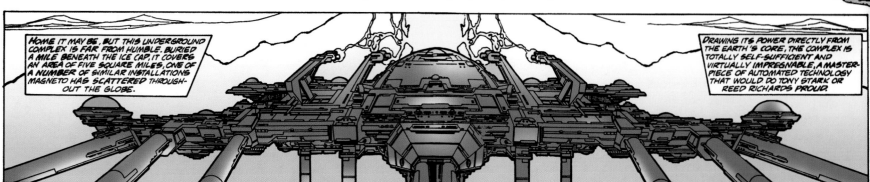

HOME IT MAY BE, BUT THIS UNDERGROUND COMPLEX IS FAR FROM HUMBLE. BURIED A MILE BENEATH THE ICE CAP, IT COVERS AN AREA OF FIVE SQUARE MILES, ONE OF A NUMBER OF SIMILAR INSTALLATIONS MAGNETO HAS SCATTERED THROUGHOUT THE GLOBE.

DRAWING ITS POWER DIRECTLY FROM THE EARTH'S CORE, THIS COMPLEX IS TOTALLY SELF-SUFFICIENT AND VIRTUALLY IMPREGNABLE, A MASTERPIECE OF AUTOMATED TECHNOLOGY THAT WOULD DO TONY STARK OR REED RICHARDS PROUD.

INTERLUDE: IN THE HEART OF THE LEGENDARY BERMUDA TRIANGLE LIES AN ISLAND RAISED FROM THE OCEAN FLOOR BY MAGNETO, MUTANT MASTER OF MAGNETISM, FOR USE AS HIS BASE.

RECENTLY, IT WAS THE SITE OF AN EPIC CONFRONTATION BETWEEN HIM AND THE X-MEN.* AFTER HIS DEFEAT...

*X-MEN *150--LOUISE.

Bermuda Triangle

Magneto's lost city base is located inside the sinister Bermuda Triangle, a region where many ships and planes have simply disappeared. Here he built a device that could trigger earthquakes and volcanic eruptions around the world. After Magneto abandoned the island, the X-Men used it as an alternative base.

Standing on one of the islands that Magneto raised from the sea is an ancient lost city. Its architecture is unlike that of any human culture. Who its architects were, whether indeed they were human, and what fate befell their civilization are all mysteries that may never be solved.

Magneto fitted Asteroid M with psionic inhibitors which neutralized Professor X's powers when he was held prisoner there.

Avalon uses Shi'ar technology stolen from the X-Men.

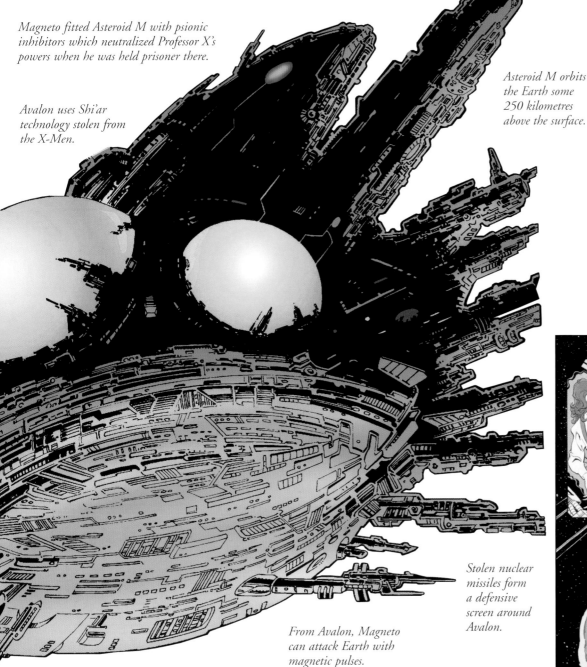

Asteroid M orbits the Earth some 250 kilometres above the surface.

Strange idols of the race that once lived there adorn Magneto's Bermuda Triangle island.

Stolen nuclear missiles form a defensive screen around Avalon.

From Avalon, Magneto can attack Earth with magnetic pulses.

The fall of Avalon

Asteroid M's enormous size made Magneto's enemies think twice before attacking it. The UN knew that if a rock that size ever fell to Earth, it would cause untold devastation across the planet. Luckily, whenever Asteroid M has been destroyed in the past, it has been smashed into small harmless pieces. Recently, Avalon was obliterated in a tremendous battle between the two mutants Exodus and Holocaust. Scott Summers and Jean Grey were aboard at the time, but escaped to safety within large sections of the base that fell to Earth. These chunks were protected from the heat of re-entering Earth's atmosphere by force fields created by two Acolytes who also survived.

BROTHERHOOD OF EVIL MUTANTS

EARLY IN HIS WAR against humanity, Magneto organized a small band of mutants to go into combat at his side. Since the world had branded him a criminal, Magneto defiantly named his team of accomplices 'The Brotherhood of Evil Mutants'. The most subservient of the group was the Toad, named both for his grotesque appearance and his superhuman leaping ability. There was also Mastermind, who could mentally create utterly convincing illusions. Lastly, there was Quicksilver, who could move at superhuman speed, and his sister, the Scarlet Witch, who could alter probability at will. Neither Magneto nor the two siblings knew at this time that he was actually their father by his estranged wife Magda.

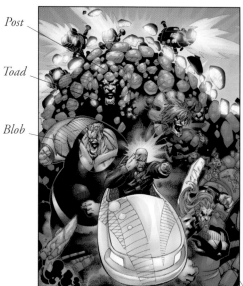

Post
Toad
Blob
Mimic

*A NEW TEAM
Mystique organized the most recent version of the Brotherhood, which included Toad, the Blob, Pyro, Mimic, and Post. At one point, this team even kidnapped Professor X to help battle a sentient version of Cerebro which was terrorizing mutants and humans.*

Making himself a leader at last, the Toad organized a short-lived Brotherhood of his own, including the Blob and Pyro, a woman named Phantazia, who could disrupt machines and super-powers, and even the reptilian Sauron.

BROTHERHOOD'S LEGACY

Time and again, the Brotherhood clashed with the original X-Men, until Magneto was captured by an extraterrestrial being known as the Stranger. Tired of Magneto's war, Quicksilver and the Scarlet Witch soon joined the Avengers Super Hero team.

Magneto later reorganized the Brotherhood three more times, adding new members such as the Blob, Unus, and Lorelei, before abandoning the concept entirely. Subsequently, the mutant terrorist Mystique formed her own Brotherhood, which she recently reactivated. Ironically, the Toad, who now bitterly hates his former master, stole Magneto's idea and also formed his own Brotherhood, but could not hold it together for long.

*MASTERMIND
Also known as Jason Wyngarde, this former carnival mentalist can psionically cast illusions, even to disguise his own appearance. He is now believed to be dead, but a woman claiming to be his daughter operates as the new Mastermind.*

*TOAD
Born in England as Mortimer Toynbee, treated as a freak since childhood, the Toad was pathetically devoted to Magneto, who contemptuously treated him as a lackey until the Toad finally turned against him.*

HOT ON HIS HEELS CHARGE HIS TEAMMATES.

BY THE NUMBERS, FREEDOM FORCE, AS I TRAINED YOU!

I WANT THIS ENDED SHORT AND SWEET.

*FREEDOM FORCE
Believing the group had become too dangerous to act as mutant terrorists, Mystique made a daring offer: the Brotherhood would operate as government agents in exchange for immunity from prosecution. Thus Mystique's Brotherhood became Freedom Force, and battled the X-Men on behalf of federal authorities. Freedom Force collapsed after an ill-fated Middle East mission.*

Destiny   Avalanche   Mystique   Pyro   Blob

Mystique's team

After Magneto's last Brotherhood collapsed, Mystique carried on its legacy by forming her own Brotherhood of Evil Mutants. Among its members were her close friend Destiny, a blind mutant who could foretell the future; Avalanche, who generates small earthquakes; Pyro, who mentally controls flame; and the X-Men's perennial foe, the Blob. They made a notorious public debut when they tried to assassinate Senator Robert Kelly, who sought to take legal action against the 'mutant menace'.

QUICKSILVER
Like his sister, Pietro Maximoff grew up in the Eastern European country of Transia. Though he resents humans' prejudice towards mutants, Quicksilver ultimately rejected Magneto's war on humanity.

SCARLET WITCH
Imbued with 'chaos-magic' at her birth, Wanda Maximoff, the Scarlet Witch, uses her mutant ability to manipulate these energies to make the most improbable events probable. She reluctantly served Magneto because he had rescued her from an anti-mutant mob.

ON SCREEN

The *X-Men* movie has its own Brotherhood of Evil Mutants, consisting of Magneto, Mystique, Sabretooth and Toad. The Toad who appears in the movie bears little resemblance to his comic-book counterpart. Although he has the bulging toad-like eyes, gone are the medieval costume he wears and the snivelling behaviour which typifies his character in the comics. Instead, the movie Toad is a very effective fighter, using his superhuman agility and leaping ability to become a powerful kickboxer. He is also able to climb sheer surfaces, a skill he shows at Westchester station and inside the Statue of Liberty. Another weapon in his arsenal is his extendible tongue which can shoot out of his mouth in the blink of an eye. He uses it to cover a target in a slimy substance that hardens quickly, as Jean Grey finds out, or it can be used to take a firm hold of something. With it, he rips off Cyclops' visor, causing devastation at the train station as Scott's force beams are uncontrollably unleashed. He also uses it to cling on to the Statue of Liberty for dear life as Storm conjures up a mini-hurricane. However, this tongue lifeline becomes the cause of his downfall, as it turns into a conduit for the lightning blast that Storm creates to blast him into the icy waters of New York Harbor.

KA-ZAR

THE ICY WASTELAND of Antarctica is the last place one would expect to find a primeval tropical jungle, much less living dinosaurs. Yet it was there that the X-Men discovered the prehistoric wilderness known as the Savage Land and its self-proclaimed guardian, the jungle lord Ka-Zar. The Savage Land was created at the behest of an enigmatic, other-dimensional race known as the Beyonders, who intended it to be a combination zoo and botanical garden. On their instructions, an alien race called the Nuwali collected specimens of Earth's fauna and flora over millions of years for this wildlife refuge. Climate-control mechanisms safeguarded the Savage Land's tropical environment from the endless winter surrounding it.

New York City zoologist Shanna O'Hara became the jungle adventurer Shanna the She-Devil. Disillusioned by civilization, Shanna moved to the Savage Land, where she married Ka-Zar and bore him a son, Matthew.

LORD OF THE JUNGLE

Lord Plunder, an English explorer, discovered the Savage Land years ago. Plunder returned there with his young son Kevin, only to be murdered by beings called the Man-Apes. As they were about to seize Kevin, the Man-Apes were attacked by a sabretooth tiger, which became the boy's protector as he grew up. Kevin named the loyal tiger Zabu, and the boy became known in the Savage Land as 'Ka-Zar', or 'Son of the Tiger'. When the X-Men first came to the Savage Land, Ka-Zar had forgotten much of the English language and behaved in an uncivilized manner. Even so, Ka-Zar became their ally, and eventually travelled to England, where he rapidly learned the ways of Western civilization. Ka-Zar later returned to the Savage Land, where he has aided the X-Men on their subsequent visits.

Sauron

On a boyhood trip to Tierra del Fuego, Karl Lykos was attacked and bitten by pterodactyls, winged reptiles that had flown from the Savage Land. Somehow the bites changed Lykos, so that he could drain the life energy from other beings. Without this life energy he could not survive. After draining life force from a mutant, Lykos metamorphosed into a predatory pterodactyl-like creature called Sauron, who now lives in the Savage Land.

The Beyonders chose one of the most inhospitable places on Earth for the Savage Land.

To South America

Savage Land and Pangea

ANTARCTICA

ANTARCTICA
The Savage Land is located on a peninsula that extends from Antarctica towards the southern tip of Chile. A long underground tunnel links the island of Tierra del Fuego to the Savage Land.

Environmental Control Equipment

Mount Flavius

Eternity Mountain Range

Shalan

Gorahn Sea

Atlantea

Mot

Zarhan

Thonos

Zuvi Land

Kazar and Shanna's home

The Savage Land
The Savage Land is separated from the rest of Antarctica by a ring of volcanoes. Alien devices create a field that refracts light, shielding the Savage Land from outside view; presumably alien machines also create artificial sunlight during the long Antarctic winter. The people of ancient Atlantis used this alien climate-control machinery to create Pangea, a much larger tropical paradise next to the Savage Land.

Prehistoric zoo
Dinosaurs still thrive in the Savage Land. The alien Nuwali have gathered specimens of plant and animal life from the beginning of the Mesozoic Era, the Age of Dinosaurs, to the end of the Pleistocene, the 'Ice Age'. Creatures from different eras inhabit different areas of the Savage Land. Dinosaurs roam the tropical interior, while woolly mammoths range along its border with Antarctica.

Thin flaps of skin form Sauron's wings.

Sauron's wing bones are extensions of his arm and finger bones.

The people of the Savage Land

Ka-Zar may be called the Lord of the Savage Land, but he makes no claim to rule its peoples. There are humans, such as the Sun People, who worship the sun god Garokk, the Fall People, led by the female chieftain Nereel, and the less civilized Swamp Men. Radiation mutated members of the Nhu-Gari race into strange, winged creatures, and there are also the Man-Apes, who resemble Neanderthal cavemen. Millennia ago, Atlantean scientists conducted genetic experiments on Man-Apes, creating the animal-like humanoid races that inhabit nearby Pangea. Since the X-Men first visited the Savage Land, its existence has become publicly known. Recognizing Ka-Zar as its representative, the United Nations has declared this paradise off limits to conquest and to commercial exploitation.

Zabu the sabretooth tiger

-- AN' SOME O' THE UGLIEST, NASTIEST MUTATES O' THEM ALL!

THERE'S OL' BARBARUS AIRIN' OUT HIS PITS ...

SLIMY AMPHIBIOUS, HOPPIN' UP A STORM ...

AN' EVEN EQUILIBRIOUS WITH HIS HOO-DOO EYES!

THEY'VE CAPTURED TWO O' THE FALL PEOPLE --

The Savage Land mutates

Magneto genetically altered some of the Savage Land natives, endowing them with superhuman powers. People who are mutated after their birth are called mutates. Led by Magneto, Zaladane, or the mutant genius Brainchild, the Savage Land Mutates have repeatedly fought the X-Men on their trips to the Savage Land. The mutates include the frog-like Amphibious, the four-armed Barbarus, Lupo, who mentally controls wolves, and Vertigo, who psionically disorientates her victims.

ZALADANE
In the 15th century, a British sailor made his way to the Savage Land after the sinking of his ship. Here he imbibed a potion that he thought would grant him immortality. And so it did, but at the price of transforming him into a living, stone-like double of Garokk, a sun god worshipped in the Savage Land. Garokk's high priestess is Zaladane, a sorceress who has made repeated efforts to conquer the entire Savage Land. She claims to be an émigré from the outside world, and has even dared to confront Magneto himself.

41

JUGGERNAUT

From the first day they met, Cain Marko was Charles' enemy. Even when they were boys, Marko was using his brute strength to bully his stepbrother.

Charles Xavier watches as Cain picks up the Ruby of Cyttorak.

THE SAGA of the Juggernaut began thousands of years ago, when eight mystical entities from other dimensions made a wager to determine which was the most powerful. Each of them decided to endow a human being with their tremendous power. These Exemplars, as the transformed humans came to be known, would plunge the Earth into war on behalf of their masters. The mystical being whose Exemplar triumphed would win the age-old contest. Many years later, when Charles Xavier was a small boy, his mother Sharon married Dr. Kurt Marko, her late husband's colleague. As soon as he moved into the Xavier mansion, Marko's son Cain began bullying the younger Charles. Cain envied and resented Charles for his intelligence, his athletic prowess, and his emerging telepathic powers. Later, while serving in the army in Korea, the two brothers discovered a temple dedicated to Cyttorak, one of the eight mystical entities. Here Cain was transformed into the Exemplar known as Juggernaut, only to be buried alive as the cave collapsed around him.

EVIL STEPBROTHER

But Juggernaut did not die. Years later he returned to make his first attempt to kill his stepbrother and the X-Men who defended him. Not being a mutant himself, deriving his power from the magic of Cyttorak instead, Cain possesses seemingly unlimited physical strength and is nearly invulnerable to injury, even without the protective force fields he can create around himself. Once Juggernaut starts moving, nothing seems able to stop him. His only weak spot is his mind, so he wears a 'psionic helmet', constructed from a mystical metal, to protect himself from telepathic attack. Although he remains one of the X-Men's greatest enemies, Juggernaut sometimes finds himself on the side of good. Indeed, he has even defied Cyttorak and thwarted the other seven Exemplars' efforts to take control of the world.

The Ruby of Cyttorak

While they were soldiers in Korea, Cain deserted under fire, and Charles followed to bring him back. Inside a cave, Cain found the long-hidden temple of Cyttorak. Marko seized a ruby from the lap of an idol and read the inscription on it: 'Whosoever touches this gem shall possess the power of the Crimson Bands of Cyttorak. Henceforth, you who read these words shall become forevermore a human juggernaut.' As Xavier watched in horror, the ruby transformed Marko into the monstrous Juggernaut.

ACHILLES' HEEL
When Juggernaut first encountered the X-Men, he easily broke through the many defences they had erected around Xavier's mansion. Nor could the X-Men themselves do anything to stop his advance. Their only hope lay in exposing Juggernaut to Professor X's mental bolts. Finally, with the help of another Super Hero, the Human Torch, the X-Men succeeded in tearing off the psionic helmet that shielded Juggernaut's mind.

Unstoppable Juggernaut

Once Juggernaut begins walking in any direction, virtually no known force can halt his advance. Not only have Cyttorak's magic energies made him almost indestructible, but Juggernaut can also surround himself with an impenetrable force field. And with his enormous strength, he can smash through any obstacle in his path, even under a hail of bullets!

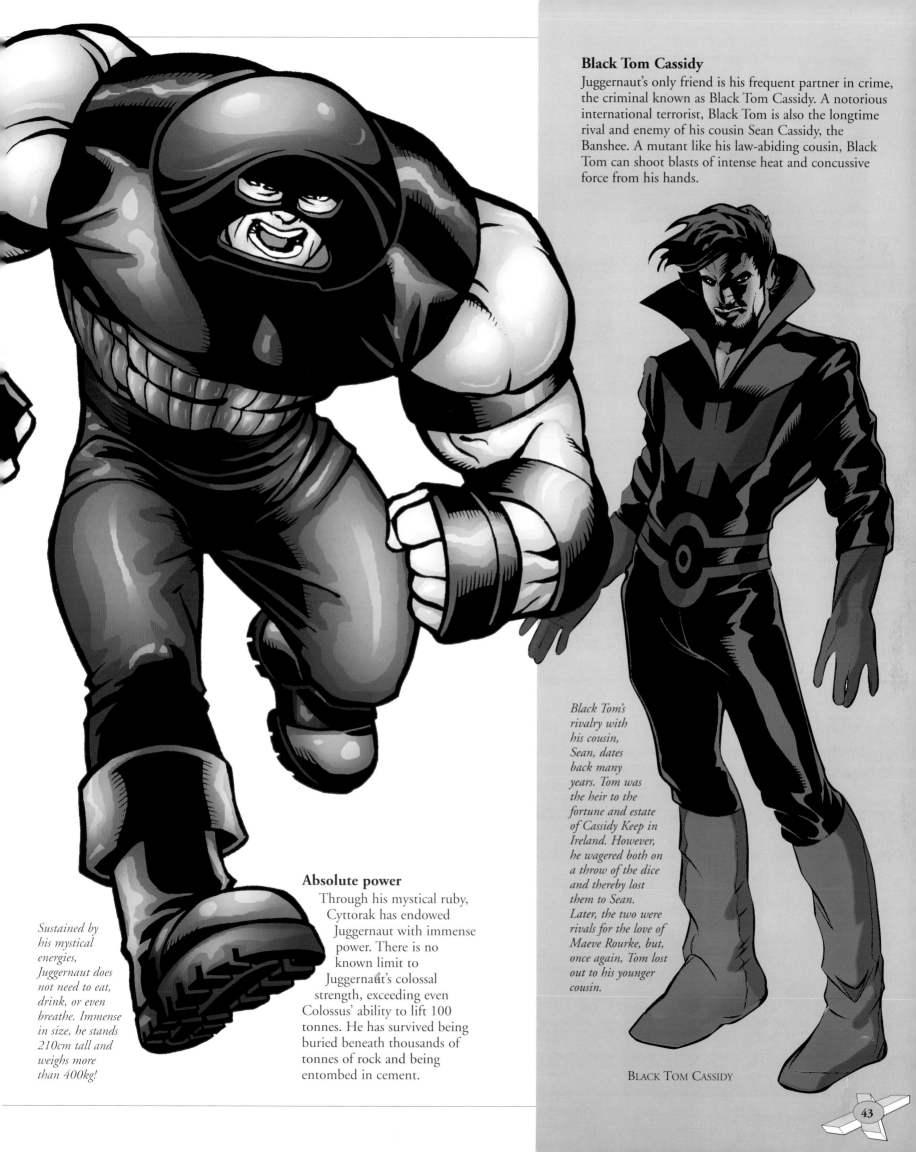

Juggernaut's only friend is his frequent partner in crime, the criminal known as Black Tom Cassidy. A notorious international terrorist, Black Tom is also the longtime rival and enemy of his cousin Sean Cassidy, the Banshee. A mutant like his law-abiding cousin, Black Tom can shoot blasts of intense heat and concussive force from his hands.

Black Tom's rivalry with his cousin, Sean, dates back many years. Tom was the heir to the fortune and estate of Cassidy Keep in Ireland. However, he wagered both on a throw of the dice and thereby lost them to Sean. Later, the two were rivals for the love of Maeve Rourke, but, once again, Tom lost out to his younger cousin.

BLACK TOM CASSIDY

Absolute power

Through his mystical ruby, Cyttorak has endowed Juggernaut with immense power. There is no known limit to Juggernaut's colossal strength, exceeding even Colossus' ability to lift 100 tonnes. He has survived being buried beneath thousands of tonnes of rock and being entombed in cement.

Sustained by his mystical energies, Juggernaut does not need to eat, drink, or even breathe. Immense in size, he stands 210cm tall and weighs more than 400kg!

43

THE SENTINELS

D R. BOLIVAR TRASK feared that mutants would someday rule the human race. That fear led him to create the Sentinels, immense robots that would hunt down mutants. Ironically, Trask himself was the father of two mutants: Tanya, who had the ability to travel through time, and became known as Sanctity, and Larry, who had the ability to see into the future. Dr. Trask created an amulet that suppressed Larry's mutant power. Trask first created a prototype, the Master Mold, and then the Mark I Sentinels. But

The world first learned of the Sentinels when Bolivar Trask unveiled them on television, only to be struck down and captured by them during the live telecast.

the Sentinels' logic led them to decide that they could best protect humanity by taking control of it. So they rebelled against Trask and made him their prisoner. Trask realized, to his horror, that it was he who had created the real threat to humanity. He therefore sacrificed his life by triggering an explosion that destroyed the Master Mold and the Sentinels. Blaming the X-Men for his father's death, Larry built the Mark II Sentinels. These could analyze any threat and determine how best to counter it, making them nearly invincible. But when his amulet was removed, the Sentinels identified Larry as a mutant and turned on him. He was killed during the battle in which the Mark II Sentinels were also destroyed.

HAND WEAPONS
A Sentinel's immense size alone makes it an overwhelming threat. But each one is also a living arsenal, which can fire destructive bolts from its hands. The Sentinels' hands can also shoot jets of knockout gas or hot steam or even unleash metal tendrils to ensnare fleeing mutants.

LETHAL VISION
If a Sentinel sees an opponent, it can destroy him simply by firing laser-like force beams from its eyes. Larry Trask's Mark II Sentinels could also spray jets of liquid nitrogen from their eyes that froze their targets on contact.

CLASSIC SENTINEL DESIGN
Most Sentinels follow Bolivar and Larry Trask's basic design. Standing over nine metres tall, the Sentinels' size and strength make them fearsome adversaries.

Human and mutant all-band spectrum organic analyzer and receiving antennae

Sensor platform and navigational unit

Liquid nitrogen spray nozzle (in eye)

Neck articulation

Central processing unit

Shoulder joint

Electric motors (muscle stimulators)

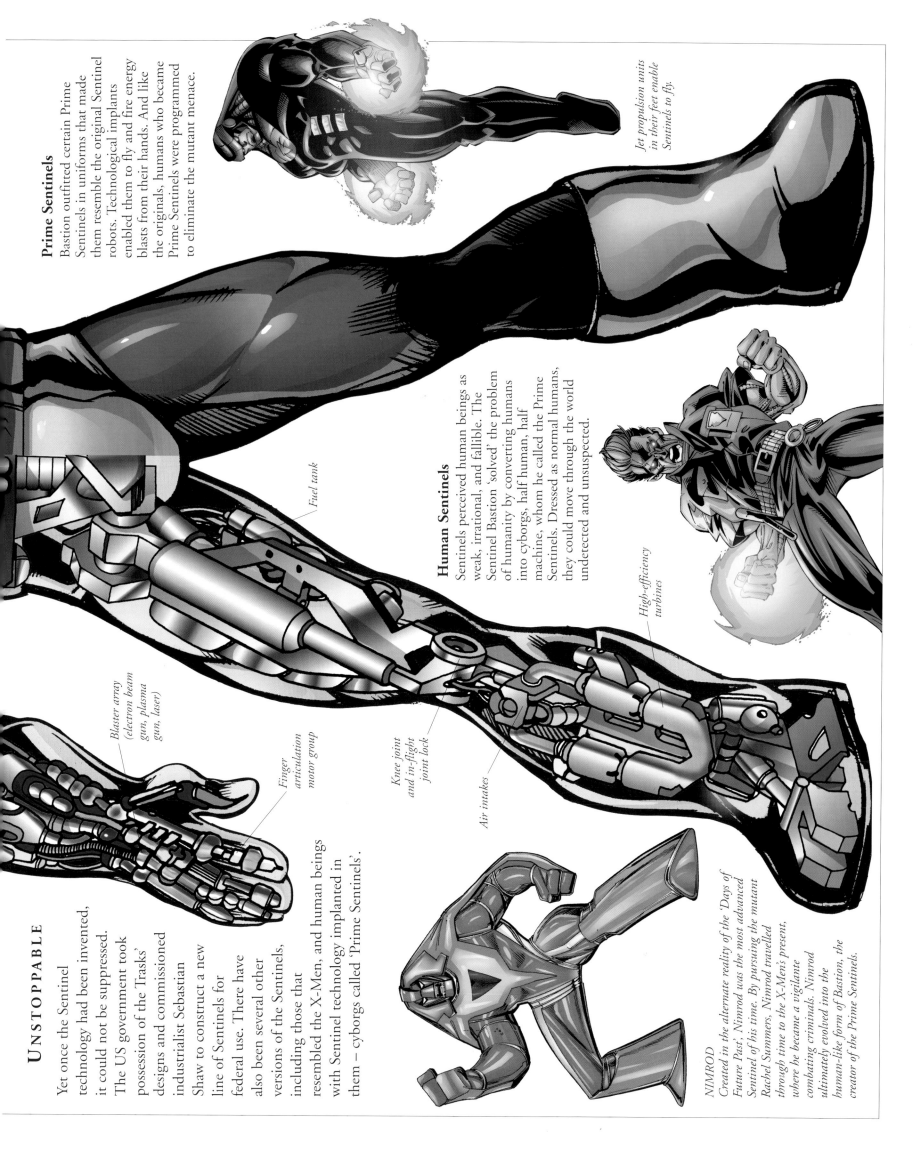

UNSTOPPABLE

Yet once the Sentinel technology had been invented, it could not be suppressed. The US government took possession of the Trasks' designs and commissioned industrialist Sebastian Shaw to construct a new line of Sentinels for federal use. There have also been several other versions of the Sentinels, including those that resembled the X-Men, and human beings with Sentinel technology implanted in them – cyborgs called 'Prime Sentinels'.

Blaster array (electron beam gun, plasma gun, laser)

Finger articulation motor group

Fuel tank

Knee joint and in-flight joint lock

Air intakes

Prime Sentinels

Bastion outfitted certain Prime Sentinels in uniforms that made them resemble the original Sentinel robots. Technological implants enabled them to fly and fire energy blasts from their hands. And like the originals, humans who became Prime Sentinels were programmed to eliminate the mutant menace.

Jet propulsion units in their feet enable Sentinels to fly.

Human Sentinels

Sentinels perceived human beings as weak, irrational, and fallible. The Sentinel Bastion 'solved' the problem of humanity by converting humans into cyborgs, half human, half machine, whom he called the Prime Sentinels. Dressed as normal humans, they could move through the world undetected and unsuspected.

High-efficiency turbines

NIMROD
Created in the alternate reality of the 'Days of Future Past', Nimrod was the most advanced Sentinel of this time. By pursuing the mutant Rachel Summers, Nimrod travelled through time to the X-Men's present, where he became a vigilante combating criminals. Nimrod ultimately evolved into the human-like form of Bastion, the creator of the Prime Sentinels.

MIMIC

CALVIN RANKIN, also known as Mimic, was the first non-mutant to join the X-Men. When he was young, Rankin accidentally inhaled an unknown chemical in his father's laboratory, which gave him the ability to copy the features and abilities of any other person. At that time, Rankin could only retain those features and abilities as long as he remained within a certain distance of the person he had 'mimicked'. At first, Mimic was the X-Men's enemy, but he later forced them into accepting him as a member until Xavier expelled him for his arrogance. Since then, Mimic has sometimes been a hero and sometimes a villain: recently he found refuge with the British Super Hero team Excalibur, but then left them to join the new Brotherhood of Evil Mutants.

MIMIC

Mimic copies Angel's wings, Cyclops' eye beams, and the Beast's large hands and feet.

A one-man team

When Mimic met the original X-Men, he gained all of their powers. He grew wings just like Angel, mimicked Beast's large hands and feet, and wore a ruby quartz visor to contain the eye beams he copied from Cyclops. He has also copied Colossus' organic metal body and even Nightcrawler's prehensile tail. Later, Mimic's powers increased so that he could retain the abilities he copied from mutants, even when he was far away from them.

CHANGELING

THE FIRST OF THE X-MEN to die in action, the Changeling is an enigma to this day. He had the mutant ability to alter his physical appearance, costume, and voice to imitate any other human being, but his true identity remains unknown. He was once the second-in-command of Factor Three, an organization of mutants bent on world conquest. Ultimately, though, he aided the X-Men in defeating the conspiracy's leader, the Mutant Master, who turned out to be an extraterrestrial being. But then the Changeling discovered that he was dying. Wishing to atone for the sins of his past, the Changeling sought out Charles Xavier, who had a task for the penitent mutant.

CHANGELING

Xavier's double

Xavier asked the Changeling to impersonate him while he secretly prepared a defence against alien invaders called the Z'nox. As Xavier, the Changeling died heroically, helping the X-Men stop their enemy Grotesk from destroying the planet. Wearing another man's face, the Changeling had found redemption at last.

POLARIS

WHEN LORNA DANE was growing up, she was careful to hide the only sign that made her different from other girls: she dyed her green hair brown. But her life changed shortly after she first met Iceman. The mutant criminal Mesmero captured Lorna and placed her in a machine that activated her latent mutant power to control magnetic forces. She then met Magneto, who claimed she was his daughter. However, Iceman discovered that Lorna's real parents had died in a plane crash when she was a baby. Once he told Lorna this, she teamed up with the X-Men against Mesmero. As for the 'Magneto' she had met, he later turned out to be an android constructed by the criminal Starr Saxon, who had hoped to trick Lorna into serving him.

Early on, Lorna tried out the code name 'Magnetrix' – but quickly discarded it!

This regal costume suited Lorna's role as 'Magneto's heir'.

Lorna no longer hides her green hair.

Polaris wore this uniform in the US government's X-Factor.

Since X-Factor's collapse, Lorna has returned to her green costume.

QUEST FOR HAVOK
Recently Lorna has been searching for the missing Havok, unaware that he has been transported to the 'Mutant X' alternate Earth.

Using magnetic powers, Polaris can fly.

A TEAM PLAYER

Lorna was attracted to Iceman, but she fell in love with Alex Summers, alias Havok. She and Alex worked with the X-Men for a while, but they eventually left to pursue graduate studies in geophysics. Later, Lorna, now using the code name Polaris, and Havok returned to become full-time members of the X-Men. Then Lorna briefly fell under the mental possession of the evil entity, Malice. The Savage Land sorceress Zaladane, who claimed to be Lorna's sister, broke Malice's hold over her, but stole Polaris' magnetic powers. After regaining these powers, Polaris served alongside Havok in the second version of the mutant team X-Factor.

Villains' pawn

Time and again the X-Men's enemies have tried to seize control of Lorna and her mutant magnetic powers. First, there was Mesmero's attempt to convince her that she was Magneto's daughter. Later, Eric the Red, an agent of the alien Shi'ar, brainwashed her into attacking the X-Men. He gave Lorna this Shi'ar costume and the code name 'Polaris'. After she regained her free will, she decided to keep both.

Warring sisters

The next villain to take control of Lorna's mind was Malice, a member of the Marauders, who exists as a disembodied mind. Zaladane inadvertently freed Lorna from Malice while stealing her alleged sister's powers. But after Zaladane was seemingly slain by Magneto, Lorna regained her stolen powers.

HAVOK

SEPARATED AFTER their parents' disappearance, Scott Summers and his brother Alex grew up apart. Unlike Scott, Alex showed no sign of being a mutant until he was captured by Ahmet Abdol, an Egyptian mutant who was worshipped as the Living Pharaoh. Alex proved to have the ability to discharge waves of force and heat, turning the air in its path into super-heated plasma. The Pharaoh discovered that Alex gained this power by absorbing cosmic rays. He imprisoned Alex in a coffin-like device that cut him off from the ambient cosmic radiation. As a consequence, the Pharaoh began absorbing the energy instead, transforming himself into the Living Monolith. Alex broke free, causing the Monolith to revert to helpless human form, but they were both captured by the Sentinels. The robots' master, Larry Trask, gave Alex the code name Havok and imprisoned him in a cell with another mutant, Lorna Dane. And so Havok met the woman with whom he fell in love.

STUDY BREAK

Havok and Lorna worked with the X-Men for a time, but moved to the Rio Diablo mountains of Arizona to do research work for their graduate studies in geophysics. Eventually they returned to their lives as costumed adventurers, first as fully fledged members of the X-Men and then in the government's revamped version of X-Factor.

Havok fires a blast of plasma at a doomed Sentinel robot.

Living Monolith
Alex's power somehow limited the abilities of the Living Pharaoh. By imprisoning Alex and blocking cosmic rays from reaching his body, the Pharaoh could attain the full extent of his own powers.

ICEMAN

BRUTE

MARVEL
WOMAN

THE FALLEN

MUTANT X
Havok was transported to a parallel Earth where he joined the Six, a team of mutants like the X-Men, but with a difference. They include Marvel Woman (Madelyne Pryor), The Brute (Hank McCoy), Bloodstorm (Ororo Munroe), The Fallen (Warren Worthington III), and Iceman (Bobby Drake).

BLOODSTORM

Chest display shows how much cosmic energy Havok has absorbed.

While trying to revamp X-Factor, Alex was seemingly killed in an explosion. He was, however, thrown into the reality of a parallel Earth where he became Mutant X, leader of the Six.

SUMMERS FAMILY TREE

BOTH ACCORDING to the science of the Victorian biologist Sinister in the past and to the prophecies of the Askani Sisterhood in the far future, the family of Scott Summers, better known as Cyclops, is destined for greatness. Within the Summers' bloodline lies the genetic potential for extraordinary mutant powers. But more importantly, the Summers family consists of a long line of heroes.

Scott's paternal grandparents, Philip and Deborah Summers, are both still alive, and run a small air transport service from Anchorage, Alaska.

Their son, Christopher, became a major in the United States Air Force. He and his wife Katherine Ann had two sons, Scott and Alexander.

Scott's first wife was Madelyne Pryor, a clone of Jean Grey created by Sinister. Their son, Nathan Christopher Summers, was transported two thousand years into the future, where he grew up to become the mutant warrior Cable. Nathan married a fellow freedom fighter, Aliya, and they had a son, Tyler.

Christopher later became Corsair, the leader of the interstellar freedom fighters known as the Starjammers.

Scott and Alex are the first known mutants in the Summers family. Scott became Cyclops, and Alex is now known as Havok. (Sinister has hinted that there is a third Summers brother, but there is as yet no evidence of this.)

Through one of the strange twists in time that run through the family's history, Scott Summers may have been responsible for its very beginning in 19th-century London. The scientist Nathaniel Essex, who would later be known as Sinister, kept unfortunates suffering from genetic deformations imprisoned in cells in his home as unwilling subjects for his experiments. Among them was a young orphan named Daniel who was mistakenly believed to be abnormal. Scott Summers and Jean Grey journeyed back in time to the London of 1859, where Jean helped free Daniel and other captives from Essex's cells. The following year Daniel and his older friend Oscar Stamp emigrated to New York City, posing as a son and his father. Oscar suggested they choose a new last name for themselves. Impressed by the kindness of Jean and Scott, Daniel took the name Summers.

Cable's genetic inheritance from Scott and Madelyne is shared by his own clone, the terrorist Stryfe.

Scott married Jean Grey, who herself was a mutant carrying tremendous genetic potential. Although her parents, John and Elaine, and her sister Sara are not mutants, Sara's daughter Gailyn and son Joey may prove to be.

The saga of the Summers family grows even more complicated when one considers the Summers of alternate realities. In the timeline of the 'Days of Future Past', Scott and Jean had a daughter, Rachel Summers, who later travelled into the far future and became the cult leader Mother Askani.

In the 'Age of Apocalypse' timeline, Sinister used genetic material from Scott and Jean to create Nate Grey, alias X-Man, perhaps the most powerful mutant alive.

In the Mutant X timeline, Havok and Madelyne Pryor married and had a son named Scotty.

Key

———	Present
———	Days of Future Past
———	Age of Apocalypse
———	Mutant X
– – –	Clones

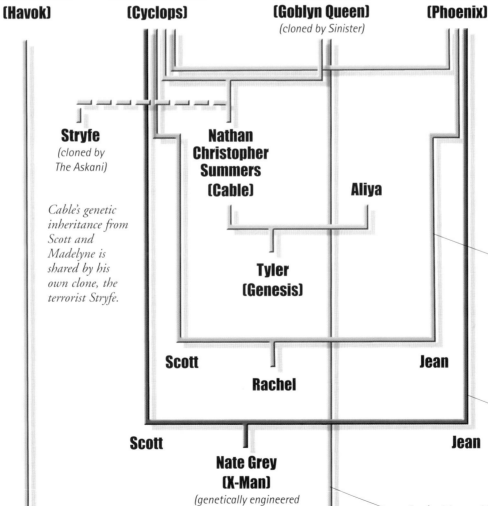

OTHER '60s VILLAINS

B Y FORMING THE ORIGINAL X-MEN, one of Charles Xavier's goals was to organize a team of young mutants who would oppose mutants who did not believe in peaceful coexistence with 'normal' human beings, but used their powers to menace society. These mutants fanned the flames of human bigotry towards the entire mutant race of *Homo superior*. Magneto and his band of criminals, known as the Brotherhood of Evil Mutants, were the most notorious of these criminals, but there were others as well, including the Vanisher, the Blob, Unus the Untouchable, and Mesmero. Xavier rescued Scott Summers from another mutant called the Living Diamond, before recruiting Cyclops into the X-Men. Then there was the Maha Yogi, a millennia-old mutant who had used his psionic powers to impersonate the magician Merlin, and the Living Pharaoh, who drew on cosmic rays to become the colossal mutant known as the Living Monolith. Others were not mutants but members of entirely non-human races. Grotesk, for example, was the survivor of an extinct race of humanoid Subterraneans.

ALIENS AND HUMANS

There were also extraterrestrial adversaries for the X-Men to battle. These included Lucifer and the all-powerful Stranger, who kidnapped Magento and the Toad and took them to his alien museum as mutant exhibits. There was also the octopus-like Mutant Master, and the alien race of Z'nox. Finally, some human beings could prove as malevolent as the evil mutants: the crimelord Count Luchino Nefaria; Sauron, a man transformed into a pterodactyl; El Tigre, who gained the Mayan god Kukulcan's powers; and even the Locust, who used genetic engineering to create colossal insects.

Eventually, Unus lost control of his power and seemingly suffocated to death within his own force field.

Blob

When he first met the X-Men, Fred J. Dukes was performing as 'the Blob' in a travelling carnival. Far from being soft and flabby, this obese mutant is superhumanly strong and nearly invulnerable. His huge body can even absorb cannon fire without harm. The Blob can make himself almost immovable at will by exerting enough gravitational force to bind himself to the ground.

WOW! HE'S TOSSIN' THE SHELLS AWAY JUST BY EXPAND-ING HIS CHEST!!

NEVER SAW ANY-THING *LIKE* IT! THE BLOB HAS A BODY LIKE SILLY PUTTY!! HE CAN DO *ANYTHING*!

Grotesk

Grotesk was once the prince of a race of subterranean beings. After a nuclear test wiped out his people and distorted his mind and body, Grotesk vowed revenge on all surface dwellers. Using a stolen device, he started to set off earthquakes. When Changeling, impersonating Charles Xavier, tried to stop him, Grotesk overloaded the machine. It exploded, killing Changeling, and the defeated Grotesk returned to his kingdom.

BUT, IT MAY *ALREADY* BE TOO LATE, FOR...

AWAY, HUMAN WORM! NO ONE SHALL STOP MY FATAL PLAN! NO ONE!!

NO... STOP!! THERE'S NO NEED FOR YOU TO WANT TO SEE THE EARTH *DESTROYED*! NO *REASON*..!

Grotesk was once known as Prince Gor-Tok.

Unus the Untouchable

The costumed wrestler Unus the Untouchable used his mutant ability to surround himself with an impenetrable force field to become a virtually unstoppable thief. The X-Men first encountered Unus when Beast was involved in a wrestling match against him. Even with Hank's acrobatic ability, he could not harm the untouchable mutant. Instead, he had to watch as his blows were simply deflected by Unus.

Vanisher

Police were helpless against the Vanisher, a mutant who could teleport himself from one place to reappear miles away. Climaxing in a spectacular one-man crime wave, the Vanisher stole defence plans from the Pentagon and brazenly appeared on the White House lawn to demand ransom. Only Professor X was able to stop him by wiping out the Vanisher's memory of his own powers.

Mesmero once briefly performed a hypnotism act in New York City.

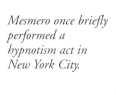

The alien race the Arcane have allegedly 'terminated' Lucifer.

Mesmero

The green-skinned mutant Mesmero wields superhuman hypnotic abilities that enable him to force his victims to do anything he commands. When he first clashed with the X-Men, Mesmero captured Lorna Dane and helped trick her into believing that she was Magneto's daughter. Mesmero once even mesmerized the X-Men into becoming performers in his travelling circus. Mesmero need only establish eye contact for a few seconds to put most people under his hypnotic control; those with strong wills can resist for only a few moments. Mesmero can give his victims a new, false set of memories and even radically alter their personalities.

Lucifer

The adversary whom the X-Men know as Lucifer was actually the advance agent for an impending invasion by his alien race, the Arcane. Lucifer crippled Charles Xavier when they first clashed. Years later, when he sought to enslave Earth, Lucifer finally met defeat at the hands of the X-Men.

THE X-MEN IN THE 1970s

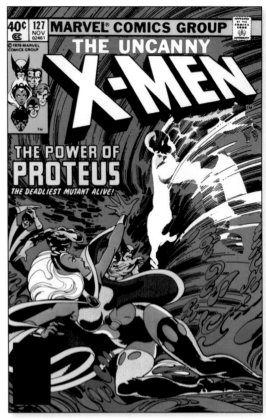

The Uncanny X-Men #127 (November 1979)
Storm against Proteus
(Cover art by John Byrne and Terry Austin)

ALTHOUGH THE ROY THOMAS-NEAL ADAMS-TOM PALMER issues of *X-Men* have long been regarded as classics, they came too late to save the series. Based on the sales of the issues before Adams' arrival, *X-Men* was cancelled with issue 66 in 1970. However, Marvel was determined to keep the X-Men alive. Only nine months after the cancellation, the *X-Men* comic returned, reprinting stories from the past. The X-Men also continued to appear as 'guest stars' in other Marvel series. Meanwhile, Marvel tinkered with the X-Men concept. In *Marvel Team-Up* issue 4, for example, the X-Men went into action in everyday clothing. The Beast was spun off into his own series in *Amazing Adventures*, in which he was given a radical makeover, becoming furry and more animalistic.

Roy Thomas came up with the idea of a new international team of X-Men. On Thomas' suggestion, writer Len Wein and artist Herb Trimpe (following a design by John Romita, Sr.) introduced Wolverine in *Incredible Hulk* issue 180, intending him as a potential future X-Man. Wein and artist Dave Cockrum then created the 'new' X-Men, who made their debut in 1975 in *Giant-Size X-Men* issue 1, intended as the first of a series of double-sized comics. That, however, was not to be. With the very next story, *X-Men* returned to the standard format, picking up the original series numbering with issue 92 (the reprints had ended with 91). More significantly, Wein turned over the scripting of the *X-Men* to a new Marvel writer, Chris Claremont. Thus began Claremont's 17-year run as writer of the *X-Men*, a record yet to be matched. The Claremont-Cockrum team quickly drew notice from discerning comic book readers of the time, introducing strong science fiction elements and intriguing character development. After two years Cockrum left to be succeeded by a newly rising talent, John Byrne, who had been working with Claremont on the martial arts series *Iron Fist*. Together Claremont, Byrne, and inker Terry Austin created a thrillingly dramatic, graphically brilliant, and highly literate run of issues that are still landmarks of the genre today. And the series fittingly changed its name to *The Uncanny X-Men*.

X-Men #104 (April 1977)
'New' X-Men against Magneto
(Cover art by Dave Cockrum)

1970

X-Men #66 (March 1970)
Final issue of original series
(Cover art by Marie Severin)

1972

Amazing Adventures #11 (March 1972)
Appearance of furry Beast
(Cover art by Tom Sutton)

1975

X-Men #94 (Aug. 1975)
First issue of new X-Men and first script written by Chris Claremont
(Cover art by Gil Kane)

Giant-Size X-Men #1 (1975)
First appearance of new X-Men
(Cover art by Gil Kane)

X-Men #64
(January 1970)
First appearance of Sunfire
(Cover art by Don Heck
and Tom Palmer)

1976

X-Men #98
(April 1976)
Sentinels against
new X-Men
(Cover art by

1978

X-Men #114 (Oct. 1978)
'The Day the X-Men Died'
(Cover art by John Byrne
and Terry Austin)

1979

Uncanny X-Men #117
(January 1978)
'Psi-War'
(Cover art by John
Byrne and Terry Austin)

REJECTED PHOENIX COSTUME

APPROVED PHOENIX COSTUME

VARIATIONS ON PHOENIX
Here are two sketches that Dave Cockrum did of possible Phoenix costumes. The rejected costume looks more otherworldly, but the final design is stronger in its simplicity.

Nightcrawler
Writer Len Wein intended Nightcrawler to be a grim, melancholy character, brooding over his demonic appearance. Chris Claremont, though, sided with artist Dave Cockrum in having Nightcrawler not only accept his mutant form but revel in his acrobatic prowess.

KURT AND ORORO
This is a sketch of Nightcrawler and Storm that their co-creator Dave Cockrum did as a gift for Chris Claremont.

THE STARJAMMER

The Starjammer
Dave Cockrum and Chris Claremont's shared interest in science fiction led to the X-Men's adventures in space during Cockrum's two stints as *X-Men* artist. Cockrum designed the Starjammers, a band of space pirates. This is his design for their starship, the Starjammer.

Face beneath the mask

Oddly, Wolverine was not shown unmasked in his initial appearances. Moreover, his co-creator Len Wein intended Wolverine to be a teenager! Speculating on what Wolverine looked like beneath his mask, John Byrne drew this sketch.

WOLVERINE UNMASKED
It was Dave Cockrum who designed Wolverine's face, one of the most distinctive in Super Hero comics. This is John Byrne's interpretation of Cockrum's design. Note how Wolverine's hair echoes the 'horns' of his mask.

POLARIS BY BYRNE
Captured and hypnotized by Eric the Red, an agent of the alien Shi'ar, Lorna Dane acquired the code name Polaris and an alien Shi'ar costume, designed by artist Dave Cockrum.

POLARIS BY
MARC
SILVESTRI

CHANGING FACES – 1970s

AS THE 1970S BEGAN, the X-Men discovered that Charles Xavier was still alive; he had been in seclusion preparing to combat an alien race, the Z'nox. Only an issue after the X-Men bested these invaders, the original *X-Men* series came to an end. The X-Men remained together, though most of their adventures during this period would not be recounted until decades later, in *X-Men: The Hidden Years*.

In *Giant-Size X-Men* issue 1, published in 1975, there came perhaps the most important turning point in X-Men history. Except for Cyclops, who escaped, all of Xavier's X-Men were held prisoner by the largest mutant they have ever encountered: Krakoa, the Living Island. Xavier travelled the world to recruit a new team of X-Men to go to his students' rescue: Banshee from Ireland, Sunfire from Japan, Thunderbird from the American Southwest, and Wolverine from Canada. The newcomers succeeded in freeing the original team. But except for Cyclops, Xavier's longtime students left the school to seek their own destinies. This new line-up was very different from the old one: they had different national and racial backgrounds, some were adults, and several did not fit easily into the team. Sunfire soon quit, the impetuous Thunderbird perished on their second mission, and Wolverine proved capable of going into a berserker rage at the least provocation. Following a battle in space against the Sentinels, Jean Grey seemed to be transformed, gaining vastly increased powers and calling herself Phoenix. Soon after, Lilandra, an alien princess, sought Xavier's help against her brother, the ruler of the Shi'ar galaxy. In response, the X-Men journeyed far into space, and Phoenix used her immense powers to save the entire universe from annihilation.

In combat with Magneto at his Antarctic base, Phoenix became separated from the other X-Men. Thinking them dead, she informed Xavier, who left Earth and became Lilandra's consort on her throneworld. Phoenix journeyed through Europe, where she began falling under the mental influence of the mutant Mastermind. However, the other X-Men had survived and took a long route home through the Savage Land, Japan (where Wolverine fell in love with a woman named Mariko), and Canada, where they fought against Alpha Flight. Phoenix and the X-Men were soon reunited in Scotland, all unaware of the tragedy that Mastermind would soon bring about.

COLOSSUS

A GIANT OF A MAN, the Russian Piotr Nikolaievitch Rasputin would deserve the name 'Colossus' even if he were an ordinary human being. However Peter, as he is known in English, is a mutant who can transform his body into an organic substance that resembles living steel, gaining superhuman strength and near-invulnerability in the process. Despite his extraordinary powers, Peter Rasputin preferred to live on a collective farm in Siberia with his parents and his beloved little sister, Illyana. It was here that Professor Xavier met him and persuaded him to join his new international team of X-Men. Young and idealistic, Colossus remained a loyal member of the X-Men for many years, finding romance with his team-mate Kitty Pryde, alias Shadowcat, and a new vocation as a gifted amateur painter.

--ENERGY RELEASED IN A MOST ASTONISH-ING MANNER!

--THE VERY AIR AROUND HIM CRACKLING WITH THE ENERGY OF HIS EXERTION--

--AND, WITHOUT HESITATION, PETER RASPUTIN IS RUN-NING, LEGS PUMPING, HEART POUNDING--

LOSS OF FAITH

However, Colossus lost faith in Xavier's dream of peaceful coexistence with humanity when Illyana succumbed to the Legacy Virus, a lethal genetic disease that strikes down mutants. Angry and frustrated, Colossus turned to Xavier's enemy Magneto and joined his band of mutant Acolytes for a time. But Colossus could not accept their ruthless methods and found refuge with his friends Kitty and Nightcrawler in the British mutant team Excalibur, before all three of them finally returned to the X-Men, where they belong.

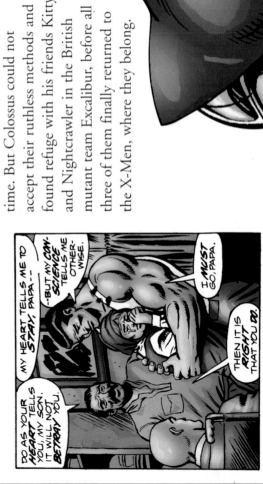

DO AS YOUR *HEART* TELLS YOU, MY SON. IT WILL NOT *BETRAY* YOU.

MY *HEART* TELLS ME TO *STAY*, PAPA--

--BUT MY *CON-SCIENCE* TELLS ME OTHER-WISE.

I *MUST* GO, PAPA.

THEN IT IS *RIGHT* THAT YOU *GO*.

JOINING THE X-MEN
Peter was happy living on a collective farm in Siberia with his family, who knew about his superhuman powers. But Charles Xavier persuaded Peter that it was his duty to join the X-Men and use his powers for the good of the entire world.

Metal man

At will, Peter Rasputin can convert his body into organic steel, making him nearly impervious to injury. He can survive an explosion of more than 200kg of TNT unharmed, and he can withstand heat of up to 5,000°C. It is believed that above this temperature his armoured body might begin to melt!

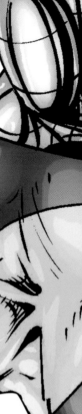

When Colossus transforms, even his eyes turn into organic steel, making them hard enough to survive the impact of a .45 calibre bullet!

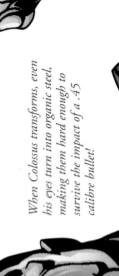

Peter, in his normal, un-armoured form, is still a giant of a man, standing 198cm tall and weighing in at a hefty 114kg!

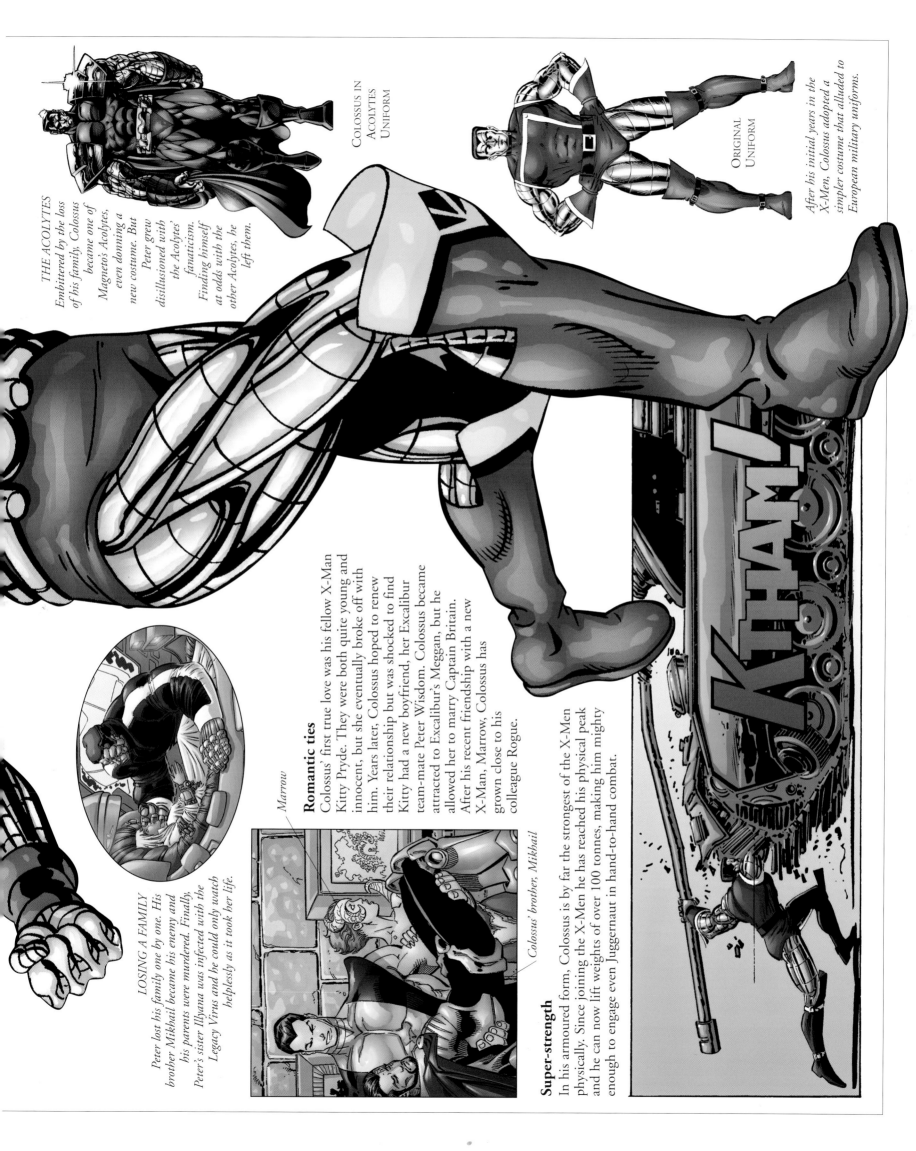

THE ACOLYTES
Embittered by the loss of his family, Colossus became one of Magneto's Acolytes, even donning a new costume. But Peter grew disillusioned with the Acolytes' fanaticism. Finding himself at odds with the other Acolytes, he left them.

COLOSSUS IN ACOLYTES UNIFORM

ORIGINAL UNIFORM

After his initial years in the X-Men, Colossus adopted a simpler costume that alluded to European military uniforms.

LOSING A FAMILY
Peter lost his family one by one. His brother Mikhail became his enemy and his parents were murdered. Finally, Peter's sister Illyana was infected with the Legacy Virus and he could only watch helplessly as it took her life.

Marrow

Colossus' brother, Mikhail

Romantic ties
Colossus' first true love was his fellow X-Man Kitty Pryde. They were both quite young and innocent, but she eventually broke off with him. Years later, Colossus hoped to renew their relationship but was shocked to find Kitty had a new boyfriend, her Excalibur team-mate Peter Wisdom. Colossus became attracted to Excalibur's Meggan, but he allowed her to marry Captain Britain. After his recent friendship with a new X-Man, Marrow, Colossus has grown close to his colleague Rogue.

Super-strength
In his armoured form, Colossus is by far the strongest of the X-Men physically. Since joining the X-Men he has reached his physical peak and he can now lift weights of over 100 tonnes, making him mighty enough to engage even Juggernaut in hand-to-hand combat.

KTHAM!

NIGHTCRAWLER

IN THE SHADOWS
Nightcrawler cannot literally turn invisible, but the thin, indigo-coloured fur all over his body enables him to blend into deep shadows as if he had disappeared from sight.

APPEARING OUT OF NOWHERE in a puff of smoke, at first Nightcrawler looks like a demon from a medieval image of hell. His yellow eyes seem to glow, his smile has fanged teeth, he is covered with dark blue fur, and he has a long, prehensile tail that ends in a point. But, in fact, Nightcrawler is Kurt Wagner, a German-born mutant with the ability to teleport himself from place to place at will. Far from being a devil, Kurt is deeply religious and sees himself as a swashbuckling romantic hero, performing incredible acrobatic feats of daring. Only recently has Kurt learned that he is the son of the mutant shapeshifter Mystique and a German aristocrat. When Bavarian villagers discovered Mystique's true mutant physical appearance and that of her newborn, they tried to kill them both. To save herself, Mystique used her powers to disguise herself as a villager and ruthlessly threw her baby into a waterfall. Miraculously, little Kurt survived and was found by the gypsy sorceress Margali Szardos, who raised him in a travelling circus. There Kurt won applause as an acrobat and high-wire performer from audiences who assumed that he was an ordinary human wearing a costume.

BAMF!!!!
When Nightcrawler suddenly disappears via teleportation, he displaces an amount of air equivalent to the size of his body, creating an odd 'bamf' sound.

SAVED BY PROFESSOR X

Kurt's world came crashing down when he fought and accidentally killed his foster brother Stefan, who had gone insane. Terrified villagers would have driven a stake through Kurt's heart had he not been saved by Charles Xavier, who recruited him into the X-Men. Nightcrawler stayed with the team for years before moving to England to help found the Super Hero team, Excalibur. When that group disbanded, Nightcrawler returned to America and to the X-Men.

CLOSE, WOLVERINE... BUT *NOT QUITE...*

COULDN'T RISK *TELEPORTING* TO JEAN'S ROOF--

-- I DIDN'T GET A *GOOD LOOK* AT IT WHEN I *FELL,* AND I CAN'T *'PORT* UNLESS I KNOW *EXACTLY* WHERE I'M GOING. BUT *THIS* WAY'S JUST AS GOOD--!

Acrobatics
Gifted with superhuman agility, Nightcrawler learned to perform feats of acrobatics in his years as a circus performer in Germany. His circus training still comes in handy today in his missions with the X-Men. He can even use his prehensile tail and his opposable toes to swing from a flagpole!

I'M RIGHT BEHIND YOU, *MEIN HERR.*

I'VE BEEN ACHING TO TRY THIS STUNT AGAIN.*

BY TELEPORTING AS FAST AS I CAN PUNCH...

...I CAN DECK ALL THESE MEN BEFORE THE FIRST ONE EVEN HITS THE GROUND!

*LAST USED IN CLASSIC #17--BOB.

Nightcrawler attacks the guards of the Hellfire Club by teleporting and punching in quick succession.

Fighting
Being able to teleport enables Nightcrawler to appear out of nowhere, strike his opponent, vanish before his adversary can hit back, and then reappear and attack from a different direction. These three Hellfire Club guards literally never knew what hit them!

AND, REMARKABLY... THEY **DO**!

VAS--? TH-THEY'RE NOT **MOVING**!

WHAT HAS **HAPPENED** TO THEM?

I HAPPENED TO THEM, KURT WAGNER.

MY NAME IS **CHARLES XAVIER**!

YOU DID... **THIS** TO THEM? BUT **HOW**--? WHY?

Just in time!

Thinking him a demon from hell, a Bavarian mob was about to drive a stake through Kurt Wagner's heart when Charles Xavier arrived on the scene. Paralyzing his assailants with his mental powers, Xavier saved Kurt's life and invited him to join the X-Men.

DASHING HERO
Seeing himself as a dashing hero, Nightcrawler has trained himself to be an expert swordsman.

He can even wield a sword with his tail!

IF YOU INSIST. BUT THE BEER PROBABLY WON'T BE AS GOOD.

WHAT THE HECK IS THAT?!

AN IMAGE INDUCER.

FLIP

KLIK

PROFESSOR XAVIER SECURED IT FOR ME FROM INDUSTRIALIST-INVENTOR TONY STARK.

Quick change

Shortly after joining the X-Men, Nightcrawler was given an image inducer, a portable device that could surround the person carrying it with a holographic image. Using the image inducer, Nightcrawler could make himself look like a normal human being when he went out in public. It was not long, though, before Kurt gave up using the device, having decided not to be ashamed of or hide his actual physical appearance.

After years of training under the guidance of Professor X, Nightcrawler can now teleport over large distances, reappearing up to 5km away!

MYSTIQUE
Nightcrawler received his indigo skin and distinctive eyes from his mother, Mystique, but none of her love. She threw her baby son to his apparent death when escaping a pursuing mob. Not until he was an adult did Kurt finally learn who his mother was – and, as a result, that his fellow X-Man Rogue was his foster sister!

...SHE MOMENTARILY **STARTLED** HER OPPRESSORS...

...ALLOWING HER TO MAKE IT TO THE GROUNDS **BEHIND** THE ESTATE.

BUT SHE WAS YOUNG, **INEXPERIENCED**.

"IN EGYPT, SHE LOST HER PARENTS TO A BOMB."

"CABLE, SHE WAS BURIED ALIVE WITH HER DEAD MOTHER'S BODY. CAN YOU IMAGINE?"

"SHE WAS JUST A CHILD, AND YET SHE MANAGED TO SURVIVE."

"SHE CARRIES THE SCARS OF THAT TIME IN HER SEVERE CLAUSTOPHOBIA."

The terrorist attack that killed her parents left the young Ororo buried alive beneath the rubble of a building. The experience traumatized the orphan and Ororo still suffers from claustrophobia to this day.

STORM

ORPHAN AND GODDESS, thief and crusader, African and American – Ororo Munroe, better known as Storm, has filled many roles during her young life. She has the mutant ability to control the weather around her. She can create rain, hail, snow, fog, and even lightning at will. Storm can also summon up winds strong enough to carry her through the air in flight. Storm's mother, N'Dare was the princess of a tribe in Kenya, and was descended from an ancient line of African priestesses, all of whom had white hair and blue eyes. N'Dare married the American photojournalist David Munroe and moved with him to Cairo, Egypt. Five years later, a terrorist bomb destroyed their home, killing Ororo's parents and leaving her trapped beneath the rubble. Orphaned at the age of five and a half, Ororo wandered the streets until she met the master thief Achmed el-Gibar. He taught her to become the best pickpocket and thief in Cairo, but when Ororo was twelve, she left the city and travelled by foot to her mother's ancestral home, the Serengeti Plains.

STORM
CIRCA
1975–1983

TO AMERICA

There in the shadow of Mount Kilimanjaro, she utilized her newly emerged mutant power over the weather to help local tribes, who worshipped her as a goddess. Ororo remained there until Charles Xavier invited her to join the second generation of X-Men. Xavier gave her the code name Storm, and to begin with, she was an innocent character, unfamiliar with Western ways. In later years, her personality went through a more combative phase, and she adopted a Mohawk haircut and leather outfit. Today, she has returned to her long hair and flowing cape. During her years with the X-Men, Storm has grown into a formidable combatant. She has served as the team's leader and remains one of the X-Men's most valuable members to this day.

STORM
CIRCA
1983–1989

STORM IN THE 1990s

The fury of Storm

Storm's powers over the weather are linked to her emotions. If she becomes annoyed, storm clouds gather. When she is angry, then she is fearsome indeed, summoning winds to carry her high into the sky, causing thunder to resound around her, and hurling lightning bolts from her hands as if she were a goddess of wrath. Ordinarily, though, Storm has a serene personality, finding peace in the natural world around her.

THE GODDESS ORORO
From her adolescence, Ororo was worshipped as a goddess by the people of the Serengeti Plains in Kenya. Here she used her powers to control the weather to ensure that her community suffered neither drought nor famine.

STORM LOSES HER POWERS
At one point US government agent Henry Peter Gyrich shot Storm with a neutralizer gun invented by her future team-mate Forge. The effect deactivated her mutant powers. Ultimately, Forge was able to restore the use of her powers.

ON SCREEN

In the *X-Men* movie, Storm has her familiar white hair and the power to control the weather that gives her her name. While in the comics Storm is often drawn as if she had no pupils in her eyes, in the movie her eyes actually turn white when she concentrates on utilizing her powers. As in the comics, Storm's ability to summon up powerful winds and bolts of lightning makes her an awe-inspiring opponent.

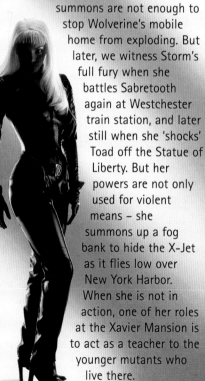

Storm is first seen in action saving Wolverine and Rogue from an attack by Sabretooth. However, the winds she summons are not enough to stop Wolverine's mobile home from exploding. But later, we witness Storm's full fury when she battles Sabretooth again at Westchester train station, and later still when she 'shocks' Toad off the Statue of Liberty. But her powers are not only used for violent means – she summons up a fog bank to hide the X-Jet as it flies low over New York Harbor. When she is not in action, one of her roles at the Xavier Mansion is to act as a teacher to the younger mutants who live there.

WOLVERINE

Logan once served as a special operative for the CIA. His partners were Victor Creed, who would become Sabretooth, and the German freedom fighter now known as Maverick.

HE'S THE BEST there is at what he does, it's said. And what he does is fight. Like the animal that is his namesake, Wolverine may be small in size but he is ferocious in battle. Yet as fearsome as he is to others, Wolverine's greatest enemy is himself. It has taken him years to master his animalistic impulses to kill, and should his control slip, he could easily give way to berserker madness. Wolverine's principal weapons are his claws which are actually bones that lie within his forearms. At will he can thrust the claws forth through the back of his hands or retract them. In the past, scientists bonded molecules of the iron alloy adamantium to the claws, making them unbreakable. He has a mutant ability to heal from injuries at exceptional speed, making him virtually unkillable, and has superhumanly acute senses of smell and hearing. Logan's past is a mystery even to himself. CIA scientists have tampered with his memory. His healing power also greatly retards his aging: no one knows how old he is. But this is what we do know.

Wolverine eagerly accepted Professor X's offer to quit working for Canada's Department H and join the X-Men.

WILD MAN

He calls himself simply Logan, and he was born in Canada. He has fought in wars as a soldier. Decades ago he was a special operative for the CIA, who ran the Weapon X project that both gave him his adamantium and drove him mad. He was an animalistic savage when he was found by James and Heather Hudson, who helped him regain his sanity. Logan worked with James in the Canadian government's Department H and became known as Weapon X, alias Wolverine. James Hudson intended Logan to lead Canada's new Super Hero team, Alpha Flight. But Logan felt guilty over his secret love for Heather. Hence, when Charles Xavier invited him to join the X-Men, Logan accepted immediately, and he has remained one of the team's central figures ever since.

DOOMED LOVE
Logan fell in love with Japanese noblewoman Mariko Yashida, but he was forced to slay her criminal father, Shingen, in combat. Finally, one of Logan's enemies poisoned Mariko, and he had to kill her to spare her a long and agonizing death.

MARIKO

Stripped of adamantium

Wolverine had come to rely on the adamantium bonded to his bones. But then the X-Men's archfoe Magneto used his magnetic power to strip the adamantium molecules from his skeleton, rendering it vulnerable once more. Many months would pass before another enemy, Apocalypse, restored the adamantium to Wolverine's skeleton before making him his slave.

ULTIMATE HUNTER
Wolverine's mutant sense of smell is so strong that he can identify people by scent and track them down like a dog or a wolf.

When he turned feral, Wolverine took to wearing a mask.

FERAL WOLVERINE

DEPARTMENT H COSTUME

SECOND X-MEN COSTUME

Changing face

Wolverine has gone through many changes in his appearance, ranging from his Department H outfit, to his reversion back into a feral state just after he lost his adamantium.

BONY CLAWS
After he lost his adamantium, Wolverine's claws appeared in their natural state: bone without metal.

Wolverine's fast healing

Perhaps Wolverine's greatest advantage as a fighter is his mutant healing ability. Although he does feel pain, he recovers from injuries with amazing speed. Gunshot wounds in non-vital areas cannot stop him. Within hours he can fully recover from an injury that would kill a human.

ON SCREEN

In the *X-Men* movie, Wolverine's past is an even greater mystery than it is in the comics. He remembers nothing about his life before the adamantium was grafted onto his skeleton, and the only clues he has to his past are the dog tags he wears. Even though the other X-Men call him Logan, his dreams are haunted by the code name that appears on these dog tags; 'Wolverine'.

He has the same healing power and the same gruff personality that he has in the comics. He also tries to woo Jean Grey, a move that brings him into conflict with Scott Summers. In the comics, Wolverine was working for the Canadian government when he joined the X-Men. In the *X-Men* movie, he is wandering the country, trying to learn about his past. Instead of being sought out by Xavier, as he is in the comics, Logan becomes involved with the X-Men through a chance encounter with the young mutant Rogue.

BANSHEE

SEAN CASSIDY takes his name, the Banshee, from a female spirit of Irish folklore, who wails to warn a family that one of its members is about to die. The X-Men's Banshee also wails. Using his ability he can create sonic vibrations that are powerful enough to shatter steel or propel himself through the air in flight. Like the banshee of myth, Sean Cassidy is familiar with tragic events. In his youth he had nothing but good fortune. He was heir to a magnificent Irish castle, Cassidy Keep and had a successful career in the international law enforcement organization, Interpol. Most importantly, he had married the beautiful Maeve Rourke, despite competition from his disreputable cousin, Black Tom. While Sean was away on a lengthy secret mission, Maeve discovered she was pregnant and gave birth to their daughter, Theresa. Then, during a visit to relatives in Northern Ireland, Maeve was killed by a terrorist bomb. Black Tom secretly rescued Theresa, planning to raise her himself.

Sean's sonic vibrations are powerful enough to propel him through the air.

BOTH SIDES OF THE LAW

Overwhelmed with grief, but ignorant of his daughter's existence, Sean left Interpol and later became a police detective in New York City. Unable to find peace of mind, he drifted into crime and was enslaved by Factor Three. The X-Men freed Banshee from Factor Three, and together they wrecked the organization's plans for world domination. Sean gratefully accepted Charles Xavier's offer of membership in the X-Men. It was in their ranks that Sean met and fell in love with the X-Men's ally, Moira MacTaggert, and was finally united with Theresa, who is now the teenage mutant heroine, Siryn. Today, Sean has left the X-Men to teach the young mutants of Generation X at Xavier's new school in Snow Valley, Massachusetts.

In Interpol
For years, Sean Cassidy served as a leading Interpol operative. But grief over his wife's sudden death turned Sean's life upside down, and he became the complete opposite of a law enforcer: a law breaker. As if in punishment for turning to a life of crime, he was captured by the group known as Factor Three, a conspiracy of mutants bent on world conquest.

AND, THE FOLLOWING SECOND...

UHH... THAT SCREECHING NOISE! THE EAR WAX ...WON'T KEEP IT OUT!

HE'S...EVEN MORE POWERFUL THAN I FEARED! FIGHT BACK, ALL OF YOU ...YOU MUST FIGHT BACK!

WE... CAN'T! THE EAR SHIELDS ONLY LESSEN THE PAIN... BUT, IT'S STILL TOO GREAT!

CAN'T... KEEP AWAKE! WE'RE ALL... PASSING OUT!

Freed by Xavier
Banshee first met the X-Men as their enemy. He had been forced to serve Factor Three, who had strapped an explosive device to his head to ensure his obedience. By disarming this device in his headband, Charles Xavier freed Sean Cassidy from a life of crime and allowed Banshee to join forces with the rest of the X-Men instead.

Banshee has carried on a long-lasting relationship with Moira MacTaggert since the days when she was Professor X's 'housekeeper'. He lived with her on Muir Island after his powers were lost.

Banshee joins the X-Men

Middle-aged Sean Cassidy was an exception to Charles Xavier's usual preference for recruiting young mutants into his school. However, the original team of X-Men had been captured by the living island of Krakoa, and Xavier needed a new team of mutants to rescue them. Cassidy enthusiastically accepted, seeing membership in the X-Men as his opportunity to go straight after his wasted years on the wrong side of the law.

Banshee's beam of sonic energy

Banshee loses his powers

While in Japan, the X-Men found themselves battling Moses Magnum, a criminal mastermind who had been endowed with the psionic power to cause earthquakes. In the fight that followed, Banshee severely damaged his vocal cords while creating a vibratory force strong enough to neutralize the energy waves that Magnum had unleashed in his attempt to destroy Japan. Sean's ability to speak soon returned, but he could not use his sonic powers again for years.

Siryn

Banshee's teenage daughter, Theresa Rourke, alias Siryn, has inherited her father's sonic powers. His cousin, Black Tom Cassidy, made her a reluctant accomplice in his criminal career. Siryn has since reformed and became a member of X-Force. Like her father, Siryn is a natural leader, and formerly headed the mutant team.

Reluctant partners

In choosing teachers for the young mutants of Generation X, Charles Xavier paired former X-Man Sean Cassidy with one of the X-Men's old enemies, Emma Frost, the former White Queen of the Hellfire Club. Unsurprisingly, these mismatched teachers are often at odds, but they have nonetheless become an effective team.

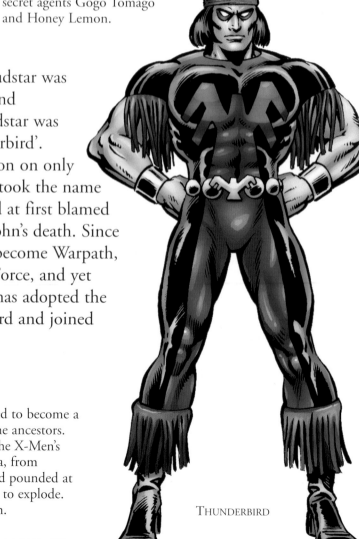
Sunfire

SUNFIRE

SUNFIRE

W HEN THE UNITED STATES dropped an atomic bomb on Hiroshima at the close of World War II, Shiro Yoshida's mother was exposed to intense radiation that altered her genes. Years later she died giving birth to her son Shiro, a mutant who could generate intense heat and flames – and even fly. Naming himself Sunfire, Yoshida vowed to take revenge on the United States for Japan's wartime defeat. The X-Men successfully stopped him from destroying the US Capitol building. Eventually, the death of Shiro's father, a diplomat, shocked Sunfire into abandoning his path of revenge. He even joined the second team of X-Men on the invitation of Professor X, but, being a loner by nature, he quit after a single mission. Since then, Sunfire has primarily used his powers on missions for the Japanese government, though he still aids the X-Men on occasion.

Shiro Yoshida is related to the Yashida crime family, which includes Wolverine's ex-fiancée, Mariko Yashida.

Sunfire displays his nationalistic pride in a costume that adapts the Japanese symbol of the rising sun.

Silver Samurai   Baymax   Sunfire   Honey Lemon

Hiro Takachiho   Gogo Tomago

Big Hero 6
Recently, Sunfire has joined Japan's first Super Hero team, known in English as Big Hero 6. Members include the Silver Samurai, the robot Baymax, boy genius Hiro Takachiho, and secret agents Gogo Tomago and Honey Lemon.

THUNDERBIRD

B ORN ON AN APACHE RESERVATION in Arizona, John Proudstar was a Native American mutant endowed with superhuman strength and endurance. After serving as a soldier in the United States Army, Proudstar was recruited by Xavier into the X-Men and was given the name 'Thunderbird'. His fellow X-Men were shocked when Thunderbird was killed in action on only his second mission with the team. Proudstar's younger brother James took the name Thunderbird and at first blamed the X-Men for John's death. Since then, James has become Warpath, a member of X-Force, and yet another mutant has adopted the name Thunderbird and joined the X-Men.

I'VE BEEN A *LONER* ALL MY LIFE, XAVIER -- AN *OUTCAST* -- DUMPED ON BY EVERYBODY I MET--

-- BUT I'M A *MAN*, XAVIER, A *WARRIOR* OF THE APACHE--

--AN' *TODAY* I'M GONNA PROVE IT!!

RAKT!

FOR GOD'S SAKE, LADDIE-- GET OFF THE PLANE!!

A hero's death
John Proudstar wanted to become a warrior like his Apache ancestors. Determined to stop the X-Men's enemy, Count Nefaria, from escaping, Thunderbird pounded at his aircraft, causing it to explode. He died a hero's death.

THUNDERBIRD

MOIRA MACTAGGERT

ONE OF THE WORLD'S leading authorities on genetic mutation, Dr. Moira MacTaggert is Charles Xavier's longtime colleague and confidante and was also once his fiancée. The daughter of Lord Kinross of Scotland, Moira met and fell in love with Xavier when they were both graduate students at Oxford University. However, Moira ended their engagement when she was forced into marriage with the late politician Joseph MacTaggert. Thereafter she had a son, named Kevin, a mutant menace with the ability to alter reality at will. Moira also raised the orphaned mutant girl Rahne Sinclair, now known as Wolfsbane. The two have grown so close that Rahne now considers Moira to be a second mother to her.

Moira Kinross MacTaggert won the Nobel Prize for her work in genetics.

Moira reluctantly kept her mutant son, Kevin, alias Proteus, confined for years on Muir Island. Once he escaped, Proteus' powers quickly incinerated his own body, and he existed as psychic energy, taking over and burning out a succession of bodies, including that of Moira's estranged husband Joe, before Colossus finally halted his rampage.

MUIR ISLAND

Today, Dr. MacTaggert operates the high-tech Mutant Research Centre on Muir Island off the northern coast of Cape Wrath, Scotland. This is the largest and most advanced facility of its kind that is owned and operated by a private individual. Here Moira conducts genetic research and confines mutants that she and Professor X consider to be dangerous. She is a staunch friend and ally of Charles Xavier and also of the X-Men, New Mutants, and the members of Excalibur, who have used Muir Island as their base of operations. Recently she has devoted herself to finding a cure for the deadly Legacy Virus, which was engineered by Stryfe; ironically, she is the only non-mutant to have become infected with this disease.

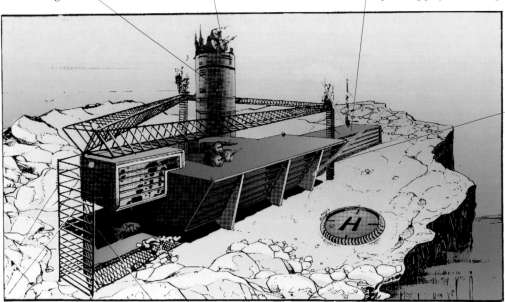

Storage stack   Communications

Mutant genome sequencing project building

LABORATORY STACK:
- *High-energy transfer*
- *Mutant pathology*
- *Archive cross-reference*
- *Large computer centre*
- *Mutant constraint analysis*
- *Hospital*

QUARANTINE When she learned that she had been infected with the Legacy Virus, Moira sealed herself in a quarantine chamber so that she could study the development of the disease under controlled conditions. Her experiments have proved fruitless, and she has since left the chamber.

THE X-MEN AIRCRAFT

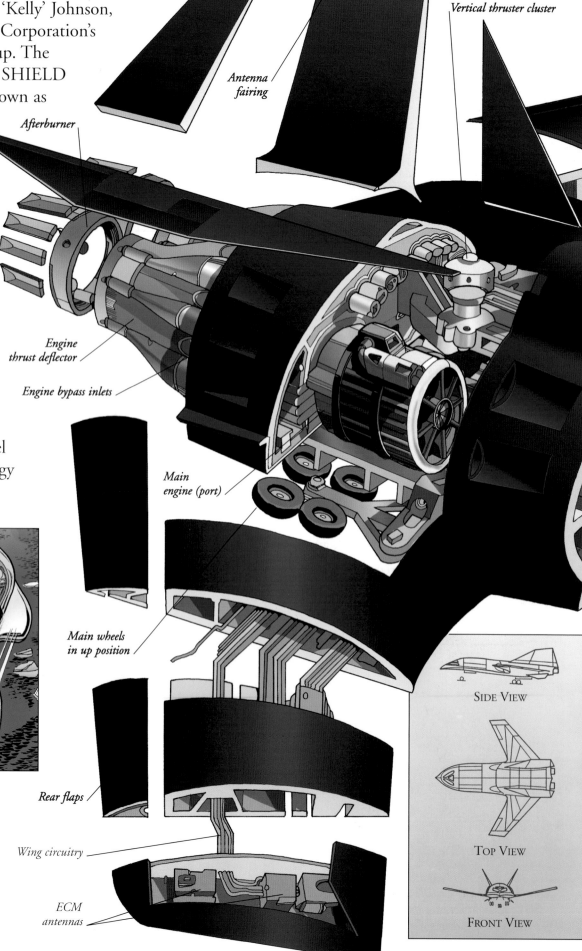

THE X-MEN'S ADVANCED jet aircraft, the Blackbirds, are based on designs by Clarence 'Kelly' Johnson, former head of the Lockheed Aircraft Corporation's Advanced Development Projects Group. The international law enforcement agency SHIELD built a number of these craft, then known as the Lockheed SHIELD (RS-150) Blackbird, but all were destroyed except for the one acquired by Charles Xavier. The Blackbird is a transonic, long-distance airplane, used in the X-Men's high-altitude reconnaissance missions. It is a VTOL (vertical take-off and landing) craft and can fly at speeds of up to Mach 4.2 at high altitudes. A mission-specific accessory pod can easily be added for unusual or pre-planned operations. The X-Men have greatly enhanced the original Lockheed model by incorporating alien Shi'ar technology and innovations devised by Forge.

Vertical thruster cluster

Antenna fairing

Afterburner

Engine thrust deflector

Engine bypass inlets

Main engine (port)

Main wheels in up position

Rear flaps

Wing circuitry

ECM antennas

SIDE VIEW

TOP VIEW

FRONT VIEW

Sentinel Skycraft

After their battle with the Sentinels, the original X-Men captured some highly advanced aircraft designed by the Sentinels' creator, Larry Trask. Originally used for transporting mutant prisoners, the craft was converted by the X-Men and used for supersonic flight across vast distances. One of the ships was unfortunately lost when it crashed in the Savage Land.

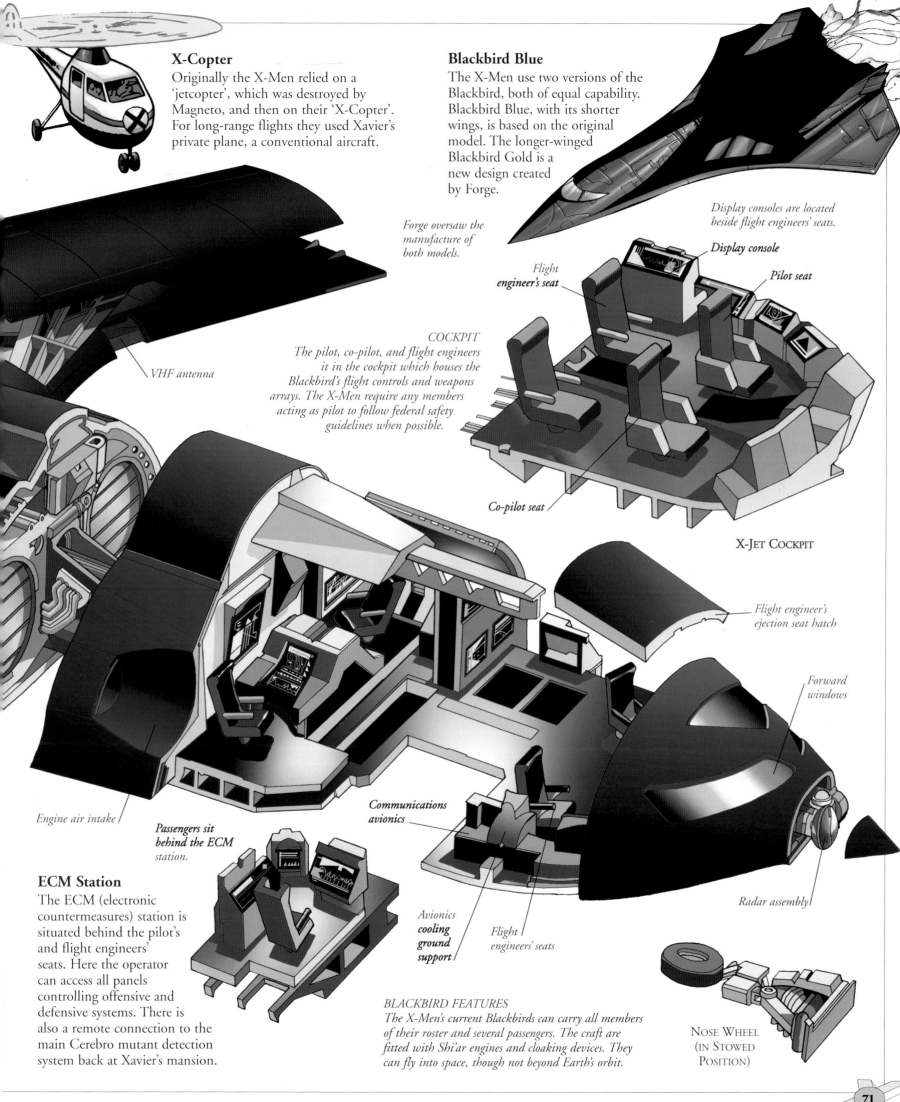

X-Copter

Originally the X-Men relied on a 'jetcopter', which was destroyed by Magneto, and then on their 'X-Copter'. For long-range flights they used Xavier's private plane, a conventional aircraft.

Blackbird Blue

The X-Men use two versions of the Blackbird, both of equal capability. Blackbird Blue, with its shorter wings, is based on the original model. The longer-winged Blackbird Gold is a new design created by Forge.

Forge oversaw the manufacture of both models.

Display consoles are located beside flight engineers' seats.

Flight engineer's seat

Display console

Pilot seat

COCKPIT
The pilot, co-pilot, and flight engineers it in the cockpit which houses the Blackbird's flight controls and weapons arrays. The X-Men require any members acting as pilot to follow federal safety guidelines when possible.

Co-pilot seat

VHF antenna

X-JET COCKPIT

Flight engineer's ejection seat hatch

Forward windows

Engine air intake

Passengers sit behind the ECM station.

ECM Station

The ECM (electronic countermeasures) station is situated behind the pilot's and flight engineers' seats. Here the operator can access all panels controlling offensive and defensive systems. There is also a remote connection to the main Cerebro mutant detection system back at Xavier's mansion.

Communications avionics

*Avionics **cooling ground support***

Flight engineers' seats

Radar assembly

BLACKBIRD FEATURES
The X-Men's current Blackbirds can carry all members of their roster and several passengers. The craft are fitted with Shi'ar engines and cloaking devices. They can fly into space, though not beyond Earth's orbit.

NOSE WHEEL
(IN STOWED POSITION)

THE STARJAMMERS

EVER SINCE Christopher Summers was a boy, he loved the adventures of the swashbuckling heroes of old novels and movies. Even as a major in the United States Air Force, he chose the call sign 'Corsair' in homage to them. Chosen for the space programme, he hoped he would soon travel into space. He got his wish, but not in the way he would have wanted. Following a visit to his parents in Anchorage, Alaska, Major Summers was flying his wife, Katherine Ann, and his sons, Scott and Alex, down the Pacific coast in his private plane when they were attacked by a Shi'ar starship. Scott and Alex parachuted to safety, but Major Summers and his wife were teleported aboard the starship and taken back to the Shi'ar throneworld. The Major was imprisoned but escaped only to find Emperor D'Ken attempting to force himself on Katherine. D'Ken murdered Katherine before Summers' eyes and then sentenced him to the mines of the planet Alsibar.

Ch'od

Raza

Hepzibah

Corsair

Fighting alongside the X-Men against D'Ken, Corsair was reunited with his son Scott, now called Cyclops.

PRISON BREAKOUT

Slowly, Christopher Summers' spirit was broken, until he encountered a female, cat-like alien who was being beaten by guards. Outraged, Summers attacked the guards, and two more prisoners, Ch'od and Raza, came to his assistance. Together, they stole a starship and escaped. Summers took the name Corsair and called his new outlaw band the Starjammers. They became space pirates, revenging themselves on the Shi'ar by attacking their spacecraft. The Starjammers helped the X-Men to stop the Shi'ar Emperor D'Ken's attempt to destroy the universe with the M'Krann Crystal. In gratitude, Lilandra unofficially put an end to the feud between the Empire and the Starjammers. After she was overthrown by Deathbird, Lilandra found refuge with the team until she regained the Shi'ar throne.

THE STARJAMMER

Interstellar pirates

The original team of Starjammers included five members. Unable to pronounce the cat-like alien's name, Corsair called her Hepzibah; she is a Mephitisoid, a member of a race conquered by the Shi'ar. Ch'od is a Saurid, a reptilian being of vast strength, and Raza is a Shi'ar cyborg and a master swordsman. Their ship's physician is a member of the insect-like Chr'ylite race whom Corsair dubbed "Sikorsky". Later, they were joined by the Earthwoman Carol Danvers, who wields cosmic powers and is known as Binary.

THE STARJAMMER
Corsair dubbed his interstellar pirate ship the Starjammer after the sailing ships on Earth known as windjammers. Its ultra-light drive enables Corsair and his companions to quickly traverse even the vast distance between Earth and the Shi'ar Galaxy.

LILANDRA AND THE SHI'AR

THE SHI'AR are an extraterrestrial race who rule an empire that extends throughout their galaxy. They have physical characteristics in common with both birds and mammals. Although humanoid in appearance, the Shi'ar have feathers instead of hair – they even have vestigial feathers on their arms. The Shi'ar Empire is one of the three great galactic empires in the known universe. The others belong to the militaristic, humanoid Kree, and the shapeshifting, reptilian Skrulls, each of whom is the dominant power in their own galaxy. The planet Earth is of strategic importance to these three rival empires, because it lies at a crossroads for starship travel between their respective galaxies.

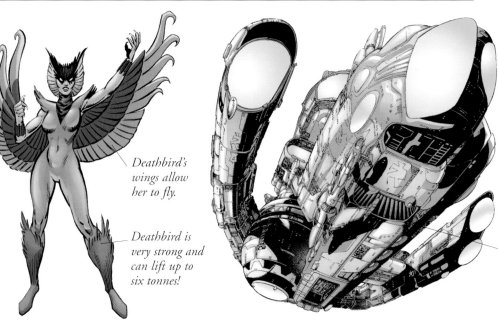

Deathbird's wings allow her to fly.

Deathbird is very strong and can lift up to six tonnes!

Lilandra's older sister, Deathbird, is an evolutionary throwback. She was exiled from the Shi'ar Empire for regicide.

*SHI'AR FLEET
The Shi'ar use various designs for their starships, including this enormous Apocalypse-class flagship. However, the most distinctive ships of the fleet are the small scout ships, which coincidentally resemble Earth insects.*

The Starjammer is dwarfed by a Shi'ar Apocalypse-class flagship.

SHI'AR RULER

The ruler of the Shi'ar, known as the Majestor or Majestrix, is based on Chandilar, the imperial throneworld. The current Majestrix is Lilandra Neramani who succeeded to the throne after her brother, D'Ken, nearly destroyed the universe by trying to harness the power of the M'Krann Crystal. She had opposed these plans, and fled to Earth where she met Charles Xavier and enlisted the help of the X-Men. Subsequently, Deathbird, Lilandra's older sister, staged a successful coup, driving Lilandra into exile. But Lilandra has since regained the throne and even won a war against the Kree. Today, Charles Xavier and Lilandra remain friends, and she continues to be the X-Men's ally.

Lilandra escaped from her brother D'Ken to Earth, where she met and fell in love with Xavier. When she ascended to the throne, she took Xavier into space as her consort.

The 'hair' on the heads of the Shi'ar is actually made up of feathers.

Lilandra, Majestrix of the Shi'ar

THE IMPERIAL GUARD

THE IMPERIAL GUARD is a legion of super-powered champions who protect and defend the Shi'ar galactic empire. Its members are drawn both from the Shi'ar race and from other alien races governed by the Shi'ar. The majority of the Imperial Guard's members are known as Borderers. They assist the governors of conquered planets in enforcing the Shi'ar imperial law. The Imperial Guardsmen pictured here, however, belong to the elite corps that protects the ruler of the Empire, known as the Majestor or Majestrix, and executes his or her orders. The praetor (leader) of this elite corps is Gladiator, the most powerful member of the entire Imperial Guard.

AGAINST THE X-MEN

When the X-Men first encountered the Imperial Guard, it was as enemies, since the Guardsmen then served the evil D'Ken Neramani, Majestor of the Shi'ar. However, now that their friend Lilandra rules the Shi'ar, the X-Men and the Imperial Guard have become allies.

Gladiator
The leader of the Imperial Guard, Gladiator is the most powerful known humanoid in the entire Shi'ar galaxy. His strength enables him to lift over 100 tonnes in Earth gravity. He can fly at speeds equal to those of starships and is virtually invulnerable except to certain wavelengths of radiation. Gladiator can also emit laser-like beams from his eyes to produce intense heat. While other Guardsmen travel in starships, Gladiator can fly unprotected through the vacuum of space for long periods without breathing.

The M'Krann Crystal
The X-Men first met the Imperial Guard on a desolate world in a distant galaxy, where the Shi'ar emperor D'Ken sought to harness the power of the M'Krann Crystal. The Imperial Guard loyally defended their emperor from the invading Earthmen. D'Ken thought he could master the Crystal's energies, but it would have destroyed the universe had Phoenix not stopped it.

FANG
Highly developed animal senses
Now deceased

WARSTAR
A mechanoid symbiote
with superhuman strength

ASTRA
Able to turn intangible at will

SMASHER
Possesses superhuman strength

D'Ken

The duty of the Imperial Guard is to serve the monarch of the Shi'ar, no matter who it may be. The Guardsmen once aided the mad emperor D'Ken against his rebellious sister Lilandra, but when Lilandra succeeded D'Ken as ruler, the Guard switched their loyalty to her.

MANTA

Can see infrared light and can generate blinding flashes of light

EARTHQUAKE

Can psionically create earthquakes

ELECTRON

Can project powerful bolts of electrical energy

SIBYL

Possesses powerful telepathic abilities

SCINTILLA

Can shrink to 1/20th of her normal size

STARBOLT

Can fire powerful bolts of energy from his hands

FLASHFIRE

Can generate powerful bolts of electrical energy

NIGHTSIDE

Can create total darkness over small areas

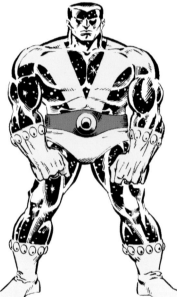

NEUTRON

Possesses superhuman strength

SHAPE-SHIFTER

Can change size and shape at will

HUSSAR

Wields a 'neuro whip'

TITAN

Can grow to gigantic size

MAGIQUE

A powerful sorceress

IMPULSE

Can fire powerful energy bolts from his visor

MENTOR

Possesses superhuman intelligence

75

ALPHA FLIGHT

THE GOVERNMENT of Canada has its own team of costumed Super Heroes, Alpha Flight. Years ago, the prime minister of Canada asked the brilliant engineer and inventor James MacDonald Hudson to aid in creating Department H, a top-secret agency within the Ministry of Defence. Hudson decided to organize a team of superhumanly powerful operatives who would go on special missions for Department H. While visiting a national park, Hudson and his wife Heather encountered Wolverine, who had reverted to a crazed, feral state. The Hudsons nursed Wolverine back to sanity, and James planned to make Wolverine the leader of his team, which would be called Alpha Flight. However, Wolverine resigned to join the X-Men, and Hudson reluctantly became the team leader instead.

WEAPON ALPHA

Wearing a battlesuit he had invented that enabled him to fly and to fire beams of force, Hudson took on the name Weapon Alpha (he would later be known as Guardian). On one of his first missions, Hudson tried to capture Wolverine and bring him back to Canada. After failing, Hudson tried again months later, along with five other Alpha Flight members. They were Sasquatch, a man who could transform himself into a legendary monster; Shaman, a Native American mystic; Aurora and Northstar, a sister and brother who moved at super-speed; and Snowbird, who could turn into any Arctic animal. Alpha Flight battled the X-Men, but Wolverine escaped. Later, Hudson and Wolverine made peace, and since then the members of Alpha Flight have worked with the X-Men.

Heather Hudson, known as Vindicator, wears a battlesuit like her husband's.

Radius is able to surround himself with a force field.

James Hudson, known as Guardian, is the leader of the group.

Sasquatch is a man who can turn himself into a super-strong monster.

Murmur can control other people's actions by touching them.

Flex can turn his limbs into sharp organic steel.

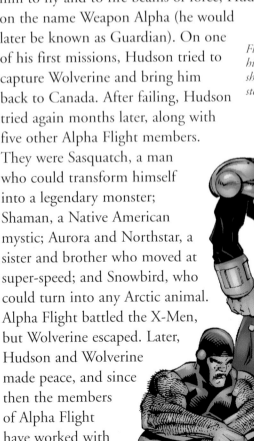

Puck is a dwarf with unusual acrobatic talents.

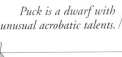
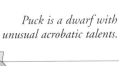

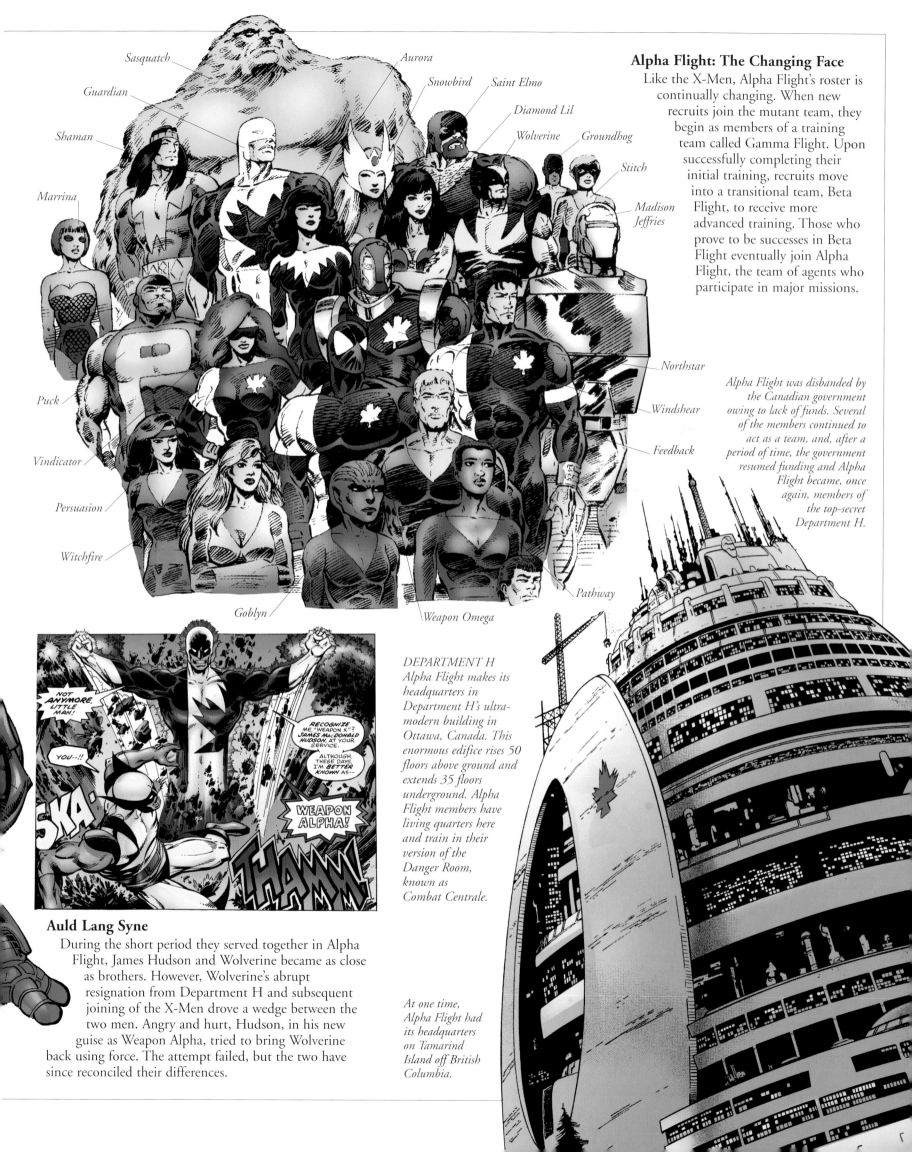

Sasquatch

Aurora

Snowbird

Saint Elmo

Diamond Lil

Guardian

Wolverine

Groundhog

Shaman

Stitch

Marrina

Madison Jeffries

Puck

Vindicator

Persuasion

Witchfire

Northstar

Windshear

Feedback

Pathway

Goblyn

Weapon Omega

Alpha Flight: The Changing Face

Like the X-Men, Alpha Flight's roster is continually changing. When new recruits join the mutant team, they begin as members of a training team called Gamma Flight. Upon successfully completing their initial training, recruits move into a transitional team, Beta Flight, to receive more advanced training. Those who prove to be successes in Beta Flight eventually join Alpha Flight, the team of agents who participate in major missions.

Alpha Flight was disbanded by the Canadian government owing to lack of funds. Several of the members continued to act as a team, and, after a period of time, the government resumed funding and Alpha Flight became, once again, members of the top-secret Department H.

DEPARTMENT H Alpha Flight makes its headquarters in Department H's ultra-modern building in Ottawa, Canada. This enormous edifice rises 50 floors above ground and extends 35 floors underground. Alpha Flight members have living quarters here and train in their version of the Danger Room, known as Combat Centrale.

At one time, Alpha Flight had its headquarters on Tamarind Island off British Columbia.

NOT ANYMORE, LITTLE MAN!

YOU--!!

RECOGNIZE ME, "WEAPON X"? JAMES MacDONALD HUDSON, AT YOUR SERVICE.

ALTHOUGH, THESE DAYS, I'M BETTER KNOWN AS--

SKA-

WEAPON ALPHA!

THAMMM

Auld Lang Syne

During the short period they served together in Alpha Flight, James Hudson and Wolverine became as close as brothers. However, Wolverine's abrupt resignation from Department H and subsequent joining of the X-Men drove a wedge between the two men. Angry and hurt, Hudson, in his new guise as Weapon Alpha, tried to bring Wolverine back using force. The attempt failed, but the two have since reconciled their differences.

OTHER '70s VILLAINS

I N ADVENTURES FIRST PUBLISHED in 1970, the original X-Men reunited with Professor X to combat a conquering alien race, the Z'nox, before clashing with the superhumanly strong Incredible Hulk in Las Vegas. Then the X-Men's original series was discontinued, and five years passed before the new X-Men team was launched. Their first adventure pitted them against the strangest of adversaries: Krakoa, a mutant entity comprising all the vegetation on a small island. A new wave of villains soon followed, including the N'garai race of demons, who could emerge from another dimension through a cairn on Xavier's estate. In Japan, the X-Men struggled against Moses Magnum, who had the power to start large-scale earthquakes. Longtime nemeses returned, including Magneto, the Juggernaut, the Sentinels, Mesmero, and Count Nefaria, the Italian crimelord responsible for the death of the new X-Man, Thunderbird. This period also introduced such formidable adversaries as the Inner Circle of the Hellfire Club, Black Tom Cassidy, Zaladane, and Proteus, all of whom are featured elsewhere in this book.

LETHAL PRANKSTER
For Arcade, it is not the money he is paid by his clients that is important, or even whether he succeeds in killing his targets. What matters to him is the sheer macabre joy he finds in tormenting his chosen victims.

Arcade's real name and past are mysteries. He once said he murdered his millionaire father for cutting off his allowance, but this may well be a lie he told to amuse himself.

THE UNHOLY THREE

The three most infamous villains who first appeared in the 1970s are featured on these pages: Arcade, Garokk, and the Shadow King. The latest series, *X-Men: The Hidden Years*, has introduced various new villains who fought the X-Men in between the original team's run-in with the Hulk and the new team's debut. Notable among them is the mutant Deluge, who controlled a storm that threatened to wipe out half of the Earth's population.

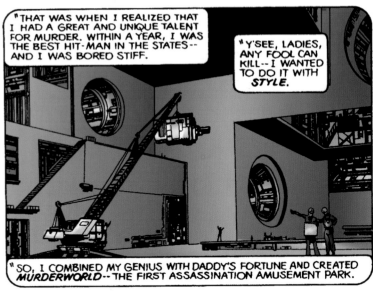

"THAT WAS WHEN I REALIZED THAT I HAD A GREAT AND UNIQUE TALENT FOR MURDER. WITHIN A YEAR, I WAS THE BEST HIT-MAN IN THE STATES-- AND I WAS BORED STIFF.

"Y'SEE, LADIES, ANY FOOL CAN KILL-- I WANTED TO DO IT WITH STYLE.

" SO, I COMBINED MY GENIUS WITH DADDY'S FORTUNE AND CREATED MURDERWORLD-- THE FIRST ASSASSINATION AMUSEMENT PARK.

Arcade and Murderworld
The most eccentric – and expensive – of assassins is known only as Arcade. For a million-dollar fee he will trap any victim in one of his Murderworlds – secret hi-tech death traps that resemble amusement-park attractions. Arcade failed to kill the X-Men when first hired by the Juggernaut and Black Tom Cassidy. But he keeps on trying, seeing the X-Men as ideal opponents in his murderous games.

--THE X-MEN ARE AS GOOD AS DEAD!

"HIS BODY BEGAN TO GLOW...

"AND WHEN THAT GLOW FADED..."

WHAT ARE YOU DOING?! NO, PLEASE-- NO!

YARRRGH!

"...UNTIL IT DISAPPEARED WITHIN A LIGHT BRIGHTER THAN THE SUN.

WHAT... MADNESS IS THIS?!

I... DIED, CONSUMED BY THE STAR-BORN FIRES THAT GAVE ME BIRTH. YET NOW... THE PETRIFIED MAN...LIVES!

Garokk

In the 1400s, a British sailor was shipwrecked off the Antarctic coast and was carried by a current into the Savage Land. There he found an idol of Garokk the Sun God and drank a strange potion from its altar. Returning to England, he found that the elixir had made him immortal at the price of slowly transforming his body into the living image of the idol. Because of his grey, rock-like skin, he is known as the Petrified Man. In recent years, he returned to the Savage Land, where he gained superhuman powers. Reverting to human form, he died of extreme old age. But then Zaladane, high priestess of Garokk, resurrected him, transforming a captive's body into that of the Petrified Man. Together, Garokk and Zaladane attempted to enslave the peoples of the Savage Land.

GAROKK'S POWERS
Garokk has the power to shoot beams of light, waves of heat, and a concussive force from his eyes. When Ka-Zar and the X-Men tried to stop Garokk and Zaladane, the Petrified Man fought an eye-blast duel with Cyclops. Garokk and Zaladane were thwarted. Years later, after a disaster turned the Savage Land into an Antarctic wasteland, Garokk sacrificed his life by using his powers to restore it to its tropical state. Whether Garokk will be resurrected again remains to be seen.

UNNNHH!

THE FORCE OF HIS EYE-BLASTS -- IT'S LIKE TAKING A SLEDGE-HAMMER IN THE HEAD.

I'VE GOT TO PARRY HIS BEAM WITH MINE EXACTLY. EVEN THE SLIGHTEST SLIP, AND HE'LL BLOW ME OFF THE DOME!

Shadow King

The first evil mutant Charles Xavier ever encountered was the Shadow King, whose telepathic powers rival his own. They met in Cairo, Egypt, when the Shadow King was inhabiting the body of Amahl Farouk. They waged a battle on the astral plane, and Xavier won, slaying Farouk's physical body. But the Shadow King lived on, taking temporary possession of new hosts, such as the New Mutants Karma and Cypher.

In the 1930s, Wolverine and the time-travellers Kitty Pryde and Rachel Summers encountered the Shadow King as Farouk, and thwarted his conspiracy, involving the Nazis, against the British throne.

"OUR EYES MET, AND IN THAT INSTANT, THE GAUNTLETS WERE THROWN. WITHOUT A WORD BEING SPOKEN, WE WERE BITTER ENEMIES."

CRUEL GRUDGE
The Shadow King's enmity towards Xavier has lasted for decades. In earthly reality the Shadow King cruelly crippled Xavier again after the professor had only just regained the ability to walk. But in their duels on the astral plain, they are free from material restrictions, and can reshape that dimension's reality as they choose.

On the astral plane, the Shadow King can assume any form he chooses.

THE X-MEN IN THE 1980s

ACCLAIMED BY AN ENTHUSIASTIC FOLLOWING, *The Uncanny X-Men* was still a cult success in 1980. With the continued collaboration of Chris Claremont and John Byrne, sales continued to grow, until, by the decade's end, it was the best-selling Super Hero comic book in America.

The team of Claremont, Byrne, and Terry Austin came to an end in 1981, but not before producing two story lines that are considered masterpieces: 'The Dark Phoenix Saga' and 'Days of Future Past'. Byrne left to write and draw Marvel's *Fantastic Four* and a new series, *Alpha Flight*, starring the Canadian Super Heroes he had created for *X-Men* in 1979. Claremont continued writing *The Uncanny X-Men* throughout the decade. Initially, Dave Cockrum returned to draw the series, but was succeeded by young artists Paul Smith, John Romita Jr., and Marc Silvestri.

Since most of the members of the X-Men were now adults, it made sense to create a spin-off title returning to the original concept of Professor Xavier training a class of mutant teenagers. Hence, Claremont and artist Bob McLeod introduced *The New Mutants* as a graphic novel in 1982. A monthly *New Mutants* comic book followed the next year and later dazzled readers with the astonishing visual experimentation of artist Bill Sienkiewicz. The most popular of the 'new' X-Men, Wolverine starred in a classic four-issue limited series in 1982 that paired Claremont with artist Frank Miller.

Alpha Flight vol.1 #1 (August 1983)
First appearance of Alpha Flight
(Cover art by John Byrne)

By 1988 Wolverine was starring in his own monthly comic book. The original X-Men regrouped in 1986 in *X-Factor*, a new series created by Bob Layton and Jackson Guice, which would reach new heights in the hands of artist Walter Simonson and his wife, writer (and former *X-Men* editor) Louise Simonson. Back in the 1970s, Claremont had co-created the Super Hero Captain Britain for Marvel's UK publications. In 1987, Claremont and British artist Alan Davis assembled a mutant Super Hero team around the Captain in the new *Excalibur* series. Thus, by the end of the 1980s, *The Uncanny X-Men* had spun off an entire family of related titles, including monthly series, limited-run series, and graphic novels. And it was still growing...

Excalibur #1 (October 1988)
First appearance of the Excalibur team
(Cover art by Alan Davis and Paul Neary)

1980

Uncanny X-Men #137
(September 1980)
'Phoenix Must Die!'
(Cover art by John Byrne
and Terry Austin)

1981

Uncanny X-Men #142
(February 1981)
'Days of Future Past'
(Cover art by Terry
Austin and John Byrne)

1983

The New Mutants #1
(March 1983)
First appearance of the
New Mutants
(Cover art by Bob
McLeod)

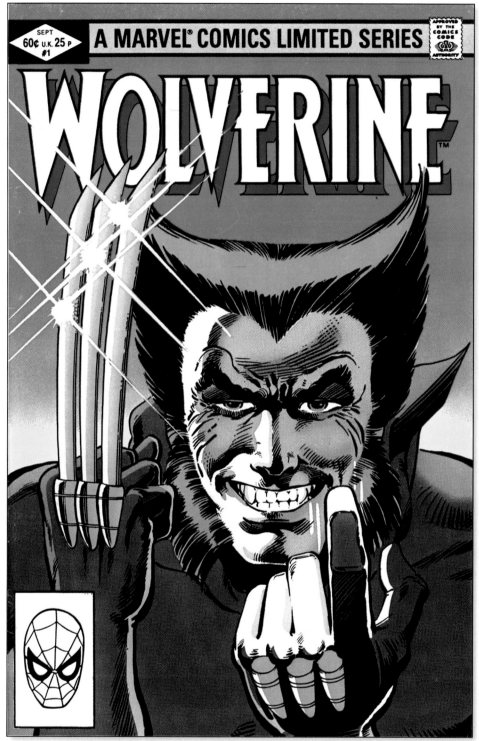

The New Mutants #18
(August 1984)
First issue with cover art by
Bill Sienkiewicz

Wolverine (limited series) #1
(September 1982)
First issue of Wolverine's first
mini-series
(Cover art by Frank Miller)

1986

X-Factor #1
(February 1986)
First appearance
of X-Factor
(Cover art by
Walt Simonson)

1988

Wolverine #1
(November 1988)
First issue of Wolverine's
ongoing series

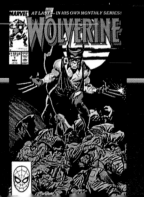

1989

X-Factor #37
(February 1989)
(Cover art by Walt

COSTUMING KITTY
Artist Mike Golden created this costume for Kitty Pryde, but she was given a more conventional, less daring uniform instead.

Sinister
Uncanny X-Men artist Marc Silvestri designed the costume and physical appearance of Sinister, making him imposing, regal, and eerily enigmatic. He would remain a mysterious mastermind until his origin was finally revealed in the following decade.

SINISTER
DESIGNS BY
MARC SILVESTRI

PSYLOCKE BY
ARTHUR ADAMS

PSYLOCKE
Arthur Adams's new costume made Psylocke look formidable (with her body armour) and mysterious (with her hood, mask, and cape).

REJECTED
SHADOWCAT
COSTUME

CHANGING FACES – 1980s

CANNONBALL
As shown in New Mutants co-creator Bob McLeod's drawing, not only was it originally intended for Cannonball to wear a mask, but also to have different powers.

EARLY VERSION OF CANNONBALL

Wolfsbane

Another new mutant, Wolfsbane, can transform into a wolf while retaining her human intellect, or into a half-human, half-wolf transitional form.

LUPINE LOOKS

WOLFSBANE HEADS
In these sketches Bob McLeod experimented with designing Wolfsbane's transitional form. She was finally given her distinctive short hairstyle in both her forms – human and half-wolf.

IN THE STORIES published throughout the 1980s, Xavier's dream won far more followers than ever before. Newcomers joined the X-Men: Kitty Pryde alias Shadowcat; Rogue, a former mutant terrorist; Rachel Summers, a refugee from a future where mutants are prisoners; the Dazzler, an entertainer who had been blacklisted for being a mutant; Psylocke; and Longshot. Xavier assembled his third generation of students, the New Mutants. Xavier's vision inspired the original X-Men to reorganize the team X-Factor, while Kitty Pryde and Nightcrawler helped to found Excalibur in England. Even Magneto temporarily became Xavier's ally, taking over as teacher of the New Mutants.

But Xavier's dream was also under assault as never before. Warning of the 'mutant menace', Senator Robert Kelly advocated a Mutant Registration Act, the first step in restricting their freedom. The X-Men learned of the 'Days of Future Past', an alternate reality in which mutants are kept in prison camps. The ancient mutant Apocalypse sought to foment war between humanity and mutantkind. An enigmatic geneticist, Sinister, engineered the slaughter of the Morlocks, a community of mutant outcasts. The X-Men discovered that the island of Genosha owed its prosperity to enslaving mutants. Xavier himself became a victim of the bigotry when he was beaten nearly to death by anti-mutant college students.

Scott Summers and Jean Grey seemed lost in a hall of mirrors. He believed that Phoenix was Jean and was devastated when she died. He soon married her exact lookalike, Madelyne Pryor, and they had a son, Nathan. But then the real Jean turned up alive; Phoenix had usurped her identity, and Madelyne, with powers of her own, became the X-Men's enemy. Wolverine underwent a spiritual crisis in Japan, finally learning to master the berserker side of his personality to defeat his enemy Lord Shingen. But on a return visit, battling the warrior Ogun, Wolverine discovered that should he drop his guard, the madness could still overwhelm him.

By the end of the decade, the X-Men seemed to have lost their way. Xavier was travelling in space with the exiled Lilandra. Some X-Men had vanished, others had disbanded the team and gone their separate ways; Wolverine wandered along the Pacific Rim with a young mutant girl named Jubilee. As a team, the X-Men were no more.

CLUB

WHEREAS the X-Men are branded outlaws, the members of the centuries-old Hellfire Club represent society's favoured elite: the wealthy, the privileged, and the famous. Few besides the X-Men know that most of the members of the Hellfire Club's Inner Circle, the Lords Cardinal, are mutants intent on dominating the rest of humanity. Founded in the 1760s in London, England, the Hellfire Club began as a meeting place for the highest ranks of British society. There they could meet to make deals and secretly indulge in pleasures that were forbidden by the morality of their time. In the 1770s two of the club's leading members, the wealthy trading company-owner Sir Patrick Clemens and his mistress, Diana Knight, emigrated to New York City, where they founded the American branch of the Hellfire Club. Today, the Hellfire Club's ranks include politicians, business leaders, socialites, and celebrities from all over the world. The general public – and even most of its members – consider the club to be a social organization with an irreproachable reputation. However, for generations the Inner Circle has been a secret cabal intent on amassing political and economic power and influence by illicit means.

SHINOBI SHAW
WHITE KING

SELENE
BLACK QUEEN

SEBASTIAN SHAW
BLACK KING

EMMA FROST
WHITE QUEEN

THE INNER CIRCLE
The Hellfire Club's most powerful members belong to its so-called Inner Circle. Members of the Inner Circle traditionally wear clothes with an 18th-century flavour for meetings and other formal occasions.

...WARREN WORTHINGTON, JR....

...HOWARD STARK...

...SEBASTIAN HIRAM SHAW...

...JOHN BRADDOCK...

PAST MEMBERS OF THE HELLFIRE CLUB
Membership of the Hellfire Club has been passed down through certain upper-class families for many generations. Hence, years ago, the club's membership included not only Sebastian Shaw but the fathers of Warren Worthington III (Archangel) and inventor Tony Stark (Iron Man), as well as a relative of Brian Braddock (Captain Britain).

London headquarters
When in London, Sebastian Shaw operates from an enormous mansion that was bequeathed to the Hellfire Club by the late Sir Henry Manners, an important member of the Inner Circle. The club's social events are held in another locale in central London.

HARRY LELAND
BLACK BISHOP

EMMANUEL DA COSTA
WHITE ROOK

JASON WYNGARDE
MASTERMIND

TESSA

DONALD PIERCE
WHITE BISHOP

FREDERICK VAN ROEHM
BLACK ROOK

MADELYNE PRYOR
BLACK ROOK

TREVOR FITZROY
WHITE ROOK

CHECKMATE

Inner Circle members hold positions named after chess pieces to denote their standing within the organization. The most powerful positions are the king and queen, and below them are bishops, rooks, and pawns. There can even be two kings and two queens at the same time, although this can lead to power struggles.

SOLDIERS
The Hellfire Club employs squads of uniformed mercenaries who act as guards at the club's Manhattan mansion and serve as soldiers on covert missions for the Inner Circle.

HELLFIRE
CLUB SOLDIERS

PRIVATE ARMY
As some of the wealthiest men and women on the planet, the members of the Inner Circle wield an economic power greater than that of many small countries. They even command a private army equipped with the latest hi-tech weapons and vehicles.

ONLY A FEW BLOCKS DOWN FIFTH AVENUE FROM AVENGERS MANSION STANDS A BUILDING THAT -- LIKE THE VAN -- IS FAR LESS INNOCENT THAN IT APPEARS.

THIS IS THE LEGENDARY HELLFIRE CLUB.

New York mansion
The Hellfire Club's historic New York mansion stands on Fifth Avenue near Central Park on Manhattan's Upper East Side. This is not only the venue for the club's renowned parties, but also the secret base of operations for Sebastian Shaw and the rest of the Inner Circle.

DARK PHOENIX

THE DARK PHOENIX SAGA is the tale of how Jean Grey, the X-Men's first female member, became a virtual goddess, possessing seemingly limitless power. It is the story of how she fell from grace into madness through the machinations of an old enemy, and of how she heroically sacrificed her life to save the entire universe. Following a battle with the Sentinels in space, the X-Men escaped back to Earth in a space shuttle piloted by Jean. The shuttle plunged through a solar radiation storm, exposing her to lethal energies. Yet when the shuttle crashed into a bay, the X-Men saw Jean rise from the waters as Phoenix. Her psionic powers had increased to potentially unlimited levels. But she soon fell victim to Mastermind, who brainwashed her into becoming the Black Queen of the Hellfire Club. Mastermind was unable to control her for long, however, and she became the insane Dark Phoenix, wreaking havoc through the cosmos. Professor X managed to return Jean to sanity, but only temporarily. Cyclops watched in horror as Jean committed suicide rather than revert to Dark Phoenix.

Black Queen
Using his powers of illusion, Mastermind made Jean hallucinate that she was a decadent woman living in 18th-century England. When Mastermind was finished, he had mesmerized Jean into becoming the Hellfire Club's ruthless Black Queen.

Jean in costume as the Black Queen of the Hellfire Club

UNLEASHED
By awakening the evil side of Jean Grey's personality, Mastermind released a force he could not control. The Black Queen turned vengefully against him, filling his mind with a vision of the cosmos that overwhelmed his sanity, and leaving him in a catatonic state. Then, before the other X-Men's eyes, Jean transformed into the insane Dark Phoenix and flew off into the depths of space.

INSTEAD OF ENSLAVING ME FOREVER, YOU SHOCKED ME AWAKE. YOU SET ME FREE.

TOO LATE.

NO! I COMPENSATED FOR THAT REACTION -- MY POWER SHOULD HAVE ...

YOUR POWER IS NOTHING!

STAR DESTROYER
Hurtling into a distant galaxy, driven by hunger for even more power, Dark Phoenix consumed energies from the core of a star, oblivious to the potential for disaster. The ravaged star exploded into a supernova, obliterating its planets and an entire alien race. The planetary system was under the rule of the Shi'ar, and a nearby Shi'ar battle cruiser attacked Dark Phoenix, seeking to avenge the slaughter. Despite the bravery of its crew, the ship was quickly annihilated.

GLADIATOR-- CONTINUE.

Royal decree

Returning to Earth, Dark Phoenix easily overpowered the attacking X-Men. But then Charles Xavier unleashed the full power of his mind against Phoenix, and Jean's true personality struggled back into control. Phoenix collapsed unconscious and awoke in Cyclops' arms as Jean, her dark side exorcized – for the moment. Suddenly, the X-Men were teleported into a starship, where the Shi'ar empress Lilandra demanded that Jean be destroyed lest she someday become Dark Phoenix once again. Invoking Shi'ar law, Xavier insisted on a trial by combat to determine whether or not Jean would live. The next day, the X-Men faced the Imperial Guard in this trial by combat amid ancient alien ruins on the Moon.

The only solution

In the midst of the battle against the Imperial Guard, Jean began reverting to Dark Phoenix. Xavier telepathically ordered the X-Men to stop her before she reached her full power. When Colossus struck her hard, Jean's true personality surfaced once more. Courageously clinging to her sanity before it disappeared again, Jean realized that the only way to free herself from the Phoenix Force was to die. Desperately, she pleaded with the X-Men and Cyclops, the man she loved, to kill her. But they could not bring themselves to do it.

TWO BEINGS-- JEAN GREY AND PHOENIX... SEPARATE...UNIQUE... BOUND TOGETHER. A *SYMBIOTE*, PETER; NEITHER CAN EXIST WITHOUT THE OTHER.

PHOENIX PROVIDES MY LIFE-FORCE, WHILE I PROVIDE A LIVING FOCUS FOR ITS INFINITE POWER.

SO LONG AS I LIVE, THE PHOENIX WILL MANIFEST ITSELF THROUGH ME. AND SO LONG AS THAT HAPPENS, I'LL EVENTUALLY, INEVITABLY, BECOME *DARK PHOENIX*.

THE PHOENIX IS A COSMIC POWER. IT CAN NEITHER BE CONTAINED NOR CONTROLLED-- ESPECIALLY BY A HUMAN VESSEL. RETURN IT TO THE COSMOS WHICH IS ITS HOME.

KILL ME!

NO!

MOURNING
Emotionally devastated, Cyclops left the X-Men for many months. Only years later would he and the other X-Men learn the truth about Phoenix.

THE AFTERMATH
Phoenix was actually a being of pure energy that had taken Jean's form. The real Jean eventually revived from suspended animation and was reunited with Scott.

SCOTT!

JEAN!

Jean's sacrifice

Jean fled into a building amid the ruins. Bidding Scott a last farewell, she telekinetically triggered an ancient energy cannon. As Cyclops watched helplessly, the blast annihilated her body. Dark Phoenix was destroyed, and the Phoenix Force was released back into the cosmos.

SHADOWCAT

Kitty was only beginning to use her mutant ability when she first aided the X-Men against the Hellfire Club.

KATHERINE 'KITTY' PRYDE was a typical 13-and-a-half-year-old teenager living in a Chicago suburb when she first did a very atypical thing: she discovered she could walk through walls. Kitty had begun to manifest her mutant ability to 'phase' through solid objects by mentally altering the vibratory rates of the atoms of her body. Her parents were approached by the heads of two different schools for 'special' students. One was Charles Xavier; the other was Emma Frost, the White Queen of the nefarious Hellfire Club. Several of the X-Men accompanied Xavier on his visit to Kitty's home, and when the White Queen captured them, Kitty helped in their rescue. Kitty Pryde soon joined the ranks of the X-Men. Initially she experimented with different costumes and code names, including Sprite and Ariel. Despite her youth, she proved so valuable a member that Xavier allowed her to remain with the older X-Men even after he organized the New Mutants, who were closer to Kitty's age. She also proved to have considerable computer skills. On a mission in outer space, Kitty first encountered a tiny alien dragon whom she named Lockheed. It followed her back to Earth and became her loyal companion.

Lockheed

Kitty once made up a fairy tale in which she portrayed the X-Men's jet, built by the Lockheed company, as a gigantic, friendly dragon. Later, on another planet, Kitty found a small creature who looked like a dragon, could fly, and even breathe flame, and she named him Lockheed. Devoted to Kitty, Lockheed is no mere pet, but an intelligent being who often appears to understand English.

SPRITE'S SECOND COSTUME

SPRITE'S FIRST COSTUME

SHADOWCAT'S FIRST COSTUME

AS ARIEL

WOLVERINE THE MENTOR

Wolverine became a mentor to Kitty and, during a stay in Japan, he gave her intensive training in the martial arts. It was then that she adopted the alias that she still uses today: Shadowcat. Shadowcat became a founding member of the British-based Super Hero team, Excalibur. During her time in the group she became romantically involved with her team-mate, former intelligence operative Peter Wisdom. Since their breakup, Shadowcat has returned to the United States and to membership of the X-Men. She is now a little older, and the naive, wide-eyed girl who first walked into Xavier's mansion is now a mature, self-reliant, and formidable young woman.

Out of phase

Originally Kitty could only make herself intangible; then she learned how to 'phase' objects, and people she touched as well. She has also learned to use her phasing ability to 'walk' on air, climbing to the top of a tall building as if she were climbing a staircase! Although Kitty can pass through any solid matter, she can still be affected by some forms of energy. An energy blast fired by Harpoon, a member of the Marauders, caused her to lose her ability to become fully tangible for months.

Kitty fails in her attempt to phase both herself and Rogue to avoid Harpoon's energy bolt.

Master warrior

One of the greatest turning points in Kitty's life came after she was captured by Wolverine's enemy, the near-immortal warrior Ogun. Once she was free, Wolverine gave her a crash course in samurai fighting techniques.

When Kitty faced Ogun for the second time, it was not as a helpless young girl, but as Shadowcat, a young woman and a formidable foe.

Kitty and Peter served together briefly in the British Super Hero team Excalibur.

Peter Wisdom

Kitty's first love was Colossus, when both were young and innocent. But when she was a few years older, Kitty moved to Britain, joined Excalibur, and fell in love with a considerably older man, ex-secret agent Peter Wisdom. This older mutant has the ability to create 'hot knives' of energy which he can throw at opponents. Perhaps because of the age difference, this contentious love affair did not last long.

DAYS OF FUTURE PAST

IN THE WORLD of the X-Men, the future may take any number of alternate directions. The path that leads to the 'Days of Future Past' sees Charles Xavier's dream turn into a nightmare in which mutants are imprisoned or slaughtered. It began when Senator Robert Kelly was assassinated by Mystique and her terrorist Brotherhood of Evil Mutants. Outraged government officials unleashed the Sentinels on the mutant population. Inevitably, the Sentinels took control of all of North America. Charles Xavier and many of the X-Men were slain, and others were confined to a concentration camp. The spirit of one of those inmates, Kate Pryde, travelled back through time into the body of her teenage self, Kitty, to prevent Kelly's assassination. Thanks to Kate's heroism, the present-day X-Men's future may take a different, better path. But they remain haunted by their knowledge of the 'Days of Future Past', knowing that unless they guard against it, a similar future could still arise.

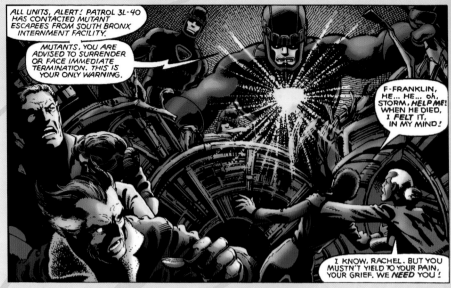

On the run

In the future, the surviving X-Men, including older versions of Colossus and Storm, devised a plan to change history. They had young mutant Rachel Summers use her psionic powers to send Kate Pryde's spirit back through time into her younger self's body. Then Wolverine helped them break out of the concentration camp in which they had been imprisoned. But they could not long escape the implacable Sentinels, who hunted them down.

Time traveller

In the X-Men's present, they had only recently welcomed 13-year-old Kitty Pryde into their team. Suddenly Kitty's soul was thrust into the future as her body was possessed by the spirit of her future self, the middle-aged Kate Pryde. Kate began telling the astounded X-Men who she was and how she had journeyed through time to stop the series of events that led to the horrors of the 'Days of Future Past'.

Future horror

Kate told the present-day X-Men that in the 'Days of Future Past' timeline Mystique and her Brotherhood killed Senator Robert Kelly to warn Americans not to take legal action against mutants. But instead the assassination inflamed anti-mutant bigotry, leading the federal government to dispatch the Sentinels to eliminate the mutant problem once and for all. The Sentinels decided that the most effective way to fulfil their task was to take control of the United States.

RESCUE MISSION
The present-day X-Men flew to Washington, DC, where they fought to stop the Brotherhood from reaching the senator. Kate anxiously watched, knowing that if Kelly was killed, the chain of events that would ultimately lead to her nightmarish future would become inevitable.

Armageddon

The future X-Men succeeded in penetrating the Sentinels' innermost sanctum, but to no avail. One Sentinel annihilated Wolverine with a single power blast, leaving only his virtually indestructible adamantium skeleton behind. Then Storm and Colossus met their own ends at the Sentinels' hands, and only Rachel was left to guard Kate's unconscious body.

MOMENT OF TRUTH
Just as the mutant Destiny fired her crossbow at Kelly, Kate 'phased' through her, upsetting her aim.

A new future

Destiny's arrow narrowly missed Kelly, and his life was saved. At that instant, Kate's spirit travelled back to the future, and Kitty's spirit returned to her teenage body. Due to the paradoxical nature of time travel, Kate found that the 'Days of Future Past' still existed. But because she had saved Senator Kelly in the present, the X-Men of our time are now following an alternate path through time, in which Xavier's dream may yet become a reality.

MYSTIQUE

THE SHAPESHIFTING MUTANT Mystique has assumed so many identities over her long life that not even she is sure of her original name. Mystique is a metamorph who can alter her form at will to impersonate other people, create new identities for herself, or even transform herself into a monster. Her power also slows down the aging process, maintaining her youthful appearance. However, she cannot duplicate the superhuman powers of those she impersonates, or increase or decrease her mass. She looks young today, yet we know she was around in the 1930s. Back then she appeared as a man, and worked in Britain as a detective named D. Raven. It was in this role that she first met Irene Adler, alias Destiny, a blind woman with the mutant ability to see into the future. The two mutants remained companions for many years until Destiny's recent death. Another of the early identities Mystique created for herself was that of billionaire financier B. Byron Biggs, a recluse who was rarely seen.

Mystique's grey-black skin and yellow eyes are genetic signs inherited by her son, Nightcrawler.

Mystique can psionically shift the atoms and molecules of her clothing to alter their appearance.

One of Mystique's latest identities is that of Ronnie Lake, who quickly became famous as the 'Model of the Millennium', a role that she relished.

MUTANT TERRORIST

Mystique once served in the Pentagon as Raven Darkholme, a Department of Defence official, until the government learned her true identity. This is one of the many guises she can slip into when need be, another favourite being her long-maintained identity as Mallory Brickman, the wife of a US senator. Many of these roles have been used by Mystique to pursue her evil goals through her own version of the Brotherhood of Evil Mutants, which she formed in outrage at the public's attempts to restrict mutants' freedom. The Brotherhood began by trying to assassinate Senator Robert Kelly, only to be thwarted by the X-Men in the first of many clashes between them. Later, Mystique and her Brotherhood worked for the government under the name Freedom Force. When it disbanded, Mystique reluctantly joined the government's new mutant team, X-Factor, before escaping and returning to her life as an outlaw.

Serving together in X-Factor, Mystique and Forge became strongly attracted to each other. Yet neither could trust the other: Forge knew Mystique was an unrepentant criminal, and Mystique resented Forge for using an inhibitor implant to keep her in X-Factor.

Weighty matters

Mystique can't alter her own body mass at will. If she impersonates someone bigger than herself, she won't weigh as much. The longer she maintains a larger form, the greater the strain she feels. So she usually prefers to take the form of people her own height and weight.

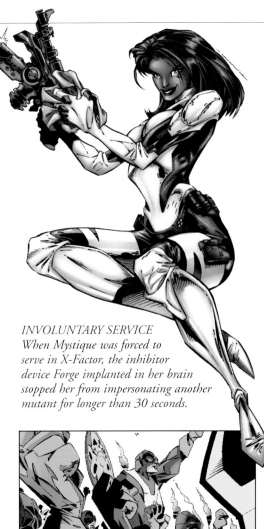

INVOLUNTARY SERVICE
When Mystique was forced to serve in X-Factor, the inhibitor device Forge implanted in her brain stopped her from impersonating another mutant for longer than 30 seconds.

Secret identity

This picture shows Mystique changing from Raven Darkholme into her true form – in the second it takes to go through a doorway! As Darkholme, she worked as the deputy director of a top-level, secret government defence agency. In this position, she learned military secrets and obtained advanced weapons for her terrorist activities.

Mystique as Mallory Brickman

WOMAN OF MANY FACES
During her life, Mystique has taken on many different identities and led many different lives. At one time, she was part of a neo-Nazi group of mercenaries, known as Hydra. Charles Xavier and Eric Lensherr, who was to become Magneto, came across this group when they were both working in a hospital in Israel. Later in life, she became Mallory Brickman, wife of US Senator Ralph Brickman. They even had a daughter, Gloria.

Bizarre family

Mystique has some of the most unusual family ties in the mutant world. Her first son, the anti-mutant demagogue Graydon Creed, was the result of an affair she had with Sabretooth. From another liaison, Mystique gave birth to Nightcrawler, whom she abandoned. Later, she fostered and raised the mutant Rogue.

STOP THE PRESS!
For a while, Mystique was a journalist on the Daily Bugle, *the same newspaper J. Jonah Jameson and Peter Parker, alias Spider-Man, worked for.*

Graydon Creed   *Nightcrawler*   *Rogue*

ON SCREEN

In the *X-Men* movie, Mystique serves as a member of Magneto's Brotherhood of Evil Mutants instead of heading the team herself. Rather than wear a costume, her entire body is covered in blue scales making her look even more inhuman. To make any of the characters she impersonates appear clothed, she simply uses her morphing power to make parts of her flesh look like clothing. The first we see of this is when Mystique is disguised as Guyrich, Senator Kelly's aide. In this guise, she helps in the kidnapping of the senator and his transformation into a mutant by Magneto's device. Mystique is later shown battling the X-Men inside the Statue of Liberty. Amidst the confusion caused by a thick bank of fog created by Storm to mask the X-Men's arrival, Mystique attacks the mutant heroes by impersonating Wolverine. The real Wolverine blocks her attack, and the two mutants begin to fight it out. But even in the same guise, Mystique cannot match Wolverine's fighting abilities. Escaping up a storm drain, she returns to the battle again, this time disguised as Storm. Once again, Wolverine confronts her, this time using his extra-sensitive smell to spot the mutant's disguise and his adamantium claws to stop her.

ROGUE

USUALLY GOOD-HUMOURED AND FEISTY, Rogue nonetheless bears the burden of a mutant power that feels to her like a curse. If Rogue's skin touches that of any other person, she absorbs all of that person's memories and abilities, leaving her victim unconscious until the transfer wears off. Rogue's plight is that she cannot control this power, and hence, she is unable to touch anyone else without triggering the transfer. As a result, she covers her entire body with clothing to prevent her skin coming into contact with that of another person. Rogue grew up in the deep South of the United States, along the banks of the Mississippi River. Her mutant power abruptly surfaced when she first kissed her friend Cody. Her mind was overwhelmed by Cody's memories, while he sank into a permanent coma. Afraid of endangering anyone else, she ran off to live as a hermit. She kept her true name a secret, so people dubbed her 'Rogue'.

"I SAID, TRYIN' TO SOUND TOUGH AS NAILS."

The young Rogue was initially suspicious of Mystique, and confronted the shapeshifting mutant when she first approached. But Mystique appealed to Rogue as a loner, revealing her true blue-skinned identity. As a result of this trust, the two grew close, and Mystique raised Rogue as if she were her daughter.

Rogue wears costumes that keep most of her body covered. Should her skin accidentally come into contact with the skin of another person, she will automatically absorb his or her memories and abilities.

SWITCHING SIDES

Another mutant, Mystique, found Rogue and raised her as a foster daughter. But Mystique also inducted Rogue into her terrorist Brotherhood of Evil Mutants. During a battle with the Super Hero Ms. Marvel, Rogue permanently absorbed her powers of flight, superhuman strength, and near-invulnerability. Mystique could not teach Rogue how to control her absorption power, so out of desperation, Rogue turned to the Brotherhood's enemy, Professor X, for help. At first, several members of the X-Men turned against Rogue, but they eventually accepted her when they realized how sincere she was. Although she still has not mastered her absorption ability, Rogue has found a new, happier, more fulfilling life as a member of the X-Men. Surrounded by her new 'family', she has developed a high-spirited personality – she even found romance, for a time, with one of her fellow X-Men, Gambit.

Rogue's personal trademark is the white streak which runs through her hair.

Teenage terrorist
Raised by Mystique, the adolescent Rogue joined the Brotherhood of Evil Mutants and repeatedly battled the X-Men as well as other Super Heroes. But Mystique did not provide the guidance the troubled girl needed to cope with her powers, and so the anguished Rogue forsook her Brotherhood to join the X-Men. Despite their estrangement, Rogue still regards Mystique as her foster mother and recently learned that Nightcrawler is Mystique's son and thus her foster brother.

FIGHTING MS. MARVEL
Usually Rogue can only absorb someone's powers and memories temporarily. The exception arose when she permanently duplicated Ms. Marvel's superpowers and even made a copy of her personality, which lay in Rogue's subconscious. Haunted by her powers, she later turned to a scientist who had developed a device that could remove her powers permanently. Rather than go through with the procedure, she destroyed the device so that it could never be used to deprive other mutants of their powers against their will.

In recent years, as Rogue has grown more comfortable with her powers and her life with the X-Men, she has favoured form-fitting costumes.

Rogue's powers
Thanks to the powers that she permanently absorbed from Ms. Marvel, Rogue can lift 50 tonnes of weight, fly at subsonic speeds, and is even bulletproof. She can absorb the memories and abilities of another person for a period sixty times longer than the amount of time her skin was in contact with her victim's flesh. Hence, one minute of contact transfers the victim's abilities to Rogue for an hour. Sometimes, Rogue even absorbs outward physical characteristics: if she touches Nightcrawler, her skin will turn blue!

Although Rogue first encountered the X-Men as their enemy, she is now a longtime veteran of the team. Due to her length of service, she was recently made one of the team's leaders; a move which took even her by surprise!

Gambit

Magneto

ROGUE AND ROMANCE
Rogue was convinced that her powers made it impossible for her ever to find fulfilment in love. But when she temporarily lost her powers, Rogue grew close to the reformed Magneto until he returned to terrorism. Later, Rogue fell in love with Gambit, but they parted after his dark past was revealed. Recently, she has become attracted to Colossus, who is immune to her powers in his metal form.

ON SCREEN

In the *X-Men* movie, Rogue does not have a past with Mystique and does not steal the mutant powers of Ms. Marvel. She has the comic book Rogue's Southern accent but lacks her sassy extroverted personality. Instead, the on-screen Rogue is more like the character when she first appeared in the comics. Withdrawn and afraid of her own mutant powers, the film shows the young Rogue roaming the country, avoiding human contact wherever possible. Her travels take her to a remote Canadian bar, where she comes into contact with another loner, the wandering Wolverine. After reluctantly giving Rogue a lift, the two are attacked by Sabretooth and only rescued after the intervention of two X-Men, Storm and Cyclops.

At first, Rogue settles in well with her new, adopted family at Xavier's Mansion. However, the other young mutants at the school shun her when she accidentally absorbs Wolverine's healing powers and renders him unconscious. Rogue runs away, only to be kidnapped by Magneto, who reveals that she is central to his plans. He needs Rogue to absorb his abilities and power a device he has built that will turn normal humans into mutants. However, the huge amount of energy needed to power the device will kill the young mutant.

PHOENIX II

IN THE ALTERNATE TIMELINE of the 'Days of Future Past', Scott Summers and Jean Grey raised a daughter, Rachel, who inherited her mother's powerful telepathic and telekinetic abilities. When Rachel was still a child, federal troops attacked the X-Men's mansion and captured her. Rachel was subsequently brainwashed and forced by her master, Ahab, to serve as a 'hound', using her telepathic powers to hunt down other mutants. The teenage Rachel finally broke free from her conditioning and rebelled against her masters, only to be placed in a prison camp with the other surviving X-Men. Later, she used her powers to travel through dimensions and time to the present-day reality of the X-Men we know. There she not only joined the team, but also discovered that, like her mother, she could access the potentially limitless power of the Phoenix Force.

MOTHER ASKANI

Rachel joined the new British Super Hero team, Excalibur. To save her team-mate Captain Britain, who had become trapped in the timestream, Rachel used her powers to exchange places with him. As a result, she journeyed two thousand years into the future and created the Clan Askani, a group of freedom fighters who opposed the tyranny of that timeline's evil ruler, Apocalypse. By defeating his operative, Councillor Diamanda Nero, Rachel severed her ties with the Phoenix Force, sending it back into outer space. Years later, as the elderly Mother Askani, Rachel transported Scott Summers' infant son Nathan to her future time, and then brought Scott and Jean Grey there to raise the child. She died soon after, but Nathan grew up to become the saviour of the era, the mutant warrior known as Cable.

Rachel manifests the Phoenix Force as a fiery bird of prey.

The Phoenix Force
The Phoenix Force is a manifestation of a primal force of the universe. Derived from the psionic energies of the minds of all living beings, the Phoenix Force has virtually infinite power. It also embodies the passion to create or (as in Dark Phoenix's case) to destroy. In Rachel's native timeline, the first Phoenix did not commit suicide, and Rachel inherited her mother's genetic ability to tap into and wield the Phoenix Force.

PHOENIX UNLEASHED
Not until after Rachel came to the present did she lay claim to the power of the Phoenix Force, although presumably she had unknowingly drawn upon it to travel through time. Rachel never learned to utilize more than a small portion of the Force to boost her own powers. But this was enough to make her a highly formidable opponent, especially when she gave way to her fiery temper. She once even returned to the 'Days of Future Past' with her fellow Excalibur members where they put an end to the Sentinels' tyranny.

'HOUND' TATTOOS
When Rachel served Ahab, her face was tattooed to mark her as one of his mutant-hunting 'hounds'. Afterwards, Rachel ordinarily used her telepathic abilities to create the illusion that her face was unmarked. But she often let her tattoos show when going into action as Phoenix.

Colossus

Kate Pryde

Franklin Richards

Rachel Summers

Storm

Magneto

THE LAST X-MEN
In her original timeline, Rachel was imprisoned in a concentration camp for mutants. Her fellow inmates included Kate (formerly Kitty) Pryde, Colossus, and Storm, all now middle-aged; Franklin Richards, the mutant son of the leader of the Fantastic Four; and their leader, the reformed Magneto, ironically now crippled as the deceased Xavier had been.

Rachel can use her powers of telekinesis to fly.

...FOR THE PERFECT VESSEL.

ONE DEAR TO ALL OUR HEARTS-- -- NATHAN CHRISTOPHER SUMMERS.

WHICH IS WHY I ARRANGED TO GRAB THE CHILD *FIRST.**

BUT HE WAS DESPERATELY ILL. I DID WHAT I COULD TO SAVE HIM FROM THE RAVAGES OF THE TECHNO-ORGANIC VIRUS.

BUT TIME WAS RUNNING OUT. AS A FAILSAFE, WE CREATED A HEALTHY CLONE.

Askani Motherhood
As Mother Askani, the now-aged Rachel had the infant Nathan Summers brought to the far future to become her people's champion. She halted the spread of the techno-organic virus that was killing the baby. But, in case he did not survive, she created his clone, who grew up to become Cable's nemesis, Stryfe.

NEW MUTANTS

TAKEN PRISONER by the alien Brood, the X-Men disappeared into outer space, and a despairing Charles Xavier assumed that his students were dead. His close friend Moira MacTaggert assured him that his dream still lived on and urged him to start over. So Xavier gathered together young mutants from around the world: Karma from Vietnam, Wolfsbane from Scotland, Sunspot from Brazil, a Native American named Dani Moonstar, and Cannonball from the state of Kentucky. When the X-Men finally returned home, they discovered that Xavier had assembled a new class of students: the New Mutants. As time went on, more newcomers were added to the mix. The New Mutants found Magma in the Amazon rainforest, and Colossus' little sister, Illyana Rasputin, became known as the sorceress Magik. The classmates' 'normal' friend Doug Ramsey proved to have a mutant talent for translating any language. The New Mutants even took in Warlock, a young extraterrestrial being who had fled to Earth to escape his tyrannical father.

LEAVING EARTH

Shortly after assembling the New Mutants, Xavier abruptly had to leave Earth with the Starjammers, and astonishingly, he turned over his school to his archenemy, Magneto. Many months before, when she was holding Magneto prisoner, Moira MacTaggert had tampered with his mind, altering his personality. Abandoning his drive for power, Magneto took over teaching the New Mutants. Little by little, however, Magneto's true personality re-emerged, and he ultimately abandoned the school. New members continued to join, including Boom Boom (now known as Meltdown), Rictor, Skids, who was surrounded by a force field, and Rusty Collins, who could generate heat and flame. But without adult guidance, the New Mutants began to drift apart. Finally, the mutant warrior from the future, Cable, reorganized the few remaining members into the nucleus of a new team. By the time Xavier returned, the New Mutants had become X-Force.

KARMA
The only adult member of the New Mutants, Xi'an Coy Mahn, alias Karma, is a Vietnamese immigrant with the mutant ability to take possession of the mind of another person. Here she is seen battling one of the X-Men's enemies, the female terrorist Viper.

Viper

Colossus' younger sister, Illyana, known as Magik, could create disks of energy that transported her through time and space. She died as a result of the Legacy Virus.

Magik was also a sorceress who could manifest her magical powers in her soulsword, a construct of mystical energy that could break spells and harm supernatural beings.

Wolfsbane · Thunderbird II · Karma · Cannonball · Catseye · Cypher · Empath · Roulette · Magik · Jetstream · Magma · Tarot

HELLIONS
Upset with having Magneto as their new mentor, the New Mutants rebelled by briefly joining their rivals, the Hellions. This was a group of teenage mutants being trained to serve the Hellfire Club by its White Queen, Emma Frost. The Hellions were based at the Massachusetts Academy, where Frost would later help instruct Generation X.

Roberto Da Costa, alias Sunspot, can draw energy from the Sun to give him superhuman strength.

Rahne Sinclair is a mutant werewolf called Wolfsbane who can transform at will.

WARLOCK AND CYPHER
Warlock's best friend was his fellow New Mutant, Doug Ramsey, code-named Cypher. Warlock could physically and mentally merge with Doug in order to combine their talents. Doug was killed on a mission with the New Mutants, but Warlock still retains his friend's memories.

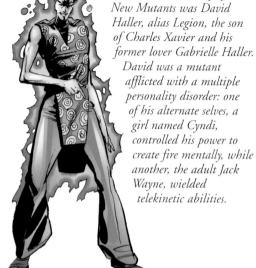

LEGION
One bizarre adversary of the New Mutants was David Haller, alias Legion, the son of Charles Xavier and his former lover Gabrielle Haller. David was a mutant afflicted with a multiple personality disorder: one of his alternate selves, a girl named Cyndi, controlled his power to create fire mentally, while another, the adult Jack Wayne, wielded telekinetic abilities.

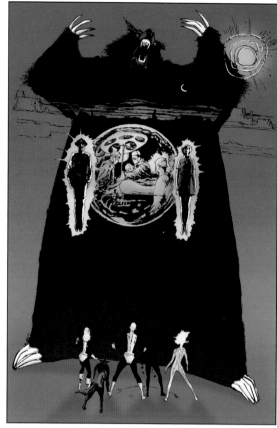

Demon bear

In one of their strangest adventures, the New Mutants battled a gigantic demon bear that had long haunted the dreams of Dani Moonstar and was now capturing innocent people. Magik's soulsword transformed the bear back into Dani's parents, whom she had long believed dead.

Danielle Moonstar has the mutant ability to manifest images from the minds of others as three-dimensional illusions.

A former coal miner in Kentucky, Sam Guthrie can propel himself through the air like a cannonball, while becoming virtually invulnerable at the same time.

Magma is a British-born mutant named Amara Aquilla. She has the power to induce small earthquakes, bring lava to the surface, and generate intense heat.

Warlock is not a mutant but a young member of an alien race called the Technarchy, whose techno-organic bodies resemble living machinery and who can change shape at will.

Joining the other side

After Charles Xavier began assembling his new class of students, mercenaries working for the Hellfire Club renegade, Donald Pierce, killed Dani Moonstar's grandfather and Roberto da Costa's girlfriend. After Xavier defeated Pierce, Dani, Roberto, and Sam Guthrie, who had been one of Pierce's mercenaries, joined Karma and Wolfsbane as the original New Mutants.

THE MORLOCKS

OUTCASTS FROM SOCIETY, the Morlocks were a community of mutants that lived in tunnels beneath New York City and its vicinity. This community was founded by the mutant Callisto who discovered the 'Alley', an enormous tunnel underneath Manhattan, which became their home. She then found Caliban, a mutant with the psionic ability to locate other mutants. Using Caliban's power, Callisto located and gathered together many other mutants who had run away from human society. Many who joined the community had been subjects of experiments conducted by the evil geneticist, Dark Beast, after he arrived in this timeline from the 'Age of Apocalypse'. These other mutants included Masque, who would grotesquely alter the faces of other Morlocks to show their rebellion against human norms.

The Morlocks' main tunnel, the 'Alley', runs the length of Manhattan. It is the centre of a network of tunnels built in the 1950s by the US government for use during a nuclear war. It is part of a tunnel system which extends into New Jersey, Connecticut, and New York State.

LIFE UNDERGROUND

At one stage, Callisto had Angel kidnapped, intending to make him her mate. To save Angel, Storm fought and won a duel with Callisto, displacing her as leader and forming an alliance between the Morlocks and the X-Men. And then the unthinkable happened. A group of mutant mercenaries, the Marauders, broke into the tunnels and massacred most of the Morlock population. Another mutant, Mikhail Rasputin, saved some of the Morlocks from the attack by taking them to another dimension. Here, Mikhail trained the survivors to avenge the Morlock slaughter by killing non-mutant humans, creating the terrorist group known as Gene Nation.

CALLISTO
A mutant with superhumanly acute senses, Callisto is a superb hunter and tracker. Although deposed as Morlock leader by Storm, Callisto has often been her ally. Since she was taken to another dimension by Mikhail Rasputin, Callisto has shown a maternal devotion towards the young Gene Nation member known as Marrow.

Among the Morlocks
Among the many known members of the Morlocks were the shapeshifter Ape; Erg; the Healer; Leech (who later worked with Generation X); Plague (who later became Apocalypse's Horseman Pestilence); Skids (who generated force fields and later joined Magneto's Acolytes); the superhumanly strong Sunder; and Tar Baby.

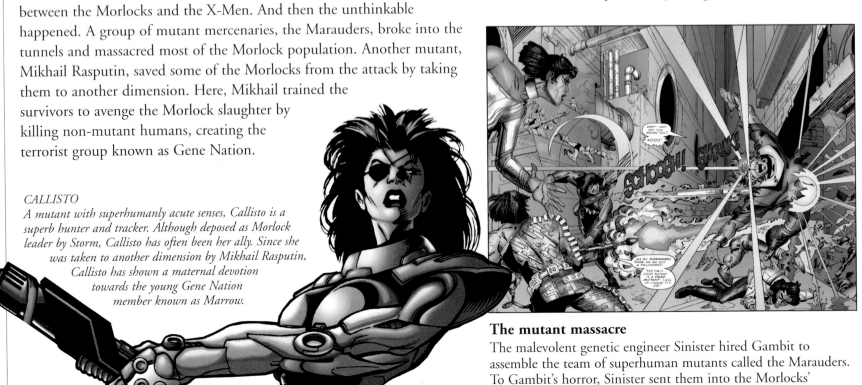

The mutant massacre
The malevolent genetic engineer Sinister hired Gambit to assemble the team of superhuman mutants called the Marauders. To Gambit's horror, Sinister sent them into the Morlocks' tunnels to exterminate their entire community. Most of the Morlocks were slaughtered, but a few escaped, some of them through the help of the X-Men and the original X-Factor.

I AM MIKHAIL RASPUTIN.

MIKHAIL RASPUTIN IN COSTUME

Mikhail Rasputin's other-dimensional citadel atop 'the Hill', overlooking the outlands.

THE SUMMIT IS ATTAINED.

THE FORTRESS SQUATTING ON ITS PEAK ATTEMPTS TO LOOK MAJESTIC, BUT SUCCEEDS ONLY IN BEING MONSTROUS.

Callisto | *Mikhail*

Morlocks' mad saviour

Mikhail was sent to Siberia to investigate a portal, through which his ship entered another dimension. When Mikhail used his powers to seal the portal, he unintentionally released energies that killed everyone else in the dimension. Eventually, the X-Men traversed the portal and brought Mikhail back to Earth. There, he sought to redeem himself by transporting the Morlocks who had survived the massacre to the other dimension.

Mikhail Rasputin

The older brother of Colossus and Magik, Mikhail was a cosmonaut in the Russian space programme. He has the mutant abilities to channel any form of energy and to psionically alter the molecular structure of matter.

GENE NATION
Raised by Mikhail to become ruthless killers, the surviving Morlocks returned to Earth as the terrorist group called Gene Nation. Marrow was their leader; and other Gene Nation members included Sack, Vessel, Reverb, Wynter, Obsidian the Dark, Fever Pitch, Integer, and Iron Maiden.

The Hill

Mikhail transported the surviving Morlocks to another dimension where he lived in a citadel on 'the Hill'. In this dimension, time passed much faster, and the children whom Mikhail had rescued grew to adulthood, while only a short period of time passed on Earth. Guilt-ridden over the deaths he had caused in this dimension when he closed the portal, Mikhail became insane and fell under the influence of an evil entity. He believed that the surviving Morlock children should become warriors to combat human cruelty. Hence, as soon as their mutant powers emerged, he sent them into the outlands and forced them to battle each other.

FORGE

THE EAGLE'S NEST
When he was designing weapons for the government, Forge lived and worked in the Eagle's Nest, a multistorey penthouse of his own design located in Dallas, Texas. Floors were suspended in space, with no visible means of support.

THE MAN KNOWN ONLY AS FORGE is characterized by dualities. He is both a mutant and a sorcerer. He is 'the Maker', an inventor, and he is a warrior. He is the hope of his Native American tribe, the Cheyenne, and he is a former operative for the United States government. And he is part man and part machine. Born with a potential for gaining extraordinary mystical powers, Forge was trained in magic from childhood by the Cheyenne shaman Naze. But Forge rebelled against his Cheyenne heritage and became a soldier, fighting in Vietnam. When the soldiers he commanded were killed in combat, the enraged Forge drew upon their spirits to summon a horde of demons to attack the enemy. After this misuse of his magic, Forge fell victim to a B-52 airstrike in which he lost both his right hand and right leg.

MAN AND MACHINE

Forge was horrified by the carnage wreaked by the demons he had summoned. He abandoned the use of sorcery and turned to his other talent: he was a mutant with an intuitive genius for inventing new forms of technology. He devised a robotic hand and leg for himself and went to work for the US government designing new and advanced weaponry. When government agents used one of his inventions that could neutralize mutant powers against Storm, he felt guilty and rescued her. Later, he reclaimed his magical powers and became the X-Men's ally against the supernatural being known as the Adversary. He eventually joined the X-Men, only to leave them and become the leader of the second version of X-Factor. Ultimately, Forge became disillusioned with the government's anti-mutant policies, and left to seek a new path in life.

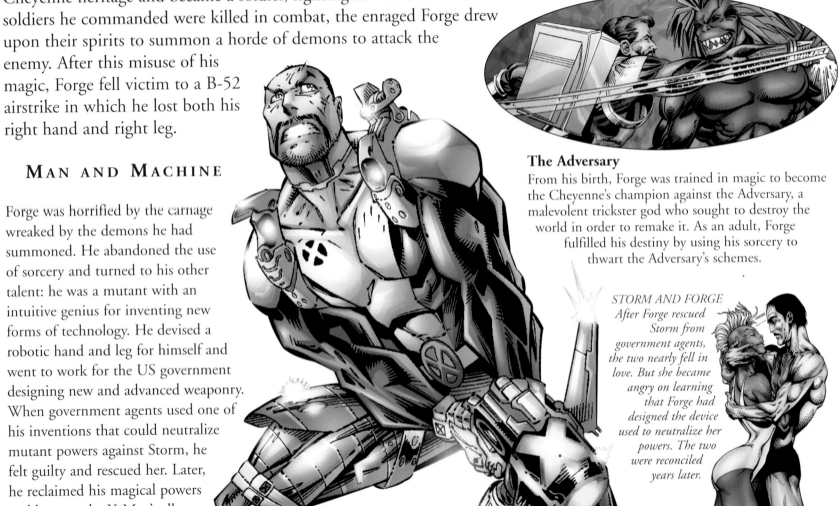

The Adversary
From his birth, Forge was trained in magic to become the Cheyenne's champion against the Adversary, a malevolent trickster god who sought to destroy the world in order to remake it. As an adult, Forge fulfilled his destiny by using his sorcery to thwart the Adversary's schemes.

STORM AND FORGE
After Forge rescued Storm from government agents, the two nearly fell in love. But she became angry on learning that Forge had designed the device used to neutralize her powers. The two were reconciled years later.

Dire Wraiths
The government first used Forge to create devices which could defeat the Dire Wraiths, a race of shape-changing aliens. Forge eventually created a powerful orbiting device. This was fired at the Dire Wraiths' home world, negating the planet's magic and depriving the Wraiths of their powers.

ALIEN RACES

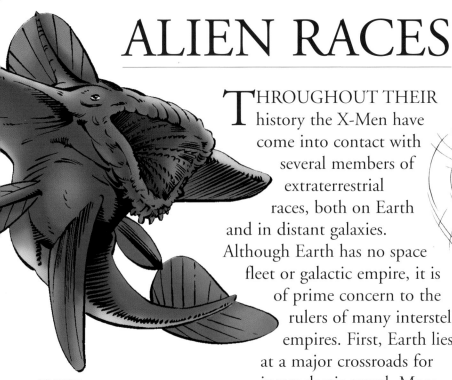

ACANTI
Resembling whales, the Acanti are sentient beings who can travel through outer space at extraordinary speeds. Hence, many Acanti have been enslaved by the Brood, who use them as living spaceships.

THROUGHOUT THEIR history the X-Men have come into contact with several members of extraterrestrial races, both on Earth and in distant galaxies. Although Earth has no space fleet or galactic empire, it is of prime concern to the rulers of many interstellar empires. First, Earth lies at a major crossroads for intergalactic travel. More importantly, in recent decades, Earth has spawned superhuman beings, including the X-Men and other mutants, whom these aliens perceive as potential threats. The original X-Men thwarted attempts to conquer Earth by the Arcane (through their agent Lucifer), the Siri (represented by the Mutant Master), and the Z'nox, without ever leaving the planet. It was when Princess Lilandra Neramani of the Shi'ar came to Earth seeking Xavier's help against her mad brother, Emperor D'Ken, that the second generation of X-Men first journeyed into outer space. The Shi'ar rule one of the three largest galactic empires in known space: the others are those of the Kree and the Skrulls. By befriending Lilandra, the X-Men became embroiled with her enemies, notably an insect-like race called the Brood.

BATTLING THE BROOD

It was when the X-Men defeated an attempt to overthrow Lilandra which was supported by the Brood, that this predatory race first learned about the mutants. The Brood captured the X-Men, seeking to make them host bodies for their young. The Brood's homeworld was destroyed during their clash with the X-Men, and the insect race has plagued the mutant team ever since, visiting Earth to find new prey. More recently, the X-Men have contended against the reptilian, shape-changing Skrulls, who have attempted to conquer the Shi'ar.

Brood

Although they resemble Earth insects, members of the Brood are over two metres long. They are cunning, vicious hunters, driven by their need to procreate. The Brood captures members of other species, each of whom acts as a host for an egg laid by the Brood Queen. On hatching, the Brood embryo merges with its host, genetically restructuring the host's body into an adult member of the Brood. Through this process, a member of the Brood can gain superhuman abilities possessed by its host.

A fully grown member of the Brood

Sidrian hunters

One of many alien races inhabiting the Shi'ar Empire, the Sidri have no native planet but instead live in deep interstellar space. These formidable beings grow additional layers of organic body armour at will within seconds and can fire force blasts from the front of their bodies. Within the Shi'ar galaxy, Sidri work as bounty hunters.

A colony of Sidri can merge together to form a single organism with a collective mind!

PSYLOCKE

ELIZABETH 'BETSY' BRADDOCK is the sister of Brian Braddock, who, as Captain Britain, is the United Kingdom's leading Super Hero. The siblings inherited the genes giving them superhuman powers from their late father, who came from an extra-dimensional realm called Otherworld. Betsy developed telepathic powers and used them in her work for STRIKE, the British division of the international law enforcement agency SHIELD. At one point, Brian persuaded Betsy to become the new Captain Britain. After she was severely beaten and blinded in combat, however, Brian resumed his role as Captain Britain.

Psylocke's psychic knife appears from her right fist.

BODY SWAP

While recuperating, Betsy was captured by Mojo, who restored her sight by giving her new bionic eyes. She was rescued by the New Mutants and became a guest at Professor Xavier's mansion. After holding her own in a battle against Sabretooth, Betsy officially joined the X-Men under the name Psylocke. Thereafter, Betsy's life took perhaps the strangest twist in X-Men history. The X-Men's enemy Spiral swapped over the minds of Betsy and the Japanese assassin Kwannon. Kwannon, now calling herself Revanche, learned that she was infected with the Legacy Virus and had herself killed. As a result, Betsy's original body died, but Betsy lived on in a new body, possessing both her own psychic powers and Kwannon's martial arts skills. Since then Psylocke's powers have undergone various changes, culminating in her recent acquisition of telekinetic powers.

Psylocke now wears this figure-hugging outfit, which offers her greater freedom of movement.

Psylocke's psi powers

Psylocke's telepathic powers not only enabled her to read minds and communicate mentally, but, like the mental powers of Professor X, she could also strike down opponents with 'mental bolts'. An energy signature resembling a butterfly sometimes appeared above her head when she used her powers. Psylocke learned to focus her powers into a 'psychic knife' which she used to stun or kill her adversary. She has now developed telekinetic powers to replace the telepathic ones she cannot use for fear of releasing the Shadow King.

PSYLOCKE'S SECOND COSTUME
After battling alongside the X-Men for a while, Psylocke changed to this new costume. Its body armour afforded her greater protection, and it had a hood and mask to conceal her true identity.

PSYLOCKE'S FIRST COSTUME

Psylocke adopted this costume, more decorative than practical, when she first joined the X-Men. Though her hair is naturally brown, she dyed it purple during her career as a fashion model.

WITH ARCHANGEL
During her early career with the X-Men, Psylocke flirted briefly with Cyclops. He, however, rejected her advances and remained staunchly loyal to his future wife, Jean Grey. Psylocke finally found romance in the arms of the winged Super Hero Archangel.

Psylocke's sacrifice

Psylocke paid a heavy price to defeat one of the X-Men's greatest enemies, the Shadow King, an evil mutant who had once inhabited the body of the Egyptian Amahl Farouk. She used her telepathic powers to imprison him on another level of reality, known as the Astral Plane, and to stop him from taking possession of other bodies. As a result, she must refrain from using her telepathic powers again. If she were to do so, she runs the risk of setting the Shadow King free.

Merging with Kwannon

Japanese crime boss Matsu'o Tsurayaba made a bargain with the enigmatic Spiral to save the life of his dying lover, the assassin Kwannon. But, to amuse her master, Mojo, Spiral double-crossed Matsu'o. She healed Kwannon's body, but switched her mind with that of Psylocke's. Thus, the woman who now looked like Kwannon had become Matsu'o's enemy. After the mind transfer, Psylocke and Kwannon, who now called herself Revanche, worked as allies, neither one certain of her true identity. But after the truth was revealed, Revanche persuaded her lover Matsu'o to kill her rather than let her die a slow, agonizing death from the Legacy Virus.

"IN BETSY'S CHAOTIC STATE, YOUR MINDS *FUSED* TOGETHER--"

"--YOU BOTH SCREAMED OUT, CUTTING THROUGH THE STILL FOG OF THE COLD NIGHT--"

ORIGINAL X-FACTOR

X-FACTOR HEADQUARTERS
X-Factor's first headquarters was a massive complex on Manhattan's East Side, financed by the wealthy Angel. Later, X-Factor moved into a colossal skycraft, which Apocalypse had used as his headquarters. This proved to be a spaceship that had been built by the Celestials, a race of all-powerful aliens.

MANY MONTHS AFTER the original Phoenix died, the real Jean Grey awoke from suspended animation and was reunited with the other four original X-Men: Cyclops, the Angel, Beast, and Iceman. By that point Charles Xavier had vanished (he was actually in space with the Starjammers), and the existing X-Men were working with Magneto. Jean proposed that the original X-Men form X-Factor in order to carry on Xavier's legacy. The Angel hired an old classmate, Cameron Hodge, who devised a new image for the team. Hiding their costumed identities, the members of X-Factor pretended to hunt down mutants in order to eliminate the 'mutant menace'. In reality, X-Factor secretly sheltered the mutants and trained them to use their powers.

At first X-Factor's members wore dark glasses and drab uniforms in their role as mutant hunters. Hence, the public did not realize that they were actually the original X-Men.

MANIPULATED

Eventually, the members of X-Factor realized that Hodge had been manipulating them to spread anti-mutant propaganda. Their foe Apocalypse abducted the Angel and transformed him into the being now known as Archangel. Cyclops, Marvel Girl, Beast, and Iceman publicly disavowed Hodge's anti-mutant campaign and proclaimed their mission to help mutants. Archangel soon rejoined the team, but ultimately the original X-Factor dissolved when Xavier returned to Earth, and X-Factor's founders all returned to the X-Men.

> **X-FACTOR**
> MUTANT INVESTIGATIONS AND *RESOLUTIONS!* NO NEED TO BE FEARFUL ANY LONGER! OUR SKILLED TEAM OF *EXPERTS* WILL AID YOU IN FINDING THE ANSWERS TO ONE OF THE MOST URGENT PROBLEMS OF OUR TIME! CALL OUR TOLL FREE NUMBER! OPERATORS STANDING BY! *VISA* AND *MASTERCARD* ACCEPTED! DON'T WAIT UNTIL IT'S *TOO LATE!*

ADVERTISEMENTS
The treacherous Cameron Hodge ran this advertisement for X-Factor in various newspapers to convey the idea that mutants were a 'problem' spreading 'fear'.

After Apocalypse genetically altered him, Archangel was briefly X-Factor's enemy.

ARCHANGEL

MARVEL GIRL

ICEMAN

CYCLOPS

X-FACTOR JET
As Warren Worthington III, the Angel could use his fortune to supply X-Factor's members with whatever they needed, including this enormous jet.

BEAST

In X-Factor's early days, Beast temporarily reverted to human form.

X-TERMINATORS
Early on, X-Factor's members only used their powers in public as the costumed 'X-Terminators'. The X-Terminators finally revealed themselves to be X-Factor to take a public stand against anti-mutant bigotry.

EXCALIBUR

FOR YEARS, GREAT BRITAIN was home to its own team of costumed adventurers. Its name not only referred to King Arthur's legendary sword, but also alluded to the 'X' in the names of the X-Men and other mutant teams. At the centre of Excalibur was Brian Braddock, who was the UK's leading costumed crusader, Captain Britain. Brian inherited his powers from his father, who came to Earth from Otherplace, an extradimensional realm ruled by a being who purported to be Merlin the sorcerer. Merlin and his daughter Roma imbued Brian with mystical energies that activated his mutant powers and decreed that he use them to serve as Britain's champion. Eventually Captain Britain met and fell in love with Meggan, a mutant shapeshifter. Brian's sister, Elizabeth, became the X-Man Psylocke. Later, Shadowcat and Nightcrawler went to Britain, where they completed their recovery from injuries sustained during the Marauders' massacre of the Morlocks.

Original Excalibur team
The original Excalibur team consisted of Meggan, a shapeshifter who flies, takes energy from the Earth, and fires it in blasts of concussive force, and Captain Britain, who has superhuman strength, the ability to fly, and a force field. There was also Phoenix II, Shadowcat, and Nightcrawler.

Two of the New Mutants, Doug Ramsey and Warlock, were believed to be dead. But then who or what was the member of Excalibur known as 'Douglock', a 'techno-organic' being who appeared to be Doug and Warlock merged into one? In time it was revealed that Douglock was the resurrected Warlock, who had gained Doug's memories.

NEW RECRUITS

When they learned that the X-Men had reportedly died in Texas, Shadowcat and Nightcrawler joined with Captain Britain, Meggan, and Rachel Summers, the second Phoenix, in founding Excalibur, to carry on Charles Xavier's vision. (As it turned out, Roma had resurrected the X-Men who had died.) Excalibur endured for years, but eventually the team dissolved: Shadowcat, Colossus, and Nightcrawler all returned to the US, but Captain Britain still stands guard over the British Isles.

TOWARDS THE END
Captain Britain, Meggan, Nightcrawler, and Shadowcat remained on the team from its start to its finish. When Captain Britain became trapped in the timestream, Phoenix II rescued him by trading places: he returned to the present, but she wound up in the distant future and became Mother Askani. Others to join Excalibur, included the mutant Kylun, the extraterrestrial Cerise, and the robot-like Widget. The most important additions in later years were Douglock, Colossus, and Peter Wisdom, a mutant and former British intelligence agent.

Captain Britain's wedding
The happiest event in the history of Excalibur also marked its ending. As their team-mates watched, Brian Braddock, alias Captain Britain, and Meggan were at long last married. But almost immediately afterwards, the team broke up, with Colossus, Nightcrawler, and Shadowcat returning to the X-Men.

APOCALYPSE

ONE OF THE FIRST MUTANTS to be born into the human race, Apocalypse is also one of the mightiest and most dangerous. Endowed with colossal strength and an incredibly long life span, Apocalypse is nearly impossible to kill. He is also a shapeshifter who can transform any part of his body into a living weapon. But Apocalypse's main threat lies in his murderous ideology of the 'survival of the fittest'. Whereas Charles Xavier and the X-Men work for peace between humanity and mutants, Apocalypse dedicates himself to enslaving or exterminating all but those he considers the strongest. Only then, he believes, can mutants grow powerful enough to dominate the planet under his leadership.

Apocalypse's 'costume' is actually part of his body which he can psionically alter at will.

The literal translation of Apocalypse's real name, En Sabah Nur, is 'The First One'.

ANCIENT EVIL

Apocalypse was born nearly five thousand years ago on the outskirts of Egypt. Fearing that the grotesque infant was a demon, his tribesmen abandoned him in the desert. A raider named Baal rescued and adopted the strange baby, seeing in him 'a god in the making'. Baal named the child 'En Sabah Nur' and raised him to believe that only the strong were worthy of survival. Believing that he was destined for greatness, En Sabah Nur laboured as a slave in the Pharaoh's city, waiting for his opportunity to overthrow the ruler. But Pharaoh Rama-Tut, who was in reality from the far future and had travelled back in time to find Apocalypse and enslave him, discovered Apocalypse first. When Nur defied Rama-Tut's orders, the Pharaoh cut him down with a weapon from the future. But En Sabah Nur did not die; rather, his full powers were unleashed. Apocalypse proved to be even more evil than the tyrant he intended to overthrow. For millennia he roamed the planet, encouraging civilizations to worship him as a god, and testing their strength by manipulating them into fighting wars of conquest. Today, he has reappeared yet again, believing world conquest to be at last within his reach.

Apocalypse sees both humans and mutants as pawns to pit against each other in battle so that he may rule the victors.

Apocalypse's powers
Apocalypse is a metamorph, capable of altering his shape and physical appearance at will. He can even increase his size and acquire virtually any superhuman physical power. Hence he can turn parts of his body into weapons or change shape to defend himself from harm. In this instance, he has turned his arm into a huge shield to protect himself from the razor-sharp feathers fired from Archangel's organic metal wings.

The rise of Apocalypse

After leading his desert raiders in slaughtering the tribe who had left the infant Apocalypse to perish, Baal rescued the mutant baby and raised him as his son. Baal believed En Sabah Nur was the being prophesied to make 'kingdoms bow at his feet'. As he was dying, Baal instructed Nur to overthrow the tyrant Rama-Tut. Surviving Rama-Tut's attacks, and rejected by Nephri, the woman he loved, En Sabah Nur turned against humankind. His incredibly long life span has enabled Apocalypse to appear throughout history in his quest to conquer the world – he will even rule the planet in an alternate future 2,000 years from now.

EGYPTIAN WARRIOR
The young Apocalypse grew into a superhumanly strong warrior. When Rama-Tut first confronted Apocalypse, the Pharaoh offered to make En Sabah Nur his heir. Nur refused and Rama-Tut ordered him to be killed, only to have his warlord defeated by the mutant. Rama-Tut fled through time into the future, leaving Apocalypse to begin his own path of conquest.

BRITAIN
After lying in suspended animation for an unknown length of time, Apocalypse awoke in 19th-century London and resumed his plans for conquest. He sought to destroy the British Empire by unleashing a plague, but was unexpectedly thwarted by his new ally, Sinister.

FUTURE APOCALYPSE
In an alternate future, Apocalypse rules the planet but only exists as a wizened figure within a robot shell. He planned to transfer his life essence into the body of his heir, Stryfe, but perished in combat with Cyclops, Phoenix, and the young Cable.

THE FOUR HORSEMEN
Apocalypse is served by his Four Horsemen, named after the unearthly figures in the last book of the Bible. The Four Horsemen are Death (a position once filled by Archangel and Wolverine), Famine, War, and Pestilence.

War is a former soldier who can explode objects by clapping his hands together.

Pestilence could infect her victims with diseases simply by touching them. She has since been killed.

Famine has the power to turn organic matter into dust.

All the Horsemen, except Death, ride mechanical flying steeds. Apocalypse can teleport steeds and riders to and from any location.

THE HOUR OF YOUR *GLORY* IS AT HAND, MY HORSEMEN!

MOUNT YOUR *BEASTS!*

SABRETOOTH

As a child, Creed remembers — or perhaps imagines — being chained up in a dark basement by his father, who considered him a freak.

IF WOLVERINE is a man who has struggled to master the animal side of his psyche, then his archenemy is the opposite: one who has surrendered utterly to the beast within. Sabretooth is a mutant predator who sees the rest of humanity as prey for him to hunt, fight, and kill. Even so, Wolverine and Sabretooth have a lot in common. Both are mutants whose injuries heal with incredible rapidity. Both also age very slowly, and due to mental meddling by their former employers, neither knows exactly how old he is. They both have superhumanly acute senses and they both have a ferocious fighting ability. But Sabretooth has sought for a long time to kill his X-Men counterpart. This vicious mutant was born Victor Creed, but, as with Wolverine, much of his past is a mystery, even to himself.

FORMER PARTNERS

Both men were once partners as special operatives for the CIA, whose 'Weapon X' programme implanted false memories into their minds and blocked real ones. More recently, Sabretooth has left the CIA and has operated as a ruthless mercenary assassin, notably with Sinister's Marauders. Although the X-Men and X-Factor have tried, no one has succeeded in restraining Sabretooth for long. He continues to stalk the globe, killing for pleasure, determined that one day he will finally destroy Wolverine.

Captured by the X-Men

At one point, Professor Xavier held Sabretooth prisoner, hoping he could help the beast overcome his murderous urges. Xavier's attempt failed and Sabretooth broke free. Later, certain US government officials placed Sabretooth in X-Factor, intending him to be a 'sleeper' agent who would kill his team-mates if it were considered necessary. He was forced to wear a restraining collar designed by Forge to prevent him from attacking the rest of X-Factor. When Sabretooth succeeded in removing it, he savagely assaulted the other members before escaping.

When Xavier kept him captive at his mansion, Sabretooth attacked Wolverine, who thrust one of his claws into Sabretooth's head, injuring his brain. No longer violent, Sabretooth enjoyed relaxing in a holographic forest. Unfortunately, his brain injury soon healed, and his psychotic personality returned.

Even as a child, Creed had fangs and claws.

Brief reversal

Recently, Sabretooth believed he had gained a decisive advantage over Wolverine when his own skeleton was laced with adamantium. At the time, Wolverine had been stripped of his adamantium by Magneto. But Apocalypse, who was intent on forcing Wolverine into serving him, removed the adamantium from Sabretooth's body and bonded the metal to Wolverine's skeleton to make him stronger.

Blood feud

In the 1960s, Logan turned against his CIA partner Creed, when Creed murdered a female agent they had been sent to rescue. The two became bitter enemies, and every year since then on Logan's birthday, Creed makes an attempt to kill him, even though it was once believed that he was Logan's father. Today, Creed hates Logan more than ever, because he resents the fact that Logan has mastered his inner demons, while Creed remains the willing victim of his own.

MARAUDER
Sabretooth wore this costume when Gambit recruited him into the Marauders, the cadre of assassins who served Sinister. Sabretooth took part in the massacre of the Morlocks, the mutant community who lived beneath Manhattan.
Afterwards, driven by his psychosis, Sabretooth became the mysterious 'Slasher', who stalked and murdered non-mutant victims in New York.

In Team X

Decades ago, Victor Creed was a member of the CIA's covert strike force, Team X. Among his partners were two other superhuman mutant agents, Logan, and David North, now known as Maverick. The CIA's Weapon X programme transformed Creed and Logan into the 'super-soldiers' Sabretooth and Wolverine. The programme also implanted false memories in Creed's mind, so that he is now uncertain which events really happened.

Over 35 years ago, Sabretooth met a woman who called herself Leni Zauber. She bore him a son, named Graydon. Leni turned out to be another long-lived mutant, Mystique, and Graydon Creed grew up to become a fanatical anti-mutant politician.

Sabretooth acts as Magneto's henchman throughout the film. We learn that he was sent by Magneto to fetch back either Rogue or Wolverine from that initial fight, and later we see him working as part of Magneto's team when they eventually abduct Rogue. During this second battle with the X-Men, Sabretooth underestimates the power of Storm, only to feel the full fury of one of her lightning bolts which throws him clear through the arrivals board of the Westchester train station. The next time the two meet, Storm is trapped by metal bands inside the Statue of Liberty. Eager for revenge, Sabretooth threatens her with the words you owe me a scream.'

ON SCREEN

In the *X-Men* movie, Sabretooth apparently meets and fights Wolverine for the first time in the course of the film. However, since the film version of Wolverine suffers from amnesia, perhaps he only thinks this is their first encounter. During their initial fight, it soon becomes obvious that Sabretooth is a mutant with amazing strength and speed. Indeed, Logan is only saved when a blast from Cyclops' visor knocks Sabretooth off the side of the mountain. Whatever the case, Wolverine and Sabretooth quickly become the same implacable enemies they have always been in the comics.

DAZZLER

WHEN TEENAGE Alison Blaire discovered that she was a mutant, she did not decide to become a Super Hero. First, she went into show business. Intent on becoming a singer, Alison realized that she could use her power to transform sound into light to create special effects for her act. She can create different light effects, ranging from a gentle glow to powerful strobe flashes of light or disorientating cascades of colour. Using these powers, Alison sought fame and fortune as the Dazzler. Virtually no one knew that she was a mutant, believing instead that her lighting effects were created by technological means. Time and again, however, Alison found herself in situations where she ended up using her powers to battle criminals.

LEAVING SHOWBIZ

When Alison publicly revealed herself to be a mutant, she was blacklisted by the entertainment industry and was only able to find work in low-paying, obscure jobs. She ended up leaving music behind to join the X-Men. Falling in love with Longshot, she went to live with him on his native world and raise their child.

Honing her skills
Through her training in the X-Men, Dazzler perfected her ability to generate and shoot laser-like beams of light from her hands which can slice through almost anything. She has also learnt how to create a protective force field of laser light around herself that can deflect or vapourize oncoming projectiles.

Dazzler practises her skills in the X-Men's Danger Room.

With a little effort, Dazzler can even create holograms of human beings and other three-dimensional objects.

YOU DID IT!

WE DID IT--TO MAKE THIS WORLD A BETTER PLACE.

Love for Longshot
After each of them had spent so long as an outcast, Dazzler and Longshot finally found true love and happiness with one another. They left the X-Men and moved to Longshot's home world.

Sound and light
When the X-Men first met the Dazzler, she was secretly using her powers to create a 'dazzling' light show for her stage act. However, guards of the Hellfire Club dressed in battle suits smashed into the club where she was performing. Dazzler used her powers to stun the guards, allowing the X-Men to escape, but only into the clutches of the White Queen!

Curiously, Dazzler cannot create light by using the sound of her own voice.

Dazzler as she appeared when the X-Men first met her.

First words

Longshot was created by the scientist Arize to incite rebellion among the slaves on Mojoworld. Longshot's first words to Mojo were, 'No one owns me'.

The only immediate difference between Longshot and humans is that he has only three fingers on each hand!

LONGSHOT

NOT ONLY IS LONGSHOT one of the few X-Men who is not a mutant, he is not even from Earth! An artificially created humanoid from another dimension, his home world, 'Mojoworld', is ruled by ruthless beings called the Spineless Ones. They coerced a scientist named Arize into creating a race of slaves for them. Arize genetically engineered a race of humanoids, hoping that they would rebel against their spineless masters. He endowed some of these humanoids with special abilities, and, as a result, Longshot has superhuman agility and the power to alter probability to give himself good luck.

REBEL SLAVE

The Spineless One called Mojo, who ruled the planet, forced Longshot to work as a stunt performer in his world's version of the movies. But Longshot broke free and became the leader of a slave rebellion. On one of his journeys to Earth, Longshot joined the X-Men and fell in love with his team-mate, Alison Blaire, the Dazzler. Ultimately, Longshot returned to his home world, and, with the help of Dazzler and the X-Men, overthrew Mojo. Alison remained there with him, and they have since had a child.

LONGSHOT'S TEAM
Among the rebels who fight for freedom alongside Longshot on Mojoworld are the Dazzler, Kragor, Demos, and the ram-headed Quark.

Longshot

Quark

LUCKY POWERS
Pulling off a stunt like this would be a 'long shot' for anyone else, but not for Longshot. He has the ability to combine his astonishing acrobatic prowess with a talent for shifting probability in his favour and literally making his own luck.

Demos

Longshot kills Mojo
After some time spent on Earth with the X-Men, Longshot returned to Mojoworld to lead a rebellion against its ruler, Mojo. The lengthy struggle between Mojo and Longshot finally ended when Longshot impaled the dictator on his sword. However, Mojo's successor, Mojo II, proved to be just as much of a tyrant.

Kragor

Dazzler

MOJO

By performing a 'dance', Spiral can teleport herself through time, space, and other dimensions.

CERTAINLY THE WEIRDEST MEMBER of the X-Men's rogues gallery is Mojo. Mojo hails from Mojoworld, a planet in another dimension. It was there that his race evolved, unable to stand because they did not have backbones. One of them, a scientist named Arize, invented a mechanical exoskeleton that enabled its wearer to stand erect. Most of the race adopted these exoskeletons, but a minority, the 'Spineless Ones', disdained using them. It was the latter group who took power, with Mojo as their ruler. Mojo demanded that Arize create a slave race to serve the Spineless Ones. Arize did so, but planned that one day the slaves that he created would rise up against their ruthless masters.

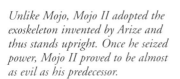

Unlike Mojo, Mojo II adopted the exoskeleton invented by Arize and thus stands upright. Once he seized power, Mojo II proved to be almost as evil as his predecessor.

LIGHTS, CAMERA, ACTION

In Mojoworld's media-oriented culture, the ruler is in charge of producing movies and television shows to keep the masses entertained. Mojo employed one of Arize's genetically engineered creations, Longshot, as a stunt man in his movie productions. But Longshot became Mojo's nemesis, leading other slaves in a rebellion. Mojo first learned of Earth when Longshot escaped to our planet, and he decided to take it over. He also tried to force the X-Men into serving as unwilling actors in his lunatic productions. It looked as if Mojo's career – and life – were finished when Longshot appeared to kill him. His successor was appropriately named 'Mojo II, the sequel'. However, the original Mojo staged an incredible comeback to wreak more chaos on Mojoworld and on Earth.

Mojo took a strange revenge on Longshot through his friend, a movie stunt woman from Earth named Ricochet Rita. Mojo had Rita transformed into a six-armed superhuman swordsman named Spiral. He then sent her back in time to fight Longshot when he arrived on Earth.

The X-Babies

Always looking for a new gimmick for his TV shows, Mojo decided to show his audience what the X-Men would be like if they were cute little toddlers! Hence, Mojo created the X-Babies, genetically engineered children with all the powers of the real mutants. Unfortunately for Mojo, the X-Babies have rebelled against the Spineless One and gave him almost as much trouble as their full-size counterparts.

THE BODY SHOPPE
Mojo makes his headquarters in the airborne Body Shoppe. Here he oversees experiments in genetic engineering. It was in the Body Shoppe, for example, that Wolverine's enemy Lady Deathstrike, was converted into a half-mechanical cyborg.

Mojo can fire bolts of plasma from his hands.

Mojo's grotesque body contains no backbone.

It's a wrap
Mojo has used the X-Men to boost his ratings on many occasions. Over the years he has kidnapped several of the mutants and even fitted Psylocke with robotic eyes that broadcast live-action feeds of the X-Men's activities back to Mojoworld.

AND... PRINT!

THAT, LADIES AND GENTLE-VIEWERS, WAS MOST DEFINITELY A WRAP!

THE END
FILMED IN
MOJOVISION

SPIDER'S LEGS
Mojo requires a robotic platform with spider-like legs to move the massive mound of yellow flesh that makes up his body.

MAJOR DOMO
Mojo depends on his right-hand man, known only as Major Domo, more than he realizes. With the personality of a loyal, sycophantic yet sardonic butler, Major Domo tries to steer a course between catering to his irrational master's mad whims and manoeuvring him into more sensible courses of action.

SINISTER

THE YEAR WAS 1859 and the place was London during the reign of Queen Victoria. Charles Darwin had published his revolutionary book, *The Origin of Species*, propounding his theory of evolution. But another scientist, Nathaniel Essex, argued that Darwin had not gone far enough. Essex's son had died due to genetic defects. Now Essex advocated controlling the mating and breeding of human beings as if they were livestock, in order to produce genetically superior children. By this means Essex believed that a superhuman race of mutants would evolve within only a century. Darwin and his fellow scientists were appalled by Essex's proposals. Even Essex's own wife, Rebecca, turned against him. After their second child died at birth, Rebecca denounced Essex on her own deathbed as 'sinister'. But by then Essex had found a patron in the ancient mutant Apocalypse, who transformed him into a superhuman being. Casting off his former identity, Essex took the name Rebecca gave him: Sinister.

SUMMERS' OBSESSION

Sent back through time by Sanctity, the daughter of Bolivar Trask, Scott Summers and Jean Grey persuaded Sinister to defy Apocalypse. After meeting them, Sinister grew obsessed with their bloodlines. Over the following century the long-lived Sinister developed genetic engineering techniques far in advance of those of today's scientists. Because of this, he secretly controlled the orphanage in which Scott Summers was confined as a boy. It was Sinister who also created Madelyne Pryor, Jean Grey's clone, so that she would give birth to Scott's son Nathan. Yet despite his efforts, Sinister has yet to take full control of one of the Summers' mutants.

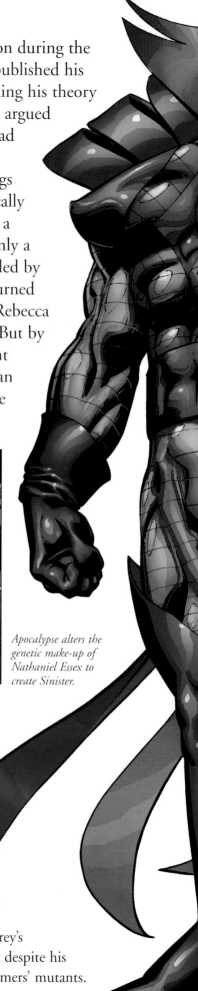

Apocalypse alters the genetic make-up of Nathaniel Essex to create Sinister.

FAUSTIAN FELLOW
Like a 19th-century version of Faust, Victorian scientist Nathaniel Essex made a bargain with evil to satisfy his thirst for knowledge. Apocalypse granted him the means to pursue his genetic theories at the price of becoming physically transformed into the inhuman creature Sinister.

Goblyn Queen and Sinister

Having created Madelyne Pryor to bear Scott Summers' mutant child Nathan, Sinister no longer needed her once he had captured the infant. But by then Pryor had become the powerful Goblyn Queen and fought back against Sinister, rescuing Nathan, before she perished in combat with Jean Grey.

Sinister's powers

Mysteriously, Sinister seems able to survive any kind of injury, no matter how destructive. Cyclops once obliterated most of Sinister's body with an optic blast, leaving only his bones behind, yet somehow Sinister recreated himself.

SINISTER'S MUTANT MASSACRE
Sinister's most notorious crime was ordering the slaughter of the Morlocks, a mutant community that lived beneath Manhattan. His agents in this and other operations are the Marauders, a team of mutants specializing in assassination. Thanks to his expertise in cloning, Sinister can replace any Marauder killed in combat with an identical double.

Releasing the Legacy Virus

Disaster followed when the mutant terrorist Stryfe tricked Sinister, giving him a canister that supposedly held samples of the Summers family's mutant genes. But the canister actually released the Legacy Virus, an as yet incurable disease fatal to mutants.

MADRIPOOR

WOLVERINE HAS MADE his second home in the Principality of Madripoor, a small island nation in the Indonesian archipelago. Like Genosha, Madripoor was a sanctuary for pirates many years ago. In fact, the pirate ethic has shaped Madripoor's history and society. Its recently deceased ruler, Prince Baran, was descended from the freebooters who settled on the island and founded the country. Just as Madripoor's rulers tolerated piracy in the past, its government today has a relaxed policy towards most business dealings that do not threaten the regime's stability. As a result, Madripoor has become one of the business capitals of the Pacific Rim. However, it is also a notorious centre for crime, especially the narcotics trade and slavery. Since Madripoor does not permit other nations to extradite criminals, the island has become a refuge for international crimelords and criminal organizations, who make payoffs to the government to ensure good relations.

Madripoor lies between Singapore, in the south of Thailand, and the island of Sumatra.

Cast of characters

One of the leading crimelords of Madripoor is Jessan Hoan, better known as Tyger Tiger, who has been Wolverine's ally and lover. Next to her on the right is her rival in crime, the late General Nguyen Ngoc Coy. The next man is Police Chief Tai, also now deceased. On the far right sits Wolverine's friend, detective Jessica Drew.

TALE OF TWO CITIES

The capital of Madripoor, also named Madripoor, is divided in two. Madripoor Hightown is one of the world's wealthiest areas, populated by the rich and powerful. Its spectacular architecture and advanced technology make it truly a city of the 21st century. However, Madripoor Lowtown is one of the most impoverished areas in the world. Lowtown is a throwback to the lawlessness of a thousand years ago: a place of rampant crime and depravity where anything can be bought. Yet certain places, such as Wolverine's Princess Bar, have a certain rough charm reminiscent of the exotic settings of old movies.

The harbour

Madripoor, the capital city of the Principality of Madripoor, is the only large city on the island. Most of the rest of the island is covered by jungle. So little land is available for farming that Madripoor has always had to depend on imported food. Fortunately, Madripoor is located near one of the major trade routes of the South China Sea. It is a major port with harbour facilities that rank among the finest in the world.

Hightown

Madripoor's Hightown stands on the bluff overlooking the harbour and the Lowtown district. Hightown rivals Tokyo and Hong Kong as one of the leading economic centres of Asia. Its gleaming skyscrapers and luxury hotels stand in sharp contrast to the impoverished slums of Lowtown.

To conceal his true identity when in Madripoor, Wolverine goes by the name of Patch, after the eye patch he wears there.

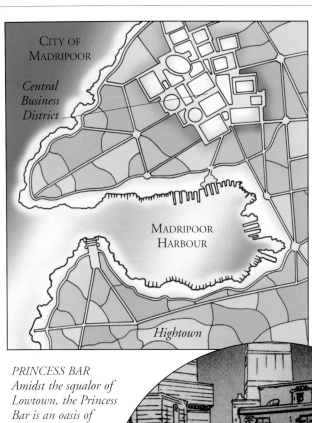

CITY OF MADRIPOOR

Central Business District

MADRIPOOR HARBOUR

Hightown

Landmarks of Hightown

Hightown's skyline is dominated by skyscrapers housing major banks and the offices of international trading firms. Here, too, is located the palace of the Prince of Madripoor, said to rival the Palace of Versailles in size and magnificence. Hightown's great hotels are the most luxurious and expensive in the world, catering to visiting businessmen and wealthy tourists. The finest of these is the Sovereign Hotel, with its incredibly costly triplex Imperial Penthouse.

Bank of Malaysia · Daewoo Building · Trade Centre · Bank of Hong Kong · Presidential Palace

Government House · Barker Plaza · Princess Bar

PRINCESS BAR
Amidst the squalor of Lowtown, the Princess Bar is an oasis of elegance and style. Frightened by Lowtown's dangerous reputation, tourists avoid the Princess Bar after dark. At night, it becomes a gathering place for local residents from both Hightown and Lowtown. The Princess Bar is also a fine restaurant with cabaret entertainment.

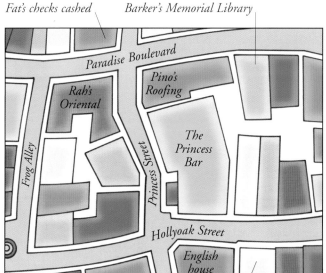

PRINCESS BAR

The men behind the Princess

The bar takes its name from a woman nicknamed 'Princess' who was somehow connected with its previous owner, a mysterious Englishman known as O'Donnell, who is now dead. O'Donnell sold a 50 per cent interest in the bar to Wolverine, who became his 'silent partner'. In Wolverine's own words, 'In Casablanca – in the good old days – everyone went to Rick's, where deals were cut and hearts broken. In Madripoor, it's the Princess Bar, where the intrigue's on a par with the food, an' comes in a lot more variety.'

Fat's checks cashed · Barker's Memorial Library

Paradise Boulevard

Rah's Oriental

Pino's Roofing

Frog Alley

Princess Street

The Princess Bar

Hollyoak Street

English house

Margie's Boarding House

INSIDE THE PRINCESS BAR
The map above shows the Princess Bar's location in Lowtown. To the right is a diagram of the interior of the bar. The most interesting — and secret — feature of which is the network of tunnels beneath the building. Known as the catacombs, they provide a means for escape from the bar.

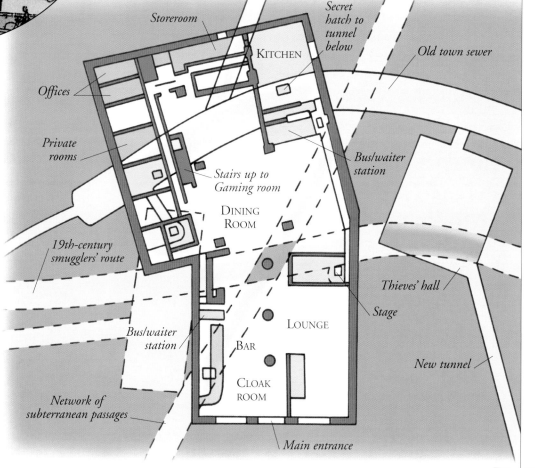

Storeroom · Secret hatch to tunnel below

Offices

KITCHEN

Old town sewer

Private rooms

Bus/waiter station

Stairs up to Gaming room

DINING ROOM

19th-century smugglers' route

Thieves' hall

Bus/waiter station

Stage

LOUNGE

BAR

New tunnel

CLOAK ROOM

Network of subterranean passages

Main entrance

GENOSHA

IKE ENGLAND in William Blake's poem, *Jerusalem*, the island of Genosha is often described as a 'green and pleasant land'. But beneath its idyllic appearance, Genosha is a sinister country with an economy based on the labour of enslaved mutants. Decades ago, the Sugar Man, a survivor from the 'Age of Apocalypse', secretly became the power behind the Genoshan government and gave it knowledge of advanced genetic engineering. The regime examined all Genoshan adolescents for signs of active or latent mutant abilities. Teenagers with such powers were genetically engineered in order to enhance or alter their abilities. These 'mutates' were then forced to serve as slaves. Worse still, Cameron Hodge used the Genoshan militia to abduct many X-Men and other mutant heroes for service in the slave economy.

Quicksilver and Polaris moved to Genosha to keep a wary eye on Magneto's activities.

Magneto Rex
Rashly, the UN believed Genosha's civil unrest would keep Magneto too preoccupied to threaten the world. But to the UN's horror, Magneto proved an adept politician who quickly established control over most of his new nation.

THE GENOSHAN CIVIL WAR

While the X-Men battled Hodge, the Genoshan militia seized control of the government, and a civil war soon erupted between the mutates and the non-mutant humans. Finally, the UN imposed a new regime with Magneto at its head. Though rebel activity persists, Magneto has restored order to most of Genosha.

APPEASEMENT
Recently, Magneto threw the planet into chaos by unleashing an electromagnetic shock wave that disrupted electrical systems around the world. Dr. Alda Huxley, shown above, persuaded the UN to appease Magneto by awarding him sovereignty over Genosha in exchange for his promise not to attack other nations. However, Huxley may secretly want to gain power in Genosha for herself.

HISTORY

The island of Genosha is located between Madagascar and the Seychelles Islands in the Indian Ocean. For centuries it was a haven for pirates, and tradition claims it was visited by the legendary Sinbad. Today, its population is almost entirely Caucasian and its national language is English. The capital city was built along Hammer Bay, whose name it shares.

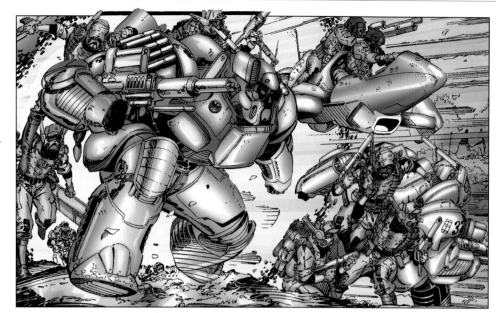

Magistrates

Before Magneto came to power, the Genoshan government operated a notorious militia known as the Magistrates. They enforced the law against mutate slaves and hunted down any who attempted to escape. The Magistrates were equipped with highly advanced weaponry, battlesuits, and assault vehicles. The oppression was so brutal that when the Magistrates seized control of the government, it sparked a spontaneous uprising among the mutates across the island.

MUTATES
Genoshan mutates were deprived of their names and identified only by the numbers tattooed on their foreheads. 'Skinsuits' were bonded to their bodies, and they were even robbed of their memories.

After the civil war, Magneto rebuilt Hammer Bay into a marvel of futuristic architecture.

The Zealot

Some Genoshans oppose Magneto's regime. The mutate known as the Zealot, shown here, preaches that Magneto is a false messiah who has taken away Genosha's independence. The people of the port Carrion Cove held out against Magneto's takeover. Even the Acolytes Fabian Cortez and Amelia Voight secretly turned against him.

GOBLYN QUEEN

Scott Summers first met Madelyne Pryor in Alaska, where she was working as a pilot for North Star Airways, the company run by his grandparents.

BY SOMEHOW OBTAINING a sample of Jean Grey's cells, Sinister created an adult clone of her. When the original Phoenix committed suicide, Scott Summers believed he had lost Jean forever, unaware that her original body lay in suspended animation in a pod at the bottom of the sea. Sinister grew his clone at an accelerated rate in his laboratory. He named her 'Madelyne Pryor' and programmed her with false memories and the desire to fall in love with Cyclops. Sinister then planned for Madelyne to bear a child, which would possess the superhuman genetic potential of both Scott and Jean. The evil mutant would then capture the child and control him as he grew up. The scheme started successfully: Cyclops married Madelyne, and they had a son, Nathan, who was destined to become Cable.

UNNATURAL BIRTH
When Phoenix died, its share of the real Jean's consciousness travelled back to Earth. This part of Jean's psyche eventually reached the clone that Sinister had created and endowed it with consciousness for the first time.

Madelyne as the Goblyn Queen

THE RETURN OF JEAN

MADELYNE'S MARRIAGE
Scott and Madelyne were married when he became convinced that she was not Jean Grey, Madelyne's exact lookalike.

When the real Jean returned, Cyclops rushed to her side. Madelyne's own psi powers began to emerge, and she took refuge with the X-Men. But then the demon N'astirh sent her dreams which aroused the dark side of her psyche. Her powers fully awakened, Madelyne became the mad Goblyn Queen and attempted to take revenge on Cyclops by sacrificing their son. Instead, Madelyne perished in combat with the original Jean. Recently, Nate Grey created a duplicate of Madelyne, a 'psionic shell' in a new physical body, who has become Nate's ally.

EVIL TWIN
Intent on destroying the X-Men along with herself, the Goblyn Queen unleashed a tremendous psychic force. But her enemies shielded themselves, and Pryor became the only victim. In one last attempt to kill Jean, the dying Pryor linked their minds together. Jean survived, and the portion of Jean's psyche which had been stolen by the Phoenix Force and had then awakened Madelyne, finally returned to Jean.

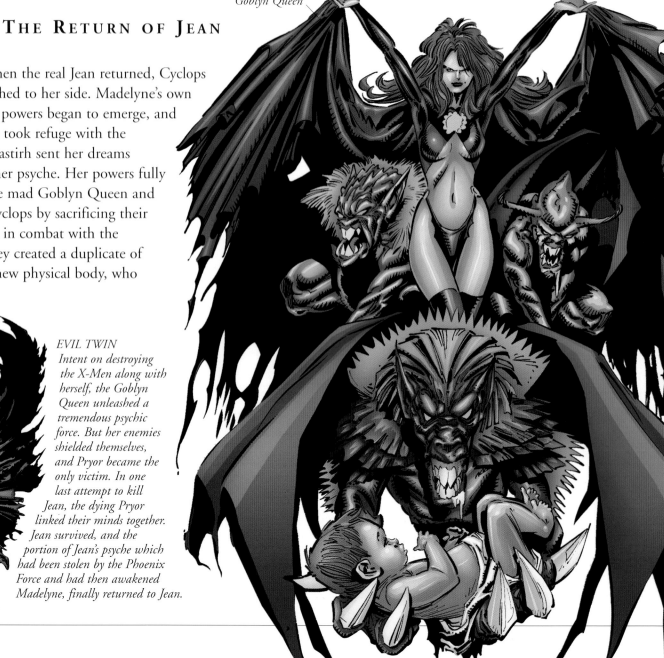

124

JUBILEE

JUBILATION 'JUBILEE' LEE, a teenage Chinese-American girl, was born in Beverly Hills, California, where she lived with her wealthy immigrant parents. However, her perfect life was destroyed in a single weekend, when her parents were mistakenly murdered by two hit men. Jubilee was sent to an orphanage, but she ran away and hid in a Hollywood shopping mall, stealing food to survive. When she discovered her mutant powers to create energy 'fireworks', she realized she could earn money by using her powers to entertain customers in the mall. Mutant hunters tried to capture her, but she was rescued by four female members of the X-Men; Dazzler, Psylocke, Rogue, and Storm. Intrigued by these mutant women, Jubilee saw them enter a teleportation portal and decided to follow them just before the portal closed.

A NEW HOME

Jubilee found herself transported to the X-Men's temporary base deep in the Australian outback. Not yet trusting the X-Men, Jubilee hid in a cavern beneath their headquarters. Here she stayed for some time and she did not emerge until after most of the X-Men had abandoned the base, and their enemies the Reavers had captured Wolverine. Jubilee helped Wolverine escape, and the two formed a close bond. He eventually sponsored her admission into the X-Men. When Professor Xavier gathered together a new class of teenage mutants, he reassigned Jubilee to this new team of youngsters, known as Generation X.

Jubilee wore this brightly coloured costume when she first served with the X-Men.

FIREWORKS
Jubilee discovered her mutant powers when she was cornered by the Hollywood Mall security police. Without realizing what she was doing, she activated her 'fireworks'. While the mall police were thus distracted, she escaped.

GENERATION X
When Professor X founded a new school to teach Generation X, Xavier reassigned Jubilee from the X-Men to the new team. At first, Jubilee was upset, believing she had been demoted, but she soon came to regard her team-mates in Generation X as her new family.

JUBILEE IN HER GENERATION X COSTUME

JUBILEE'S POWERS
Jubilee has the mutant ability to generate what she calls 'fireworks'. These are globules of energy that follow her mental commands. She can make these globules take various shapes and she can also make them explode. She can temporarily blind a person with sparkles of energy, or create an explosion that is powerful enough to shatter metal objects.

WOLVERINE AND JUBILEE
Belying his gruff demeanour, over the years Wolverine has become a father figure to several youngsters, including his Japanese ward Akiko, Kitty Pryde, and most recently, Jubilee. After they first met in Australia, Jubilee accompanied him when he travelled through Asia. After joining the X-Men, Jubilee continued to work with him on his missions away from the team.

THE X-MEN IN THE 1990s

*X-Men: The Hidden Years #1
(December 1999)
(Cover art by John Byrne and Tom Palmer)*

A S THE 1990s BEGAN, the popularity of *The Uncanny X-Men* continued to soar under the new creative team of writer Chris Claremont and artist Jim Lee. In 1991, Claremont and Lee launched a new companion series, titled simply *X-Men*. Sales for the initial issue reached over seven million, setting a new record that has yet to be broken in American comic books. At the close of 1991, Claremont finally ended his amazing marathon as the *X-Men*'s writer, 17 years after he had begun. A number of writers followed him on the two *X-Men* titles, including Fabian Nicieza, Scott Lobdell, Mark Waid, Steven Seagle, and Joe Kelly. Among the many *X-Men* artists of the 1990s were Whilce Portacio, Brandon Peterson, Adam and Andy Kubert, John Romita Jr., Joe Madureira, Chris Bachalo, Carlos Pacheco, and Alan Davis.

The X-Men's fame spread internationally through foreign-language editions published in other countries. There were even new *X-Men* stories created in 'manga' style for Japan. Moreover, in 1992, the X-Men moved beyond comics into their first animated television series, which became the top-rated children's series on the Fox network.

The rest of the *X-Men* comic books continued to expand as well. Under artist Rob

*Rogue #1 (January 1995)
(Cover art by Mark Wieringo and
Terry Austin)*

Liefeld, the New Mutants were reorganized into a commando squad in *X-Force*. The team's popular new leader was spun off into his own series, *Cable*. And now that the New Mutants had 'grown up' it was time to start yet another class of teenage mutants, known as *Generation X*, created by Scott Lobdell and Chris Bachalo. Once its original members had rejoined the X-Men, writer Peter David organized a new mutant team for *X-Factor*, a series that gave way to *Mutant X*. Other characters to receive their own monthly series included Gambit and the assassin Deadpool. There was even a series about mutants of the future called 2099. Perhaps the greatest surprise took place during the 'Age of Apocalypse' story line, in which all of the ongoing *X-Men* titles were replaced for three months by different series taking place in an alternate reality!

As the 1990s ended, the *X-Men* titles consolidated their classic past with new directions for the future. After a long absence, Chris Claremont returned to write both the *X-Men* and *Uncanny X-Men* titles. John Byrne and inker Tom Palmer collaborated on *X-Men: The Hidden Years*, presenting new stories with the original X-Men set immediately following Neal Adams' issues of two decades before. And the year 2000 brought the first live-action *X-Men* movie, introducing Marvel's mutants to both a new medium and a new century.

1991

1993

1994

*X-Force #1
(August 1991)
(Cover art by Rob Liefeld)*

*Cable #1 (May 1993)
First issue of Cable's
ongoing series
(Cover art by Art Thibert)*

*Generation X #1
(October 1994)
(Cover art by Chris
Bachalo and Mark
Buckingham)*

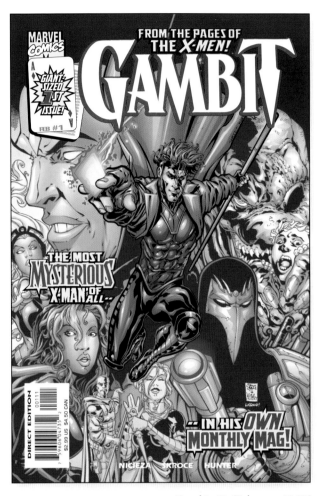

Gambit #1 (February 1999)
First issue of Gambit's
ongoing series
(Cover art by Steve Skroce)

Mutant X #1 (November
1998)
(Cover art by Tom Roney
and Andrew Pepoy)

1995

X-Man #1
(March 1995)
'Age of Apocalypse'
(Cover art by Steve
Skroce)

1998

X-Men: The Manga #1
(March 1998)

1999

X-Men Children of the
Atom #1
(November 1999)
Retelling of the X-Men's
origins
(Cover art by Steve Rude)

Gone since 1985, Xavier returned to the X-Men in 1991.

Omega Red drains his victims' life forces.

Omega Red
Making his debut in the fourth issue of the new *X-Men* series, Omega Red is a Russian mutant 'super-soldier' whose main weapons are coils made of a metal called carbonadium. These extend from his wrists to ensnare his victims.

EARLY OMEGA RED DESIGN BY JIM LEE

As Jim Lee's drawing shows, Xavier could walk when he returned to the X-Men. Soon afterwards, he became crippled again.

OMEGA RED IN ACTION

Omega Red's body gives off lethal chemicals.

FABIAN CORTEZ
The first issue of the new X-Men *series introduced Magneto's new mutant Acolytes, including Fabian Cortez, who soon proved to be treacherous.*

JIM LEE'S DESIGN FOR THE ACOLYTE CORTEZ

Rogue
Jim Lee's sketch of Rogue illustrates a short-lived fashion trend in 1990s comics: artists gave Super Heroines skin-tight costumes and then put bulky leather jackets over them!

ROGUE BY JIM LEE

Storm in the 90s
Jim Lee's early 1990s design for Storm evoked both her short-haired 1980s look and her original costume. Storm grew her hair back to its full length.

Note Storm's earrings, shaped like lightning.

STORM DESIGNS BY JIM LEE

EARLY 1990s STORM BY JOHN BYRNE

CHANGING FACES – 1990s

Early in the 1990s, the scattered X-Men were reunited as Xavier at last returned to Earth; even his original students allowed X-Factor to dissolve and returned to his side. There were more additions to the X-Men's ranks as the decade progressed: Gambit, Jubilee, Bishop, Cannonball, Joseph, Maggott, Marrow, and Dr. Cecilia Reyes.

But there were tragedies as well. Apocalypse infected Cyclops' son Nathan with a lethal 'techo-organic' disease. To save the infant's life, Scott let Nathan be transported to the far future. There Nathan grew up to become Cable, who returned to the X-Men's own time and moulded the New Mutants into the commando team X-Force. Wolverine's fiancée Mariko was killed, and the bestial side of his personality temporarily resurfaced.

Tensions between humanity and mutantkind escalated. Genosha was riven by civil war between humans and their former mutate slaves. There arose a new anti-mutant political organization, the Friends of Humanity, whose leader, Graydon Creed, might have become President of the United States had he not been assassinated. The US government organized a new X-Factor, but its members rebelled at hunting down other mutants. When Xavier gave in to rage in a new battle with Magneto, the dark sides of both mutants' minds merged and formed the fearsome psionic menace Onslaught. Onslaught conquered Manhattan before the X-Men and their allies vanquished it. To take action against the 'mutant menace', the governments of the United States and other major nations sanctioned 'Operation: Zero Tolerance', a paramilitary organization headed by Bastion. This fanatic even held Xavier prisoner until he overreached himself, and the American government shut 'Operation: Zero Tolerance' down. Magneto resumed his assaults on the nations of the world; finally, in hopes of appeasing him, the United Nations granted him rulership of Genosha. Worst of all was the creation of an alternate reality, the 'Age of Apocalypse', in which Apocalypse took control of North America, 'culling' those he deemed to be genetically unfit.

Yet there were still signs of hope for the future. Charles Xavier gathered together another new class of teenage mutants, Generation X. Best of all, Scott Summers and Jean Grey were finally married in a celebratory day on which it seemed as if Xavier's dream had at last become a reality.

CABLE

CABLE IS A MAN of two different times. He serves as a living 'cable', linking the destiny of the turbulent present with that of a war-torn future. Although he is the ultimate warrior, he suffers from a strange 'techno-organic' disease that has turned much of his body into organic metal. Possessing vast mutant telepathic and telekinetic powers, Cable must continually divert his mental energies to stem the spread of this disease or it will kill him.

Back when Scott Summers believed Jean Grey was dead, he married her lookalike, Madelyne Pryor, and they had a son, Nathan Christopher Summers. Seeking to destroy the child, Apocalypse infected him with a 'techno-organic' virus. To save his son's life, Scott gave him to a time-travelling member of the Askani, who carried Nathan two millennia into the future. Here, the Askani Sisterhood halted the progress of the disease. Mother Askani, the head of the cult, later transported Scott and Jean into her time to raise the child. Once Nathan had grown up, he led the freedom fighters of the Clan Chosen against the New Canaanites.

BACK TO THE PRESENT

Eventually, Cable, as Nathan became known, journeyed back to the time of his parents to pursue his primary mission: to stop Apocalypse from conquering the Earth. His archenemy, Stryfe, also travelled to our present time. Early on, Cable led a mercenary team called Six Pack, which included his companion Domino. Later, Cable remoulded the New Mutants into a mutant commando team, X-Force. Cable has recently joined the ranks of the X-Men, while continuing his quest to change the future for the better by safeguarding the present.

Spread of the virus

Infected by the evil mutant Apocalypse with a techno-organic virus, the infant Nathan began metamorphosing into a hideous jumble of organic metal and circuitry. Whereas Colossus gains even more power by turning into living metal, if the techno-organic virus had ever completed transforming Nathan's body, it would have killed him.

Organic metal arm

Cable's war spear

Stryfe

When Mother Askani brought Nathan to the future, she had him cloned in case he should die. However, Apocalypse stole the clone, named him Stryfe, and raised the child to be as cruel and ruthless as himself. Literally Cable's evil twin, Stryfe has been his continual nemesis both in the far future and in the present day.

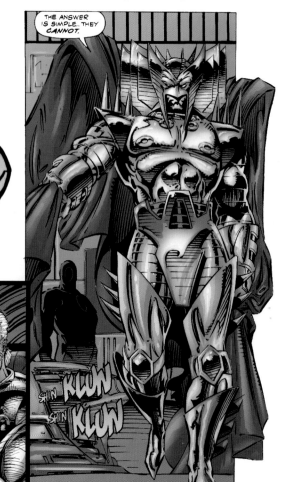

Kane   Cable   Grizzly

Domino   Hammer   George Washington Bridge

Six Pack

Before founding X-Force, Cable led the mercenary squad called Six Pack. They consisted of Kane, a cyborg also known as Weapon X; Domino, Cable's longtime friend and confidante with the ability to adjust the probability of events in her favour; Grizzly, a superhumanly strong fighter; Hammer, the team's hi-tech expert; and George Washington Bridge, a top soldier who is now a leading officer with SHIELD.

Genesis

In the distant future, Stryfe kidnapped and brainwashed Cable's son, Tyler. Sent to the present to kill his father, Tyler took the name Genesis and sought to become Apocalypse's heir. But Tyler overreached himself by driving Wolverine temporarily insane, and was slain by the clawed **feral mutant.**

CABLE'S WIFE DIES
In the future, it was Stryfe who set off the bomb that killed Cable's wife, Aliya. She had called herself 'Jenskot' in honour of the legendary X-Men, Jean Grey and Scott Summers.

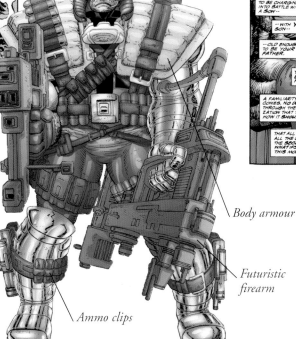

Body armour

Futuristic firearm

Ammo clips

Armoured Cable

The consummate soldier of the future, Cable sometimes wears so much body armour that he appears more machine than man. Ironically, much of his flesh has turned into organic metal, and it is only through sheer willpower that Cable keeps the techno-organic disease with which he is infected from completely transforming and killing him.

Cable and father

The life of Cable is a prime example of the paradoxes of time travel. Born in the present, he was taken two thousand years into the future where he was raised by his time-travelling parents, Scott Summers and Jean Grey. And now Cable has returned to the present where he has teamed up with the X-Men, including Scott and Jean. Here, he can fight side by side with his parents – despite having aged into a man old enough to be Scott's father!

GAMBIT

UNLIKE OTHER X-MEN, Remy LeBeau, alias Gambit, walks on both sides of the law. Coming from the Cajun culture of New Orleans, Gambit takes pride in his talents as a thief. He is also a mutant with the ability to charge objects with kinetic energy generated by his body. Gambit's trademark weapons are the playing cards he throws: imbued with energy, they explode on hitting their targets.

Remy was stolen by the Thieves' Guild, whose leader, Jean-Luc LeBeau, took an interest in the infant. LeBeau placed him in a street gang to learn how to steal, and then adopted the boy and trained him to become the master thief he is today.

A homeless boy living on the streets of New Orleans, Gambit was eventually adopted by Jean-Luc LeBeau, the leader of the legendary Thieves' Guild. Under his foster-father's tutelage, Remy grew up to become a master thief himself. As part of a peace agreement between the Thieves' Guild and their rivals, the Assassins' Guild, a marriage was arranged between Remy and Bella Donna Boudreaux. Her brother, Julien, objected to the marriage and challenged Remy to a duel. When he wounded Julien, Remy was forced to leave the city to prevent a guild war. Turning his back on his past, Gambit travelled the world, plying his trade as a thief.

LIFE OF CRIME

Gambit's freewheeling life of crime led him to his deepest shame. Under the instructions of Sinister and an as-yet unrevealed character, Gambit organized a team of mutants called the Marauders and led them into the Morlocks' tunnels. The Marauders slaughtered the Morlocks, and, despite being unaware of Sinister's deadly intentions, Gambit has been haunted by guilt ever since. He later encountered a young Storm and aided her against the Shadow King. She eventually sponsored Gambit for X-Men membership. He saw this as a chance to atone for his past sins, but hoped that nobody would discover his darkest secret. Inevitably, the X-Men learned of his link with Sinister, and Gambit left the team in shame. He has since made his peace with his team-mates and rejoined the group. Gambit still works as a thief, stealing from criminals for the thrill of the hunt.

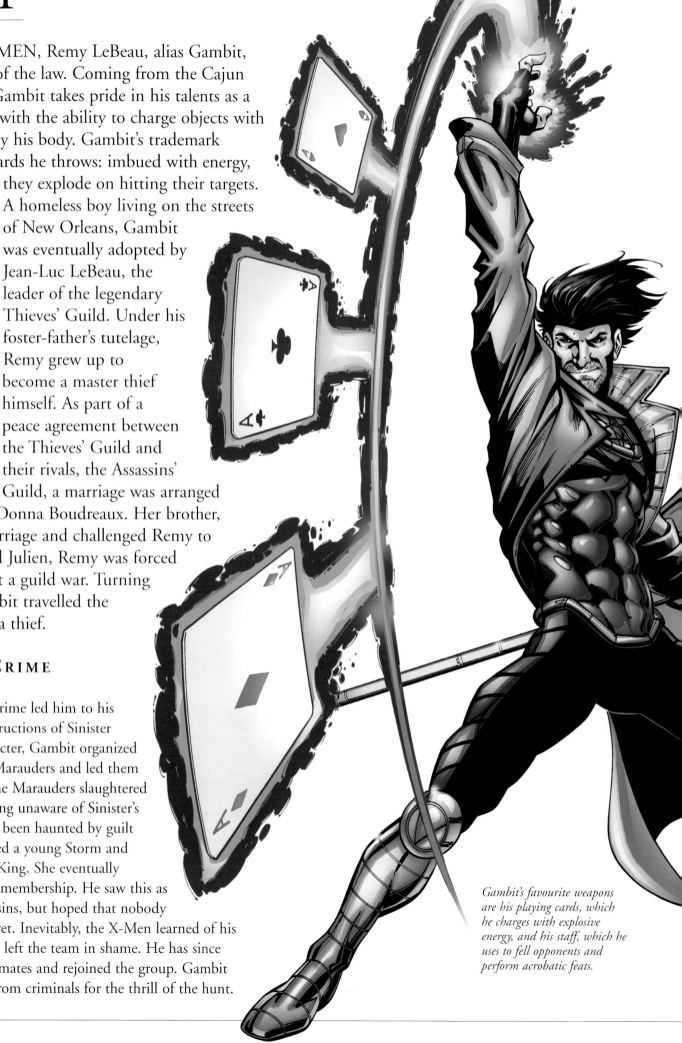

Gambit's favourite weapons are his playing cards, which he charges with explosive energy, and his staff, which he uses to fell opponents and perform acrobatic feats.

Gambit's powers

Gambit has the ability to tap into the potential energy contained within an object and transform it into kinetic energy. When Gambit thus charges an object with kinetic energy and throws it at a target, the object releases this energy explosively on impact. Usually he charges cards with his hands, but here he turns a wad of gum into a deadly weapon by spitting it at X-Cutioner.

Scrambler / Malice / Scalphunter / Vertigo / Harpoon

Sabretooth / Gambit / Riptide

KILLING THE MORLOCKS
When Sinister hired him to assemble the team of mutant mercenaries known as the Marauders, Gambit concerned himself only with his fee. But when the Marauders massacred the Morlocks, Gambit realized he bore partial responsibility, and for years it remained his darkest secret.

For better or for worse...

Remy and Bella Donna Boudreaux had loved each other since childhood. His foster father, Thieves' Guild leader Jean-Luc LeBeau, arranged their marriage with the head of the Assassins' Guild, Bella Donna's grandfather, to forge peace between the two parties. But when the Thieves' Guild exiled Remy, Gambit left Bella Donna behind, refusing to let her share his punishment.

Gambit in the future

Over 70 years from now, in the alternate future timeline in which Bishop was born, he knew Gambit as the frail and ancient man known as the Witness. Said to be the last survivor of the original X-Men, the aged Gambit had witnessed the betrayal of the X-Men by one of their own members. After coming to the X-Men's own time, Bishop suspected that Gambit himself had been the traitor until he learned how Xavier's mind had spawned the entity known as Onslaught.

BELLA DONNA
After Gambit left her, Bella Donna allied herself with the immortal mutant Candra, who endowed her with various powers, including the ability to discharge bolts of energy. No longer sane after nearly dying, Bella Donna succeeded her late father Marius as head of the Assassins' Guild and became Gambit's enemy.

Gambit and Rogue

Gambit and Rogue were passionately in love, but several obstacles stood in their way. She cannot control her mutant power to absorb the memories and abilities of anyone whose flesh she touches. Any physical contact with Gambit would render him unconscious! When Rogue did finally touch him, she discovered Gambit's deep guilt over his role in the massacre of the Morlocks.

WEAPON X

WOLVERINE HAS CLAWS because he is a mutant, but he was not born with the adamantium that makes his skeleton virtually indestructible. Adamantium is an artificial alloy of iron, and it was infused into his body by the scientists of the Weapon X project. Under the name Logan, Wolverine had already been working for the CIA alongside fellow agents like Victor Creed, the future Sabretooth. The CIA established Project X in order to convert men into 'super-soldiers' with unusual abilities. The project facilities were set up in Windsor, Canada, through a secret agreement with the Canadian government. Presumably Logan was chosen for the project because the CIA knew he was a mutant whose superhuman healing ability would enable him to survive the process. Logan was abducted and brought to the project laboratory. Here, in a process called 'Experiment X', molecules of adamantium were bonded to Logan's skeleton. But the process traumatized Logan, leaving him with the mentality of a savage beast. After undergoing brutal tests, Logan turned against his captors and escaped into the wilderness.

The Professor

Carol Hines

Dr. Cornelius

The Scientists

Experiment X was overseen by a ruthless scientist known simply as the Professor. Little is known about this man, except that he was working for some higher power and used dubious means to acquire his staff. One of these was Dr. Abraham Cornelius, who was wanted by the FBI for questioning regarding so-called 'mercy killings'. The Professor blackmailed Cornelius into joining the Experiment X staff and overseeing the adamantium bonding process. Their meek assistant, Carol Hines, came from NASA. She proved to have a conscience and was appalled by what her superiors did to Logan. Several years later, the Professor was killed by another victim of his experiments.

FEED.

STEADY.

CARDIOTACH?

HIGH. HIGHER THAN WE EXPECTED.

The Experiment

Logan was captured by three agents, who needed stun guns to subdue him. Unconscious and his body shaved of hair (which, thanks to his mutant powers, began to grow back rapidly), Logan was immersed in a tank of unknown fluids. There the project scientists infused adamantium molecules into his body, binding them to the organic molecules which made up his bones. It was during this process that the Professor and the other scientists discovered that Logan was, in fact, a mutant.

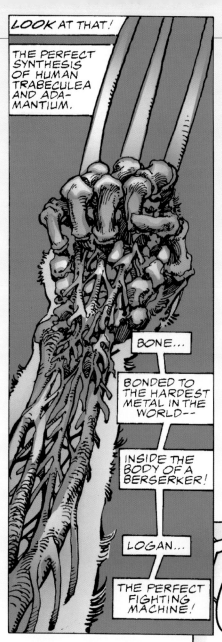

LOOK AT THAT!

THE PERFECT SYNTHESIS OF HUMAN TRABECULEA AND ADAMANTIUM.

BONE...

BONDED TO THE HARDEST METAL IN THE WORLD--

INSIDE THE BODY OF A BERSERKER!

LOGAN...

THE PERFECT FIGHTING MACHINE!

Hand of a killer

The bonding process proved a success, and Logan's skeleton was infused with molecules of adamantium, as this image of Logan's arm, fist, and claws shows. However, the process affected Logan's psyche, unleashing the bestial side of his character and turning him into a feral, ferocious killer.

Through this helmet and sensors, which were implanted into Logan's body, the scientists could control Logan's every move. That is, until the sedatives wore off, and Logan broke free.

THE PUPPET
Removed from the tank once the bonding process was complete, the deeply sedated Logan was hooked up to machines that controlled his every movement. He was now no more than the Professor's puppet. But the Professor underestimated Logan's mutant power to heal himself. Once he shook off the tranquillizers' effects, the devices could do nothing to stop him.

At the insistence of the Professor, Logan was laden down with heavy batteries, which gave the controlling machine a radius of 16 kilometres.

PAYBACK
The Professor's tests toyed with Wolverine's psyche, mixing reality with illusion. The feral Wolverine thought he had confronted his tormentors and slain both the Professor and Cornelius. But this was a fantasy they had somehow fed into his mind. Even in this delusion, the savage Logan recognized Carol Hines was not his enemy and would not kill her.

The tests

The Professor and Dr. Cornelius subjected their new 'Weapon X' to a series of trials by combat, pitting him against wolves, a bear, and even a tiger. Each time, naked and unarmed save for his claws and his sheer ferocity, Wolverine triumphed. Once he had escaped from the Project X compound, Logan roamed the wintry forests living as a wild animal. Eventually, he was found by James and Heather Hudson, under whose care he regained his human intellect. But Project X also intended that its subjects be unaware of what they had become until the CIA needed to use them. Hence, the project had wiped out much of Logan's memory and implanted false memories instead. As a result, even though Wolverine learned about the project years later, he still does not recall much of his past.

I WILL NOT SULLY THE NATURE OF SCIENTIFIC ENDEAVOR WITH... WAGERS, CORNELIUS.

YEAH, WELL-- THAT'S JUST 'CAUSE YOU'D HAVE LOST A BUNDLE.

YOU UNDERESTIMATED YOUR PRIZE, PROFESSOR--

LOGAN WAS SET-UP...!

I'D SAY HE CAME THROUGH A-I, WOULDN'T YOU?

DIDN'T FAZE HIM!

THEN WE JAMMED HIS PSYCHE WITH HIS FEAR OF MUTANTISM.

--INSTEAD HE TURNED AROUND AND BRUTALIZED THE LOT OF US!

WE GAVE HIM A CHANCE TO ESCAPE.

BUT HE DIDN'T RUN--

X-FORCE

Cannonball

Jesse Aaronson

Domino

Moonstar

AS A TEAM, the New Mutants were in severe decline. Their founder, Charles Xavier, was in space with the Starjammers; their teacher, Magneto, had abandoned them and returned to his life as an outlaw; and several of the students were gone. It was then that Cable, the mutant warrior from the future, intervened. Xavier had intended only to train the New Mutants in the use of their powers; although they fought various adversaries, they did not actively seek them out. Cable, however, believed that he had to prepare these young men and women for what he saw as the coming war against their enemies. He intended to mould the New Mutants into the soldiers of his new team, X-Force. His original roster included New Mutants Cannonball and Boom Boom. In addition were Warpath, the brother of the deceased X-Man Thunderbird, Shatterstar, a warrior from the future of Longshot's world, and Feral, a cat-like Morlock.

MUTANT COMMANDOS

The youngsters of X-Force were also joined by an adult: Domino, Cable's former partner from his days as a mercenary. Other young mutants joined over time, including former New Mutants Sunspot, Rictor, and Moonstar, Banshee's daughter Siryn, the Morlock Caliban, and Jesse Aaronson, alias Bedlam. Cannonball was promoted into the X-Men, but he felt uncomfortable in the older team and returned to X-Force. Cable himself finally left the group to pursue his own interests, and the X-Force members travelled across the United States, settling in San Francisco. Recently, they gained a new leader, former British intelligence operative Peter Wisdom, who has gone even further than Cable in turning X-Force into a commando squad.

CALIBAN
Caliban was named by his father after the grotesque creature in Shakespeare's play, The Tempest. *A mutant with the power to sense other mutants nearby, Caliban went to live among the Morlocks. Before Caliban joined X-Force, Apocalypse vastly increased his size and strength and gave him the role of Death, one of Apocalypse's Four Horsemen.*

JESSE AND DOMINO
Jesse Aaronson can disrupt electrical and mechanical devices. Domino served alongside Cable in his mercenary group, Six Pack. As well as being a superb athlete, Domino also has the ability to shift luck in her favour.

Copycat

The Domino who first joined X-Force was not really Domino. She was actually Vanessa Carlysle, a mutant shapeshifter also known as Copycat. She had been blackmailed into infiltrating Cable's new team by his evil son Tyler. Copycat also has the dubious distinction of being Deadpool's former girlfriend. Appropriately for a shapeshifter, Vanessa now works as an actress.

Peter Wisdom

Peter Wisdom was an operative for Black Air, a British intelligence agency, but he quit, appalled by its cruel treatment of mutants. Being a mutant himself, he joined the Super Hero team, Excalibur, where he met and fell in love with Kitty Pryde. After he and Kitty split up, Wisdom left Excalibur and England and took over as leader of X-Force. He intends to use this new team to uncover crimes against humanity perpetrated by the intelligence community and others.

Cable's team

X-Force's original line-up included Boom Boom, Cable, Cannonball, Domino, Feral, Shatterstar, and Warpath. Feral later became X-Force's enemy and was imprisoned for murder. Trained to be a master swordsman on Mojoworld, Shatterstar's spirit now inhabits the body of an Earthman. James Proudstar, alias Warpath, is the younger brother of the original Thunderbird and has the same mutant abilities. At first seeking vengeance on the X-Men for his brother's death, James joined the Hellions as Thunderbird II. He later joined X-Force, taking the name Warpath.

Sunspot

Warpath

Boom Boom

Warpath

Cannonball

Shatterstar

Feral

Cable

Domino

Siryn

Meltdown

MELTDOWN AND SIRYN
Since joining X-Force, Boom Boom changed her name to Boomer and then to Meltdown. She can create explosive balls of energy, called 'time bombs'. Siryn has the same sonic powers as her father, Sean Cassidy, alias Banshee.

RICTOR
The mutant code-named Rictor can generate powerful waves of vibrations, resembling small earthquakes, through any object he comes into contact with. He was taught how to cope with these powers by the original X-Factor team and he then went on to join the New Mutants. However, believing that Cable had murdered his father, Rictor joined the team Weapon: Prime, whose mission it was to capture the time-travelling mutant. But Rictor learned that it was Stryfe who was the true killer, and he decided to join up with Cable in X-Force.

X-FACTOR II

X-FACTOR HEADQUARTERS
Originally, X-Factor II was based in the upscale Georgetown section of Washington DC. Later they moved to Falls Edge, a high-tech facility located in the Blue Ridge Mountains of Virginia (shown here). Havok and his allies later used a building in New Jersey as a base.

WHILE CHARLES XAVIER travelled into space with the Starjammers, the original X-Men founded the first X-Factor as a means of carrying on his legacy. When Xavier came back to Earth, the five founders returned to the X-Men, and the original X-Factor ceased to exist. However, Dr. Valerie Cooper, a US government official, decided to organize a new team under that same name. This X-Factor would be a team of mutants who would go on special missions for the government. Cooper believed that the new X-Factor could create a positive public image for mutants. Xavier and Cooper persuaded veteran X-Man Havok to lead the team. Among Cooper's other recruits were Havok's longtime girlfriend Polaris, the former New Mutant Wolfsbane, and Quicksilver. Another member was Jamie Madrox, the Multiple Man who could create duplicates of himself at will. Finally, there was Guido Carosella, the former bodyguard of the mutant rock star Lila Cheney, who took the unpretentious code name 'Strong Guy'. The mutant inventor Forge briefly replaced Cooper as the team's government liaison, before joining X-Factor himself.

Wildchild   *Sabretooth*

Mystique   *Shard*   *Forge*   *Polaris*

Forge's team

Forge found himself leading an unusual X-Factor roster. The founding members were gone except for Polaris. The strangest new recruit was Shard, Bishop's deceased sister from the future who had been resurrected as a living hologram. Val Cooper's superiors insisted that X-Factor take on three other newcomers. One was Wildchild, a veteran of Alpha Flight. Possessing animalistic agility, senses, and claws, Wildchild at times struggled to overcome his bestial side. The outlaw Mystique was given an implant that restricted her morphing powers. The government placed Sabretooth in X-Factor as a 'sleeper agent'.

CHANGING FACE

Before long, the founding members left, and new recruits arrived, including Mystique, Sabretooth, Shard, and Wildchild. When X-Factor members realized that the government was using them to hunt down other mutants, they faked their own deaths and went underground. Disillusioned, Havok pretended to turn outlaw in order to stop the schemes of Dark Beast. Later, he became leader of three mutants from the future: Archer, Fixx, and Greystone. Havok was attempting to put X-Factor back together when he was hurled into the alternate reality of 'Mutant X'. With Havok gone, X-Factor was no more.

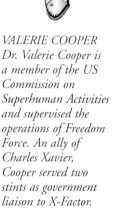

VALERIE COOPER
Dr. Valerie Cooper is a member of the US Commission on Superhuman Activities and supervised the operations of Freedom Force. An ally of Charles Xavier, Cooper served two stints as government liaison to X-Factor.

Archer, Greystone & Fixx

These three mutants hail from the same future as Bishop. All three were XSE agents who became disillusioned with the security force and formed their own group, Xavier's Underground Enforcers (XUE). The spirits of all three have since travelled back in time to the present day where they occupy the bodies of deceased humans. Archer has the ability to become a being of pure energy, while Fixx has strong telekinetic and psychic abilities that manifest themselves as little fairy-like figures. Greystone is the strongest of the three, and can grow to gigantic proportions.

Founding members

X-Factor II's original roster comprised of Havok, Polaris, Quicksilver, Wolfsbane, Strong Guy, and Multiple Man. Jamie Madrox, the Multiple Man, creates a duplicate of himself when he is struck, or even if he snaps his finger or stamps his foot; he can absorb his double back into himself at will.

Quicksilver

From the superhumanly fast Quicksilver's point of view, virtually everyone else moves at a snail's pace. After quitting his father Magneto's terrorist Brotherhood, Quicksilver joined the Avengers, a leading Super Hero team. The hot-tempered Quicksilver served in X-Factor during a period of estrangement from his wife and fellow Avenger, Crystal. He eventually returned to her, their daughter Luna, and the Avengers.

Quicksilver can run up to 280 kilometres per hour, and can react five times faster than a normal human!

STRONG GUY
Guido Carosella, alias Strong Guy, absorbs kinetic energy and converts it to superhuman strength. Storing such energy too long in the past has grotesquely distorted his huge body. Before joining X-Factor, Guido worked as bodyguard for the mutant rock star Lila Cheney.

Strong Guy

Multiple Man

Polaris

Multiple Man

Havok

Wolfsbane   *Multiple Man*

BISHOP

Bishop was tattooed 'M' for 'mutant' when he was a child in a prison camp.

THE MUTANT KNOWN only as Bishop never dreamed that someday he would be a member of the X-Men. Born half a century from now, Bishop grew up admiring the long-dead X-Men as heroes from legend. As a teenager, he discovered his own mutant ability to absorb kinetic energy and redirect it through his hands as a concussive force. Bishop became a lawman, hoping to follow in the X-Men's footsteps. But through an amazing twist of fate, he became an X-Man himself. Bishop and his sister Shard were born in a mutant prison camp in an alternate future ruled by the Sentinels, who were finally overthrown. Bishop and Shard were inspired by the stories their grandmother told them about Xavier's now-legendary team of mutant heroes. After she died, Bishop and Shard were protected by her friend Hancock, until he was murdered by mutant criminals. Bravely, the teenage Bishop used his newly emerged powers to fight back. The two XSE agents who finally stopped the murderers were so impressed by Bishop that they invited Bishop and Shard to become cadets in the XSE. Eventually they became full officers.

BACK IN TIME

When Trevor Fitzroy and a number of other mutant outlaws escaped through time into the past, Bishop and his XSE partners, Malcolm and Randall, followed. Some of the outlaws killed Malcolm and Randall, and Bishop found himself stranded in the present day. To his astonishment, Bishop not only met the X-Men, who were his childhood heroes, but was even inducted into their ranks by Charles Xavier himself. Since then, Bishop has not only served in the X-Men, but has also had adventures in the distant Shi'ar Galaxy and even visited a future time far beyond his own.

Inspired by the work of Charles Xavier, mutants of the future founded Xavier's Security Enforcers (XSE), an organization through which mutant lawmen brought criminal mutants to justice.

HARDENED FIGHTER
In his own time, Bishop was ruthless towards his enemies. When the X-Men first met Bishop, they were horrified to see him slaughter mutant outlaws from his future time. In the X-Men, Bishop learned not to act as judge, jury, and executioner, and the X-Men discovered that Bishop was deeply loyal towards his allies.

Bishop's weapons and powers

If an enemy fires virtually any kind of energy at Bishop, he can absorb it into his body and direct it back at his adversary at full force through his hands. He also carries specially developed XSE weaponry, which uses future technology to fire laser beams and plasma charges.

SCHRAAKK

GLOWING HAND
Bishop's hand glows before he releases the energy stored within his body through it.

When Bishop first arrived in our present, he was wearing his XSE uniform. Since joining the X-Men, he has created new outfits to wear into combat.

Xavier Security Enforcers

After they became officers in the XSE, Shard was promoted to become Bishop's commanding officer. Bishop remained content with staying at a lower rank where he could patrol the streets with his friends and fellow XSE officers, Malcolm and Randall. It was with these officers that Bishop travelled back in time to our present day, pursuing Trevor Fitzroy and the other escaped mutant criminals.

Hancock and Shard

Bishop and his sister Shard were raised by their grandmother at first and then, after her death, by her friend Hancock. However, Hancock was murdered by mutant criminals named Billboy and Halftrack. Amazon and Recoil, the XSE agents who stopped the two murderers, were so impressed by Bishop's fighting skills that they offered him a position in the XSE as a cadet.

Bishop

Randall

Malcolm

Shard

Fitzroy

Although he was one of Bishop and Shard's fellow cadets in the XSE, Trevor Fitzroy became one of the most dangerous mutant criminals of his time. By draining the life energy of others, Fitzroy can open portals through time. Incarcerated, Fitzroy led a mass prison break and used his power to escape into the X-Men's present, along with other mutant outlaws. Bishop, Malcolm, and Randall went back through time in pursuit. Later, Bishop journeyed to another alternate future, where he battled Fitzroy in the latter's new identity, the Chronomancer.

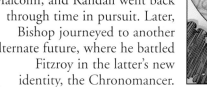

DEADPOOL

W OLVERINE IS NOT the only victim of the experiments of the Weapon X Project. As a joint operation by the CIA and the Canadian government's Special Weapons Development Branch, known as Department K, the Weapon X Project's purpose was to create 'super-soldiers' for both governments. Among the Project's subjects were the members of the CIA's special commando squad, Team X, which included Logan and Victor Creed. The Project intended to suppress its super-soldiers' memories of their own powers until these powers were needed. Hence, it interfered with some of the super-soldiers' memories and implanted false ones, making their past a mystery to all but the government agencies involved.

The scarred Deadpool calls his mask his real 'face'.

Deadpool sometimes carries two swords on his back.

DEADPOOL

Not all of Weapon X Project's subjects were as 'successful' as Wolverine, and many others were deemed failures. The most notorious of these is the character known as Deadpool. He was a mercenary who called himself Wade Wilson; his real identity is unknown. Discovering that he had a virulent form of cancer, Wade volunteered for the Weapon X Project, hoping that it could cure him. However, the Project consigned Wilson along with other subjects of failed genetic experiments to a facility headed by Dr. Killebrew. This evil scientist used these 'failures' as test subjects for his cruel experiments. The victims took bets in a 'deadpool' on which of them would survive the experiments the longest. During his time at Dr. Killebrew's facility, the healing factor that the Weapon X Project had given Wade was activated by his passion for vengeance against his captors. He escaped from the Project and became a costumed mercenary, calling himself Deadpool. It was later revealed that Wade Wilson was not Deadpool's real name, merely an identity he had stolen from a man he thought he had killed. The real Wade Wilson had, in fact, survived and returned to become Deadpool's nemesis T-Ray.

DEADPOOL UNMASKED
The healing factor that the Weapon X Project gave Deadpool cured his cancer, but at the price of permanently scarring his face and entire body. The Project also gave him the ability to regenerate entire severed limbs and body organs, even including his heart.

THIS JOKE WILL KILL YOU!
Not wholly sane, Deadpool continually chatters away in a stream-of-consciousness patter full of jokes and references to pop culture trivia, whether he is by himself or in the midst of a life-or-death battle.

DEADPOOL'S YOUTH
As with many Weapon X subjects, very little is known of Deadpool's past. His real name might have been Jack, a young tearaway who grew up to become one of the world's toughest mercenaries.

OTHER SUBJECTS OF THE WEAPON X PROJECT

WHEN LOGAN JOINED the commando squad known as Team X, he found himself teamed up with a number of other mutants. In addition to Victor Creed, there was David North, who took the code name Maverick, John Wraith, who became known as Kestrel, and the mysterious Silver Fox. Based in Alberta, Canada, Team X was sent on covert missions around the world.

Victor Creed   John Wraith

David North   Logan

TEAM X
Logan (the future Wolverine) and Victor Creed (the future Sabretooth) were both members of the CIA's special operatives squad, Team X. Another member, John Wraith, code-named Kestrel, can vanish at will. The CIA also recruited a German named Christopher Nord into Team X. Nord had made an impressive reputation as a freedom fighter against communists during the Cold War. On moving to the US, he changed his name to David North.

Team X went on missions for the CIA in the 1960s.

KANE
Garrison Kane used to be a member of Cable's mercenary team, Six Pack. Later, Kane succeeded Wolverine as the new 'Weapon X' working for Department K. He had been converted into a cyborg, part man and part machine. When he was transported into the 40th century by Cable, Kane received new cyborg parts that utilized the advanced technology of that time before he returned to the present.

MAVERICK
After Team X was disbanded, David North became the costumed mercenary known as Maverick. He is a mutant with the power to absorb kinetic energy and to rechannel it at will. He has continued his mercenary career despite recently being infected with the Legacy Virus. His mutant powers have caused his disease to go into temporary remission.

Maverick also has the same age-suppression factor as Wolverine and Sabretooth.

SILVER FOX
Wolverine remembers being in love with a character called Silver Fox, who was supposedly murdered by Sabretooth. Decades later, Silver Fox turned up alive as a member of Team X. However, Wolverine does not know whether these memories are real, or false ones implanted by the Weapon X Project.

Silver Fox betrayed the members of Team X and went on to join the subversive organization Hydra.

X-MEN 2099

MOUNTAIN BASE
For a time, the X-Men of 2099 took over a base in the mountains of New Mexico that once belonged to their foe, Master Zhao. Later, they became the protectors of Halo City, built in California as a safe haven for mutants. When Halo City was submerged by the rising ocean, the X-Men led a mutant migration to the Savage Land.

IN THE TERRIFYING alternate reality of 2099 AD, powerful corporations dominate every aspect of life in America – and mutants are not tolerated. A generation of mutants was almost entirely wiped out a few years previously, in the Great Purge. The few survivors were turned into outcasts by the corporations. But amid such persecution there arose a messianic figure, a mutant and former criminal named Xi'an Chi Xan. Known as the Desert Ghost, this mutant had the power both to punish and heal. With his left hand he could disintegrate matter, but with the touch of his right hand he could heal injuries. Inspired by the life of Charles Xavier, Xi'an intended to reunite his scattered people, the mutants. To this end he gathered together a new team of X-Men. Prominent among them was Shakti Haddad, code-named Cerebra, who had the psionic ability to sense the presence of other mutants, much like Xavier's Cerebro device.

MUTANTS OF 2099 AD

Xi'an's mutants are a varied bunch. Krystalin can create crystals from thin air. Meanstreak can move at superhuman speed. Metalhead's body takes on the properties of any metal he touches. Timothy Fitzgerald's body releases absorbed energy that makes him glow and his skeleton become visible – hence his name, Skullfire. Bloodhawk can change at will into a red-skinned humanoid with bat-like wings that enable him to fly. Although he initially refused to join Xi'an's X-Men, he became their ally.

X-Nation 2099
X-Nation is a team of extraordinary teenage mutants who live in the Xavier Shelter for Indigent Children, an orphanage in Halo City. There they are tutored by Cerebra. Among them is Clarion, who turns sound into force; December, possibly a relative of Emma Frost; the cyborg Nostromo; Twilight, who controls anything within her 'sphere of influence'; the giant Uproar; the shapeshifter Willow; and Wulff, who has claws.

Battle charge
The X-Men of 2099 faced bizarre adversaries such as the Freakshow, grotesque products of failed experiments in genetic engineering. Brimstone Love and his Theatre of Pain enslaved human beings and tormented them for their clients' entertainment. Weirdest of all was the shapechanger Halloween Jack, a psychotic genius who made Las Vegas his personal domain.

Bloodhawk   Krystalin   Desert Ghost   Skullfire   Metalhead   Cerebra   Meanstreak

PHALANX

THE X-MEN have never encountered an alien race more deadly than the Phalanx. These techno-organic beings – creatures whose nervous systems are composed of organic circuitry – were actually created on Earth by human scientists. Their bodies are structured like machinery and the entire race has a single, collective consciousness. The Phalanx infect people with the transmode virus, which converts them into techno-organic beings and assimilates them into the Phalanx collective. This evil race was born when scientists experimented on the remains of the New Mutant Warlock, who was a member of the Technarchy, a society of techno-organic beings. Technarchs feed by using the transmode virus to convert organic life forms into Phalanx and then draining their life away.

INTERSTELLAR INFECTION

Scientists originally infected volunteers with the transmode virus in a bid to create techno-organic versions of the Sentinels. However, the result of these experiments – the Phalanx – wanted to convert all life on Earth into techno-organic beings. Since the Phalanx could not assimilate mutants due to mutants' genetic structure, they instead tried to kill them. The X-Men succeeded in destroying most of the Phalanx once, but they have since spread into space, threatening the Shi'ar empire.

Phalanx in space

An army of Phalanx once attacked and conquered the Throneworld of the Shi'ar Empire, making its ruler, Lilandra, their prisoner. Gladiator of the Shi'ar Imperial Guard sought the help of the X-Men, who travelled to the Throneworld in a Shi'ar starship. One of the X-Men, Beast, devised a means of tearing the machine parts of the Phalanx from their organic parts, and thus destroyed them.

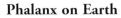

Phalanx on Earth
The Phalanx's aims on Earth were furthered by a number of human assistants. Dr. Stephen Lang, who had once built the Sentinels, was kidnapped by scientists and cybernetically linked to the Phalanx. Though he retained his free will, Lang saw the Phalanx as a means for humanity to evolve to a level higher than mutants and then to eradicate them. X-Factor's enemy Cameron Hodge was assimilated into the Phalanx and helped direct its actions. Notable among the many unwilling humans to be assimilated was Jean Grey's older sister, Sara.

WARLOCK
After being killed by Cameron Hodge, Warlock was resurrected as a member of the Phalanx in the likeness of his deceased friend, Doug Ramsey. Though his memory was gone, 'Douglock' helped the X-Men defeat the Phalanx.

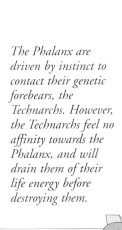

The Phalanx are driven by instinct to contact their genetic forebears, the Technarchs. However, the Technarchs feel no affinity towards the Phalanx, and will drain them of their life energy before destroying them.

147

GENERATION X

THE PHALANX once sought to capture members of the 'next generation' of teenage mutants to use them as test subjects. By experimenting on their young captives, the Phalanx hoped to find a means of converting mutants into techno-organic beings, like themselves, whom they could then assimilate. After the X-Men defeated the Phalanx, Charles Xavier decided the teenage mutants should be organized into a new class and taught how to use their powers. However, this time Xavier chose not to teach them himself; he was already fully occupied overseeing the large number of X-Men. Instead he chose two new headmasters: Sean Cassidy, alias Banshee, and the X-Men's former enemy, Emma Frost, the White Queen. Xavier took over the Massachusetts Academy, the private school Frost had headed, and turned it into the new Xavier's School for Gifted Youngsters, while Xavier's mansion became the Xavier Institute for Higher Learning.

XAVIER'S NEW SCHOOL
The Massachusetts Academy, the new Xavier's School for Gifted Youngsters and the base for Generation X, is located in the town of Snow Valley, amid the beautiful Berkshire Mountains of western Massachusetts.

A native of the Pacific island of Samoa, Mondo lived an idyllic life there until he joined Generation X. Mondo's mutant power enables his body to copy any form of matter. But Mondo ended up allied with Black Tom Cassidy as an enemy of his classmates.

Artie and Leech
The Massachusetts Academy recently took in two mutant children, Artie Maddocks and Leech. Artie communicates by creating visual images of his thoughts, while the green-skinned Leech is a surviving Morlock who can neutralize the powers of any mutant near him.

THE NEW CLASS

The students of Generation X come from diverse backgrounds, yet they have bonded into a surrogate family. Two come from wealthy families. Jubilee, an Asian-American from Beverly Hills, was transferred to the new team from the X-Men, while Monet St. Croix, code-named M, is an aristocrat from Monaco. Two others grew up in poverty. Paige Guthrie, known as Husk, is Cannonball's sister from the coal mining regions of Kentucky, and Angelo Espinosa, known as Skin, grew up in the Latino barrio of East Los Angeles. The other members of this diverse group of mutants include Englishman Jonothon Starsmore, alias Chamber, and Everett Thomas, code-named Synch, an African-American.

Chamber, Husk, and Skin
When Chamber's power to fire telekinetic blasts first arose, it destroyed half his face. Husk can shed her outer skin, revealing a new form with superhuman attributes, such as the hardness of diamond or the strength of steel. Skin has two extra metres of flesh which he can use to grapple objects.

Chamber

Husk

Skin

M

Synch

M, Synch, and Emma Frost

The egocentric M possesses superhuman strength, telepathy, and can fly. Synch can put himself 'in synch' genetically with another mutant, thereby imitating that mutant's powers. Once the X-Men's enemy and part of the Hellfire Club, Emma Frost has since joined Generation X. Guilty over her failure to prevent the deaths of her former students, the Hellions, she seeks to redeem herself through teaching Generation X.

Chamber

M

Banshee

Synch

Emma Frost

Husk

Skin

Jubilee

Penance's razor-sharp skin can cut through nearly anything.

Penance

Tom Corsi

Tom Corsi was a policeman in Salem Center. The demon bear that battled the New Mutants captured Corsi and local nurse Sharon Friedlander and transformed them into superhumanly strong Native Americans. Corsi and Friedlander then worked for Charles Xavier, and recently Sean Cassidy persuaded Corsi to teach Generation X.

Emplate

The strangest and most persistent of Generation X's adversaries is the creature called Emplate, a mutant who subsists on the genetic material of other mutants. After 'feeding' on another mutant's DNA, Emplate temporarily gains his victim's superhuman powers. If he is denied this sustenance, he is thrown into a pocket dimension where he is the subject of constant torture. The first victim Emplate killed to satisfy his hunger was his own mother. It was later learned that Emplate is actually Marius St. Croix, the brother of Monet, alias M. At one point, Marius and Monet merged, forming the dangerous, single entity known as M-Plate.

THE AGE OF APOCALYPSE

THE ALTERNATE REALITY known as the 'Age of Apocalypse' reversed the premise of the 'Days of Future Past'. Whereas in the 'Days of Future Past' timeline, mutants were the victims of oppression, in the 'Age of Apocalypse' evil mutants, led by Apocalypse, enslaved the human population of North America. It began in our X-Men's reality, when Charles Xavier's son, Legion, journeyed back in time twenty years to assassinate Magneto before he could begin his war on humanity. Instead, Legion accidentally killed Xavier, creating an alternate timeline in which no one had been able to stop Apocalypse from conquering the continent. In this new timeline, the lives of each of the X-Men and other familiar characters became radically different. Following the climactic battle, this entire timeline was obliterated. Only four characters survived by escaping into our X-Men's timeline: one hero – Nate Grey, the X-Man – and three menaces – the Dark Beast, Holocaust, and Sugar Man.

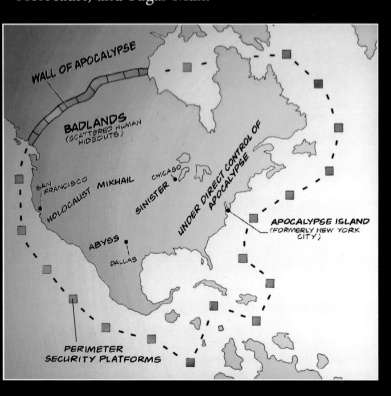

As Legion aimed his blade of psychic energy at Magneto, Xavier hurled himself between them, receiving the lethal blow himself.

Xavier's sacrifice
Hoping to change his father's life for the better, Legion went back in time to kill Magneto before he could become Xavier's enemy. But Legion did not realize that Xavier would sacrifice his own life to save his friend.

Magneto
Seeing Xavier die trying to save his life changed Magneto forever. He vowed to devote his life to bring about Xavier's goal of peace between mutants and humans. As a result, it was Magneto who founded the X-Men in this timeline, and he who became Apocalypse's enemy.

MAGNETO'S FAMILY
In this alternate reality, Magneto proved to be a good father to his son, Quicksilver. Magneto also married another of his X-Men, Rogue and they had a son, whom Magneto named Charles in memory of his fallen friend.

Bishop was sent back in time by Magneto to stop Legion from killing Charles Xavier. Magneto also slew Apocalypse, ending the evil ruler's tyranny.

Gambit and the X-Ternals
Gambit became the modern-day Robin Hood of the 'Age of Apocalypse'. He led the X-Ternals, a band of mutants which included Jubilee, Sunspot, and Strong Guy, who stole from Apocalypse's elite to help the poor. Magneto assigned Gambit and the X-Ternals to travel to the Shi'ar Galaxy to steal the powerful M'Krann Crystal.

THE RESISTANCE
By the close of the 'Age of Apocalypse', Magneto's X-Men stood united with other allies, including Logan, now known as Weapon X, and Cyclops, who was Sinister's adopted son.

Dark Beast
Henry McCoy in the 'Age of Apocalypse' timeline was a sadistic, warped genius, who took pleasure in subjecting human victims to painful genetic experiments, earning him the code name Dark Beast. He escaped into the normal X-Men timeline when the 'Age of Apocalypse' timeline was obliterated.

Apocalypse
Once in control of North America, Apocalypse implemented his philosophy of 'survival of the fittest' on a colossal scale. He set about his programme of 'cleansing' humanity's gene pool of all he considered weak and unfit to live. Through continual 'cullings' of the population, Apocalypse threatened to wipe out the human race.

XAVIER SAVED
When Bishop chanced to leave his own time and arrive in the 'Age of Apocalypse' timeline, he was baffled to discover that Magento, and not Xavier, was in charge of the X-Men. Using the power of the M'Krann Crystal, Magneto sent Bishop back in time to prevent Xavier's death. Bishop plunged Legion's psychic blade into Legion's own chest, preventing him from killing Xavier or Magneto.

Four Horsemen
In this timeline, Apocalypse's Four Horsemen were Abyss, Holocaust, Mikhail Rasputin, and Sinister. But Sinister secretly plotted against Apocalypse, creating Nate Grey to use as a living weapon against him.

TYRANT'S END
In their final battle, Magneto literally tore Apocalypse's body apart with his magnetic powers.

X-MAN

CREATED IN THE Age of Apocalypse timeline, Nate Grey, the X-Man, is one of the few of that reality's mutants to survive its end. Genetically engineered from the DNA of Scott Summers and Jean Grey, Nate Grey is, in effect, the Age of Apocalypse's counterpart to Cable. Free from Cable's techno-organic disease, Nate Grey has enormous powers of telepathy and telekinesis that make him potentially the mightiest mutant on Earth. Indeed, his abilities are so vast in scope that they are too much for his adolescent body to contain. Hence, unless a cure is found, his mutant powers will inevitably kill him while he is still young. It was Sinister of the 'Age of Apocalypse' who genetically engineered the child he named Nate Grey, intending to use him as a living weapon against the tyrant Apocalypse. By coincidence, Nate was freed from captivity by Cyclops, unaware that he was the boy's 'father'. Instead, Nate found a father figure in his world's version of Forge, until Forge was murdered by Sinister.

Having created Nate from gene samples, Sinister grew the boy at an accelerated rate inside a nutrient bath in a birthing chamber, releasing him sometimes to check on his development.

TIMELINE TRAVELLER

Ultimately, Nate Grey encountered his genetic parents and aided them and their allies in the overthrow of Apocalypse's dictatorship. Although the Age of Apocalypse timeline was doomed to oblivion, the strange powers of the M'Krann Crystal somehow spared Nate, transporting him to the restored timeline of the X-Men. Used to the bleak, devastated world of his origin, Nate found his new world beautiful but strange. At first, Nate found himself at odds with Cable and the X-Men, but recently he has been welcomed into their ranks. Now, as before, Nate's goal is to do whatever he can to prevent his new world from suffering the same fate as the dystopian Earth into which he was born.

Last battle

In the climactic battle that ended the 'Age of Apocalypse', Nate Grey drove a shard of the all-powerful M'Krann Crystal into the chest of his enemy Holocaust. Unexpectedly, it transported them both into the X-Men's normal reality, making them two of the only survivors of their native timeline.

MADELYNE PRYOR
When Nate ended up in the current X-Men's timeline, he found himself very alone. Longing for companionship, Nate subconsciously used his prodigious powers to tap into the remaining psionic energies of Jean Grey's deceased clone, Madelyne Pryor, and created a new body for her. Although the Madelyne Pryor now active on Earth is not truly the original Madelyne, but a 'psionic shell', she still has all of her powers, personality, and memories.

X-Man unleashed

Young and fiery-tempered, once Nate is provoked he can launch into a nearly unstoppable fury. Recently, Nate has learned self-control in his new role as a latter-day 'shaman', using his psionic powers to aid others.

Meeting his maker

As the 'Age of Apocalypse' timeline drew to its close, Nate Grey finally confronted his maker, Sinister, who then revealed how he had created Nate to kill Apocalypse. Enraged that Sinister had murdered his father figure, Forge, Nate unleashed his powers against Sinister, leaving him mortally wounded. Yet Nate found no satisfaction in revenge, but only a sense of loneliness in this barren world.

Using his amazingly powerful telekinetic abilities, X-Man can propel himself through the air in flight.

FIRST APPEARANCE
When Nate first arrived from the 'Age of Apocalypse' timeline, he wore this uniform.

Cranial implants

Threnody

Originally, the Sinister of this timeline used the mutant Threnody as a pawn to track down Nate Grey. On finding X-Man, Threnody switched allegiances and even became Nate's girlfriend. She is, however, haunted by her own power, the ability to turn dying breaths into destructive energy. Unfortunately, she is unable to control this ability without help, and she has been responsible for the deaths of several innocent people. Threnody has now been fitted with cranial implants which allow her to store the energy she collects for as long as she likes.
Nate made the mistake of removing these implants, and the resulting blast destroyed a hotel.

Before she was fitted with the cranial implants, Threnody accidentally killed an elderly couple who were looking after her.

ONSLAUGHT

With Xavier's telepathic abilities, but not his self-restraint, Onslaught could unleash the full, terrible force of Professor X's psychic power.

ALTHOUGH HE FOUNDED the X-Men, Charles Xavier has come the closest to destroying them. On two occasions, the evil side of Xavier's psyche has briefly manifested itself as a separate astral being. During a battle between the X-Men and Magneto, Xavier lost his temper and used his mental powers to wipe out Magneto's memory. The moment he did so, the dark side of Xavier's mind, containing all his suppressed rage at humanity's bigotry towards mutants, contacted its counterpart in Magneto's soul. A new, malevolent being, Onslaught, was created. This being combined not only the superhuman powers of both Magneto and Professor X, but also their full, unrestrained capacity for evil.

SENTINEL LEADER

Onslaught used an army of Sentinels to take control of Manhattan. This was his first step in punishing humanity for its oppression of mutants. Finally, as the X-Men turned their full power against him, other Super Heroes – the Avengers and the Fantastic Four – hurled themselves into Onslaught, and destroyed him from within.

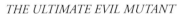

THE ULTIMATE EVIL MUTANT
Though Onslaught was unwittingly formed from the minds of Xavier and Magneto, he took on a life of his own and existed independently of his creators; his body and armour being composed of pure psionic energy. For a time, Onslaught was perhaps the mightiest being on Earth. His devastating attack on Manhattan inflamed human bigots' hatred of mutants, and set the stage for Bastion's anti-mutant 'Operation: Zero Tolerance'.

UNWILLING SLAVE
Onslaught added to his already immense power when he kidnapped Franklin Richards, the young son of two members of the Fantastic Four. By holding Franklin prisoner inside his body, Onslaught could draw upon Franklin's mutant powers to restructure reality. Likewise, Onslaught captured Nate Grey, alias X-Man, to gain Nate's powerful psi abilities.

Captive Xavier
Onslaught also held Charles Xavier captive and stripped him of his telepathic powers. Xavier, X-Man, and Franklin were all finally freed from Onslaught, but Xavier felt responsible for the being's creation and surrendered himself to the government. Xavier can never be certain that someday he will not unwittingly create another Onslaught.

BASTION

THIS MYSTERIOUS MAN saw himself as humanity's last 'bastion' of defence against the mutant menace. But, though he himself did not know it at first, the man who called himself Bastion was actually a Sentinel robot in human guise. He originated as Master Mold, an immense Sentinel designed by Bolivar Trask. After the Master Mold was demolished by the Banshee, one of its components was found by Nimrod, an advanced Sentinel that had travelled from the future. The Master Mold's programming infiltrated Nimrod's systems, reconstructing it into a combination of both robots. Dazzler blasted this amalgam into a dimensional portal created by the Siege Perilous. Magical forces then transformed the robot into the form of an adult human, with no memory of his true origins. However, he was still driven by his original programming – to capture and destroy all mutants.

SENTINELS
Bastion offered 'miracle cures' to patients in his Prospero Clinic, where he secretly converted them into warrior cyborgs called the Prime Sentinels. Claiming that 'the only way the Sentinels can protect Man is to be Man', he later planned to turn all humans on Earth into Sentinel cyborgs that would exterminate all mutants.

BODILESS MENACE
When his body was wrecked by an explosion, only Bastion's head survived. The head was recovered by a menace called Mainspring, who deleted its Bastion and Nimrod personas, and gave it a new body and a new name: Template.

BASTION'S TRUE FORM
After learning he was a robot, Bastion assumed his true, robotic form, resembling Nimrod. He was soon demolished in a battle with Cable and Machine Man.

ZERO TOLERANCE

Bastion assembled an international paramilitary force called 'Operation: Zero Tolerance' to put an end to the 'mutant menace'. He succeeded in capturing various X-Men and taking over Xavier's mansion. Appalled by his actions, the president of the United States had Bastion arrested, and government scientists soon discovered that Bastion was an android. Bastion has since escaped to menace all of humanity, most recently under the new name of Template.

Base of operations
In a secluded part of New Mexico lies a military installation once known as Hulkbuster Base. Originally built to contain the Incredible Hulk, this bunker, which extends hundreds of metres beneath the ground, once served as Bastion's base of operations.

When he appeared like this, Bastion could persuade government officials that he was an ordinary human like themselves.

MARROW

MARROW IS AN X-MAN with a disturbingly different mutant power: detachable bones grow right through her skin. She is a second-generation member of the Morlocks, an enormous community of mutants who lived in a system of tunnels beneath the streets of Manhattan. (The Morlocks took their name from the underground race in H. G. Wells' novel *The Time Machine*.) Like the other Morlocks, her parents were outcasts from human society because they were mutants. This group of pariahs found refuge in the tunnels and abandoned bomb shelters that lie under New York City. It was here that Sarah, the future Marrow, was born.

Recently, Marrow learned how to retract her exterior bones into her body, making herself appear more attractive.

MORLOCK TERRORIST

Some time after her birth, a group of mutant mercenaries, known as the Marauders, slaughtered most of the Morlocks on the orders of Sinister. Sarah was still a child then, but Colossus' mutant brother, Mikhail Rasputin, transported her and other survivors of the attack to another dimension, known as 'the Hill'. Here, time moves more quickly than it does on Earth. As a result, when Sarah returned to Earth, she had grown up and was called Marrow. She was also the leader of a terrorist army called Gene Nation. This group of second-generation Morlocks was determined to take revenge on humanity for oppressing mutants. To stop Marrow, Storm was forced to rip out her heart. However, Marrow survived because her mutant anatomy had given her a second heart. She returned to battle the forces of Operation: Zero Tolerance. Seeking to turn Sarah away from vengeance, Callisto, the Morlocks' former leader, sent her to live with the X-Men. Since then, Marrow has slowly overcome her hostility towards the rest of the world and learned to adjust to life as a member of the X-Men.

BONY GROWTHS
Sarah's largest detachable bones protrude from her back. Bones also sprout from other parts of her body, including her forehead, shoulders, arms, legs, and waist.

When Marrow removes a bone, a new one grows in its place.

Removing a bone always causes Marrow pain.

Marrow can hurl her sharp bones as if they were throwing knives.

Life in the X-Men

Marrow was embittered by the harsh life she lived, first in the Morlocks' dark tunnels, and then fighting for survival in the dimension Mikhail Rasputin took her to. Despite Marrow's hostile attitude, Wolverine decided to become her mentor when she joined the X-Men. He succeeded in training her to work as a member of a team. As Marrow slowly mellowed, she grew close firstly to Gambit, and later to Colossus.

JOSEPH

A FEMALE MUTANT named Astra created a genetic duplicate of her old enemy Magneto, but one who was physically in his early twenties. Astra sent her creation to kill Magneto, but during their battle in Guatemala, Magneto succeeding in knocking him unconscious. The double was found, his memory gone, by a nun, Sister Mary de la Hoya. A child at her orphanage named him Joseph. Sister Mary sent Joseph to the United States to find the X-Men, who assumed he was Magneto himself, somehow grown younger. Willing to give him a second chance, they made him an X-Man. The real Magneto returned, manipulating the Earth's magnetic sphere to disrupt the world's electrical systems. Joseph nobly sacrificed his life to repair the damage to the magnetosphere, thwarting Magneto's attempt at world conquest.

THIS IS FOR THE BEST, CHARLES. DURING ALL OF MY SHORT LIFE, I HAVE SEARCHED FOR PEACE OF MIND... ...A SENSE OF SELF-WORTH... A PURPOSE TO MY VERY EXISTENCE. KNOWING I HAVE STOPPED MAGNETO'S MADNESS -- -- AND SAVED ALL OF YOU TO PURSUE YOUR DREAM OF PEACE -- -- HAS GIVEN ME MY LIFE VALUE.

HEROIC SACRIFICE
Over time, Magneto has set mental limits on his magnetic power so that it will not consume him. Astra created Joseph without such limits. When countering Magneto's damage to the Earth's magnetic field, Joseph used so much power that it burned out his body, aging and finally destroying him.

MAGGOTT

U NQUESTIONABLY the X-Man with the strangest – and most disgusting – mutant power is Maggott. As a child in in South Africa, Japheth suffered from a mysterious ailment that made it almost impossible for him to digest solid food. When he was twelve, he realized that he was a financial burden to his parents and drove into the desert to die. He was found by Magneto, who activated Japheth's mutant power, releasing two giant slug-like creatures from his abdomen. When they were out of his body, his skin turned blue. Japheth discovered that the slugs were his digestive system. He could no longer eat like a normal human: the slugs eat for him, and then burrow into his body. Somehow, the hole they make when entering and leaving his body seals immediately. Now calling himself Maggott, he briefly served in the X-Men after Operation: Zero Tolerance.

Maggott was a sickly, lame child when the two slug-like creatures, then quite small, first left his body.

MAGGOTT AS AN ADULT

EANY AND MEANY
Maggott has a symbiotic relationship with the two slug-like creatures which he has nicknamed 'Eany' and 'Meany', shown here curled around his wrists. He cannot survive without them; Eany and Meany are really parts of his own body. The slugs seem to be able to consume any form of matter.

OTHER '90s VILLAINS

GRAYDON CREED
This man headed the Friends of Humanity, a political party of fanatical anti-mutant die-hards, who terrorized mutants. Creed's hatred increased when he learned that his own parents, Sabretooth and Mystique, were mutants! Creed's campaign for the presidency ended in his assassination.

Exodus served Magneto as his herald, and once led the Acolytes in his absence.

TWO OF THE X-MEN'S greatest adversaries, Apocalypse and Sinister, were introduced in the 1980s, along with Sinister's Marauders, the alien Brood, Magus, Mojo, Spiral, and Madelyne Pryor as the Goblyn Queen. There were others as well. Wolverine's persistent nemesis, Lady Deathstrike, was only one of the many members of a group of villains known as the Reavers. These were cyborgs: humans who had had parts of their bodies replaced with mechanical devices, giving them superhuman abilities. Donald Pierce, a cyborg himself, took command of the Reavers during his period of estrangement from the Hellfire Club. Then there were the twins Andrea and Andreas von Strucker. They were the genetically enhanced children of a notorious Nazi war criminal, and together they operated as terrorists under the code name Fenris.

DISPLACED IN TIME

The 1990s brought a new wave of enemies who were even more malign than their predecessors. Three of them were fugitives from the nightmarish 'Age of Apocalypse' timeline: the Dark Beast, Nemesis, and Sugar Man. Another, Graydon Creed, was a dangerous anti-mutant bigot who sought to become president of the United States by appealing to people's fear and suspicion of mutants. Equally dangerous were Exodus and his fellow members of the Acolytes who, in their own way, were as fanatical as Creed. They worshipped Magneto as a prophet of a new age in which mutants ruled the world.

Exodus

In the 12th century, Bennet du Paris was a Crusader in the Holy Land. While seeking a legendary 'tower of power', du Paris was found by Apocalypse, who unleashed Bennet's latent mutant powers. Thus he became Exodus, with the abilities to fly and discharge energy bolts. Apocalypse cast Exodus into suspended animation, from which he has recently awoken.

Sugar Man

The grotesque Sugar Man was transported from the 'Age of Apocalypse' to our X-Men's reality, but 20 years in the past. He secretly supervised the genetic experiments that created Genosha's mutant slaves.

NEMESIS
In the 'Age of Apocalypse' this mutant was called Holocaust. On arriving in this reality, he took the name Nemesis. By feeding off the life forces of his victims, he can release enough power to devastate the planet.

The Dark Beast retains the grey fur that the X-Men's Beast originally had.

Spiral laced Lady Deathstrike's skeleton with adamantium and replaced her fingers with extendable adamantium claws.

Lady Deathstrike let Spiral convert her into a cyborg: part human, part machine.

The Dark Beast had to turn his grey fur a blue-black colour when he impersonated the X-Men's Beast.

Lady Deathstrike

Yuriko Oyama's late father, a scientist, devised a process for binding adamantium molecules to human bone. Convinced that his secret had been stolen and used on Wolverine, Yuriko became the samurai Lady Deathstrike, determined to kill Wolverine and claim his skeleton.

X-Cutioner

Charles Xavier once worked closely with FBI agent Fred Duncan. But after Fred's death, his protégé, federal agent Carl Denti, became a vigilante, hunting down and executing mutants he considered to be evil. As the X-Cutioner, Denti is perfectly willing to kill the X-Men.

Dark Beast

He is known as the Dark Beast, the Black Beast, or simply McCoy. He is what Henry McCoy, the mutant Beast, became in the 'Age of Apocalypse': a sadistic genetic engineer who conducted horrific experiments on his human captives. McCoy travelled 20 years into the past of our X-Men's timeline and created the Morlocks through his experiments. In his most daring plot, he once took the X-Men's Beast prisoner and impersonated him.

The X-Cutioner adapted his armour and weapons from the Sentinel, Shi'ar, and Z'nox technologies that had been collected by his late mentor, Fred Duncan.

" BUT WHEN A MUTANT GOES BAD -- WHEN THEY GO ROGUE -- WHEN THEY KILL... HOW ARE YOU GOING TO BRING THEM TO JUSTICE? THEY'VE GOT SO MUCH POWER...

"SO I USE DUNCAN'S FILES. I USE HIS AC-QUIRED WEAPONRY LIKE THE SHI'AR PSI-LANCE.

"AND I KEEP A MASK OVER MY FACE SO NO ONE KNOWS FEDERAL AGENT CARL DENTI IS THE X-CUTIONER.

"AND I STAY ALIVE."

X-MEN COMICS 2000

THE X-MEN family of comics underwent a revolution in the year 2000 and found different directions to take into the new century. After an absence of nine years, Chris Claremont returned to writing *X-Men* and the *Uncanny X-Men*. British writer Warren Ellis devised new story lines for other X-Men-related series, including *Cable*, *Generation X*, *X-Force*, and *X-Man*. The X-Men's cast of characters went through some surprising changes. Apocalypse sought to rejuvenate his ancient body by taking over the body of Nate Grey. Cyclops saved Nate, but physically merged with Apocalypse himself and then seemingly ceased to exist. When this happened, the X-Men presumed that both Cyclops and Apocalypse were dead.

Chris Claremont and artist Leinil Francis Yu took over as X-Men's *creative team with the hundredth issue. Claremont returned to the* Uncanny X-Men *with issue 381, teamed with artist Adam Kubert.*

MAKING CHANGES

In honour of his father, Cable joined the X-Men. Phoenix no longer had telekinetic powers, but Psylocke did. The religious Nightcrawler studied to become a priest. Gambit became leader of the Thieves' Guild. Magneto ruled Genosha, while a demon, known as Blackheart, replaced Sebastian Shaw as the Black King of the Hellfire Club.

Redesigning the X-Men
The X-Men continually evolve with the times, in part by adopting new costumes as fashion changes. Artist Leinil Francis Yu sketched numerous proposals for the X-Men's new looks, some of which are shown here. Some were accepted, some modified, and some rejected. The group portrait on the opposite page shows the final versions.

ARCHANGEL IN ARMOURED COSTUME

REVOLUTION
In the X-books, X-Force became a commando squad led by Peter Wisdom, and Generation X sought to protect endangered teenagers. With Apocalypse seemingly dead, Cable found a new role defending those in need.

X-Man took on a new role, acting as a shaman, or mystic, who guards the Earth.

NEW LOOK FOR STORM

Yu later shortened Kitty's hair.

NIGHTCRAWLER DESIGN SKETCH

SHADOWCAT DESIGN

Yu further changed Kurt's look.

GAMBIT IN 2000

COLOSSUS' NEW COSTUME

After learning that her absorption power did not affect Colossus' metallic form, Rogue fell in love with him.

The Beast's new costume covers up most of his fur.

BEAST'S NEW LOOK

X-Men in 2000

The X-Men's new roster includes Beast, Cable, Colossus, Gambit, Nightcrawler, Phoenix, Psylocke, Rogue, Shadowcat, Storm, and Wolverine. On the far left stands another member, Neal Sharra, the new Thunderbird. Unlike his namesake, he is not a Native American, but comes from India. He has the mutant power to turn his body into plasma, the super-heated state of matter.

ARTHUR ADAMS
2-2000

WOLVERINE ORIGIN

Wolverine: The Origin *was drawn by Adam Kubert. Digital painting was by Richard Isanove.*

NOT EVEN WOLVERINE himself knew the truth about his origins. His mutant healing factor may have caused this memory loss, by suppressing his most painful childhood memories. The *Origin* limited series, which was plotted by Paul Jenkins, Bill Jemas, and Joe Quesada, at last provided a solution to this mystery. Around the end of the 19th century in Alberta, Canada, lived a boy named James Howlett. The wealthy Howletts took in a red-haired orphan, Rose, to be his companion. James's father John subsequently fired the groundskeeper, Thomas Logan, who bore a suspicious resemblance to the adult Wolverine. When James witnessed Logan and his son Dog murder John, James's claws emerged for the first time, and he killed Thomas Logan.

INTO THE WILD

Rejected by his family as a freak, James fled with Rose to Canada's northern frontier, where they worked at a quarry. Needing an alias for James, Rose dubbed him "Logan." At the quarry Logan grew strong and self-reliant. Dog tracked Logan down and they fought, but when Rose tried to stop Logan from killing Dog, she fell onto his claws and died. Having lost the woman he loved, Logan turned his back on civilization to roam the wilderness.

Young James Howlett
As a boy, James was frail and sickly, frightened by the horrific events that befell him. Wolverine's mutant healing factor greatly slowed his aging once he reached adulthood.

James (renamed Logan) and Rose found refuge at the quarry.

RUNNING WITH THE WOLVES
In northern Canada the other, wilder side of James's personality grew stronger and stronger. He spent days running and hunting with the wolves. After Rose's tragic death, James—now Logan—went off with the wolf pack.

Claws of Bone
As a young man, James was appalled by the claw-like bones that suddenly protruded from his fingers. In years to come, his claws would be infused with adamantium and become his deadliest weapons.

X-STATIX

O NLY A SHORT TIME AGO, most mutant humans either posed as "normal" humans or hid from the rest of humanity in order to avoid persecution. However, the X-Statix found an unexpected way to exist in human society: they became celebrities. Created by writer Peter Milligan and artist Michael Allred, the team was originally known as the new X-Force. Unlike other super hero teams, the mutants in X-Statix perform their heroic deeds for fame and fortune. They appear on television, promote products, and license merchandise bearing their images. There is only one downside to their lives as media stars: the team's high mortality rate.

U-GO GIRL

THE ORPHAN

THE PRICE OF FAME

In their first issue, *X-Force #116*, almost the entire team, including their leader Zeitgeist, was killed in action. The only survivors were Edie Sawyer, alias U-Go Girl (who could teleport), Tike Alicar, alias the Anarchist (whose sweat generates energy blasts), and the enigmatic Doop (who videotapes missions). More recruits were soon enlisted, including a new leader, Guy Smith, alias Mr. Sensitive or the Orphan (whose senses are incredibly acute), Bloke, Phat, Saint Anna, and Vivisector. However Bloke, Saint Anna, and U-Go Girl all perished on subsequent missions. The new X-Force changed its name when the new *X-Statix* series began in 2002. The new roster consisted of the Orphan, the Anarchist, Dead Girl, Phat, new recruit Venus Dee Milo, Vivisector, and Doop. Only time will tell how long any of them will manage to survive.

The Horn was a character who was designed for early concept sketches for the new X-Force.

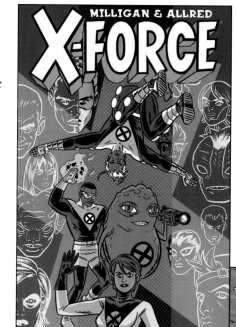

X-Force
Prominent X-Force members include the Orphan (at top), the Anarchist (center left), Doop (center right), and U-Go Girl (bottom).

At left, the original X-Force, with Zeitgeist (front center): all are now deceased.

Bloke died on a mission to South America—he was struck down by rockets fired by the armed forces of The People's Republic of Bastrona.

X-TREME X-MEN

THE THIRD X-MEN series, *X-Treme X-men*, was created by longtime X-Men writer Chris Claremont and artist Salvador Larroca and premiered in 2001. Its premise was that Storm persuaded a number of X-Men—Beast, Bishop, Psylocke, Rogue, Sage, Thunderbird—to leave the Xavier Institute to help her search the world for the missing volumes of the *Libris Veritatus*, the Books of Truth. Written by the deceased, precognitive mutant Destiny, these diaries allegedly revealed the future history of humanity and of mutantkind.

DEATH OF PSYLOCKE

Disasters befell the team: Psylocke was killed in combat by a mysterious adversary named Vargas, who also sought Destiny's diaries. Rogue's powers literally went "rogue," as she randomly manifested the abilities she had absorbed in the past. However the team gained a new mutant ally: Heather Cameron, alias Lifeguard, who developed whatever ability she needed to perform a rescue.

X-TREME X-MEN
The original lineup of the X-Treme X-Men included the Beast and Bishop (in back), Storm, Psylocke, Thunderbird and Rogue (in front), and Sage (not shown).

BEAST'S NEW LOOK
Soon after helping found the X-Treme X-Men, the Beast returned to the Xavier Institute. When he next accompanied the X-Treme X-Men on a mission, he looked very different. In NEW X-MEN he had mutated further, becoming more catlike in appearance.

Thunderbird
The new Thunderbird, Neal Shaara, is a mutant from India who can generate plasma, a super-heated form of matter.

Sage
As Tessa, Sage was Charles Xavier's spy in the Hellfire Club. She is a mutant with a computer-like mind.

ULTIMATE X-MEN

IN 2000, MARVEL launched its "Ultimate" line of comics, presenting an alternate version of the Marvel Universe. The first modern Marvel comic, *Fantastic Four #1*, appeared in 1961; the X-Men debuted in 1963. It was believed that potential new readers might not want to start buying series that were nearly forty years old. But in the "Ultimate" comics, including *Ultimate X-Men*, the sagas of Marvel's classic characters start anew in the 21st century from their beginning.

ALTERNATE HISTORY

Writer Mark Millar and pencilers Adam and Andy Kubert were the initial creative team on *Ultimate X-Men*. These X-Men first appeared in a darker, more violent world than the originals. Magneto had launched terrorist attacks on New York and Washington; Sentinels were killing mutants. Xavier formed the X-Men "to stop a war" between mutants and humankind.

Ultimate X-Men

The initial roster of X-Men in the "Ultimate" universe included (left to right) Iceman, Marvel Girl (Jean Grey, with a very different fashion sense than the original), Cyclops, Storm, the Beast, and Colossus.

MAGNETO
In the "Ultimate" universe it was Magneto who crippled his former ally Charles Xavier. This Magneto calls humankind a "parasite" who "occupies land which evolution intended Homo superior to inherit."

WOLVERINE
Sent by Magneto to infiltrate the X-Men and murder Xavier, the "Ultimate" Wolverine instead became a loyal member of Xavier's team.

NEW X-MEN

A NEW ERA FOR the X-Men began in the year 2000. In that year, Mystique destroyed Muir Isle, killing Moira MacTaggart, who had succeeded in finding a cure for the Legacy Virus. Having begun advocating peace with mutantkind, Senator Robert Kelly was assassinated by a fanatic. However, the greatest change came in 2001 in *X-Men*, now written by Grant Morrison, drawn by Frank Quitely, and retitled *New X-Men*. Charles Xavier's twin sister, Cassandra Nova, suddenly usurped mental control of her brother's body and revealed him to the world at large as not only a mutant but the leader of the X-Men.

A PUBLIC INSTITUTION

Charles Xavier soon reclaimed his body from Cassandra's control. However her public exposure of the X-Men may have been a blessing in disguise. Xavier could now publicly declare his school to be a sanctuary for mutants. He had soon assembled a larger student body of mutants at the Institute than ever before. A multi-billionaire, he created the Xavier Corporation, reaching out worldwide to help mutants. Xavier and the X-Men now dealt openly with the media, academia, and governments in promoting his dream of peaceful coexistence between mutants and the rest of humanity.

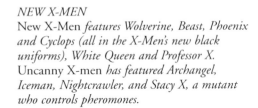

Professor X Walks
When Xavier's mind returned to his body, he discovered he could walk, thanks to Xorn, a mutant with healing powers.

NEW X-MEN
New X-Men *features Wolverine, Beast, Phoenix and Cyclops (all in the X-Men's new black uniforms), White Queen and Professor X. Uncanny X-men* has featured Archangel, Iceman, Nightcrawler, and Stacy X, a mutant who controls pheromones.

DEATH OF COLOSSUS
Colossus heroically injected himself with the cure for the Legacy Virus. His death catalyzed the vaccine and released it into the atmosphere, saving those infected all over the world.

DESTRUCTION OF GENOSHA
Cassandra Nova's body was stillborn, but her consciousness survived and eventually constructed a new body. She ordered the Sentinels to massacre the 16 million mutants of Genosha, over half the known human mutants on Earth. Eventually, after usurping Xavier's body, Cassandra's mind was trapped in a synthetic brain.

X-UNIVERSE

EXILES
The Exiles (including Blink, Morph, and other-dimensional versions of characters like the Mimic, Sasquatch and Sunfire) contend against menaces in various alternate timelines and realities.

Ｔ HE ARRIVAL OF the 21st century brought major changes for established characters and numerous new series. Havok had returned to the X-Men's reality after the original *Mutant X* series ended. Generation X disbanded, but some members joined the Banshee's mutant police force, X-Corps, as shown by writer Joe Casey in *Uncanny X-men*. In *Mechanix*, co-created by Chris Claremont, Kitty Pryde began a new life as a college student in Chicago. In *Chamber*, the title character became one of the openly mutant students at New York City's Empire State University. After Apocalypse was seemingly destroyed, Cable turned to new missions in *Soldier X*.

CHAMBER

MUTANTS IN AMERICA

New series depicted a variety of fates for mutants in today's world. In various *Weapon X* comics, the program was revived with Aurora, Kane, Marrow, Sabretooth, Sauron and others as agents. *Morlocks* showed a community of mutants hiding from persecution, *Muties* focused on the plight of mutants living among humans, while *The Brotherhood* depicted mutants who had become terrorists. By contrast, the new *X-Factor* series centred on members of the FBI's Mutant Civil Rights Task Force, which investigates hate crimes against mutants.

Agent X
Alex Hayden, one of the world's most dangerous and mysterious mercenaries, has taken the alias Agent X since, as his series states, "the letter X stands for an unknown quantity."

THE WORLD OF THE X-MEN

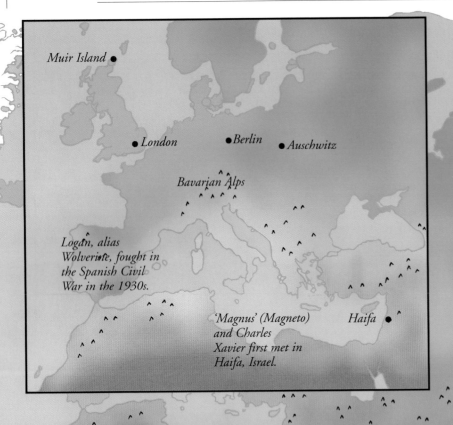

Muir Island

London • Berlin • Auschwitz

Bavarian Alps

Logan, alias Wolverine, fought in the Spanish Civil War in the 1930s.

'Magnus' (Magneto) and Charles Xavier first met in Haifa, Israel.

Haifa

Europe and the Middle East

The Hellfire Club originated in 18th-century London and now has other bases in New York City and Hong Kong. Apocalypse transformed Nathaniel Essex into Sinister in 19th-century London. Recently, the UK has been the home of Captain Britain and Excalibur. Charles Xavier and Moira MacTaggert met as students at Oxford University. Dr. MacTaggert's Mutant Research Centre is located on Muir Island, off the north coast of Scotland. Nightcrawler was born in Bavaria, Germany, while Maverick was based in Berlin. The Banshee's ancestral castle stands in County Mayo, Ireland. The young Magneto was once incarcerated in the concentration camp at Aushwitz, Poland, where his family members were murdered. To the east, Peter, Illyana, and Mikhail Rasputin were born on a collective farm near Lake Baikal, Siberia.

JAPAN

KOREA

Tokyo

Osaka

Cairo • Akkaba

Charles Xavier's legs were paralyzed by Lucifer during their clash in Tibet.

TIBET

INDIA

VIETNAM

Mt. Kilimanjaro

MADRIPOOR

GENOSHA
Magneto's island dominion

Africa

One of the oldest known mutants, Apocalypse was born in Akkaba Egypt, roughly five thousand years ago. It was in Cairo, Egypt, that Charles Xavier first battled the Shadow King, in the latter's guise of Amahl Farouk. As a child, Storm lived as a thief in the Egyptian capital before returning to her mother's homeland near Mount Kilimanjaro. Ahmet Abdol, the Living Monolith, was born in Cairo. Magneto's domain, Genosha, lies off Africa's east coast, and the X-Man Maggott was born in South Africa.

SOUTH
AFRICA

Asia and Australia

Cain Marko, Xavier's step-brother, became the Juggernaut while serving in Korea. Tokyo, Japan, is the ancestral home of the powerful Yashida family, which includes Sunfire, the Silver Samurai, and Wolverine's late fiancée Mariko. It is also the base of the Super Hero team Big Hero 6. Lady Deathstrike was born in the southern city of Osaka. The island of Madripoor, the haven for criminals where Wolverine owns a bar, is located between Singapore and Sumatra. The X-Men were once temporarily based in the Northern Territory of Australia, and Pyro of the Brotherhood of Evil Mutants was born in Sydney.

Northern Territory

AUSTRALIA

Sydney

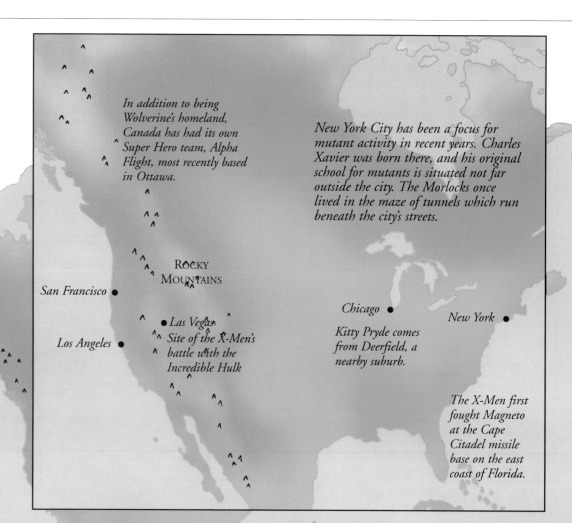

Anchorage, Alaska is where Scott Summers, alias Cyclops, was born and where his grandparents operate an air freight business. It is also where Scott first met the clone of Jean Grey, Madelyne Pryor.

In addition to being Wolverine's homeland, Canada has had its own Super Hero team, Alpha Flight, most recently based in Ottawa.

New York City has been a focus for mutant activity in recent years. Charles Xavier was born there, and his original school for mutants is situated not far outside the city. The Morlocks once lived in the maze of tunnels which run beneath the city's streets.

ROCKY MOUNTAINS

San Francisco

Chicago

New York

Las Vegas
Site of the X-Men's battle with the Incredible Hulk

Los Angeles

Kitty Pryde comes from Deerfield, a nearby suburb.

The X-Men first fought Magneto at the Cape Citadel missile base on the east coast of Florida.

North America

Mutants have been particularly active in North America, not least because Charles Xavier's two schools for mutants are located on the East Coast, in Salem Center, New York, and Snow Valley, Massachusetts. Various mutant teams have been based around the continent, including the second X-Factor, which was situated in the Washington, DC area, the Defenders, who were based in the Rocky Mountains, the Champions, who were established in Los Angeles, and X-Force, which is currently based in San Francisco.

BERMUDA TRIANGLE

Two of Magneto's bases are located on islands in this mysterious area.

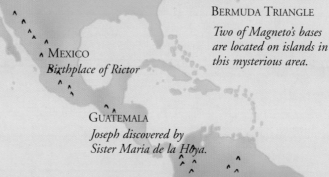

MEXICO
Birthplace of Rictor

GUATEMALA
Joseph discovered by Sister Maria de la Hoya.

● SAMOA
Birthplace of Mondo

South America

Roberto DaCosta, alias Sunspot, was born in Rio de Janeiro, Brazil. His fellow New Mutant Magma and her enemy Selene both lived in Nova Roma, a city modelled after Ancient Rome, hidden deep in the Amazon jungle.

BRAZIL

Rio de Janeiro

Antarctica

The Savage Land, home to Ka-Zar, is located on the continent of Antarctica, where it is separated from the glaciers by a ring of volcanoes. Magneto's Antarctic base was located beneath a nearby volcano.

ANTARCTICA

The Savage Land

CHILE

In Tierra del Fuego, an island south of Chile, the young Karl Lycos was bitten by a Savage Land pterodactyl – an incident that triggered his transformation into Sauron.

TIERRA DEL FUEGO

THE ANIMATED SHOW

The animated X-Men comprised Cyclops, Jean Grey, Beast, Storm, Rogue, Gambit, Jubilee, Bishop, and Wolverine.

IN THE 1990s, the X-Men moved from the pages of comic books and onto TV screens. There had been an unsuccessful attempt in the late 1980s to launch an X-Men animated series through a pilot episode, 'Pryde of the X-Men'. But it was not until 1992 that the first X-Men animated series made its debut. It was produced by the Saban animation studio and Graz Entertainment for the Fox network in the US. Aimed at an older, more sophisticated audience than most Saturday morning animated shows, the X-Men series took story lines and character concepts directly from the comics, even adapting the 'Dark Phoenix Saga' and 'Days of Future Past'. This animated series ran for 76 episodes between 1992 and 1997.

X-MEN: EVOLUTION

The year 2000 saw the start of a new animated television series, *X-Men: Evolution*. This series depicted Cyclops, Jean Grey, Nightcrawler, Rogue, Kitty Pryde, and a new character, Storm's nephew Spike, as teenagers at the Xavier institute. Storm and Wolverine work with Professor X, and the local high school's principal is Mystique.

Around the world
Animation episodes were set in Genosha, Japan, Germany, Africa, and even outer space. On the left, Wolverine takes on Barbarus and Lupo, two of the Savage Land mutates.

THE ANIMATED X-MEN

Variations on a theme

The animated series came up with variations on the original story lines from the *X-Men* comics. As in the comics, Jubilee first encountered the X-Men at a shopping mall. But this time the X-Men had to save her from a squad of attacking Sentinel robots.

Height chart

The show's many animators have to draw the characters in a consistent style. This model shows the comparative heights of Cyclops, Storm, Jubilee, and Professor X.

CYCLOPS

STORM

JUBILEE

PROFESSOR X

Cast of characters

The Fox animated series ranged far beyond its core group of X-Men to feature other heroes from the X-Men universe. Archangel, Iceman, Colossus, Nightcrawler, Cable, Longshot, Dazzler, Forge, Quicksilver and the Scarlet Witch, Ka-Zar, Maverick, and even Cannonball and Shard all made significant guest appearances. Alpha Flight turned up to try and capture Wolverine. The Starjammers and Lilandra showed up in episodes set in outer space. Even Captain America guest-starred in one of the final episodes.

VILLAINS
Among the many villains who appear in the Fox television series are Magneto, Apocalypse, Juggernaut, Sinister, Sabretooth, Mojo, the Sentinels, the Shadow King, D'Ken, Proteus, Sauron, Garokk, the Friends of Humanity, and the Phalanx.

Magneto used his Asteroid M base on the show.

MAGNETO

JUGGERNAUT

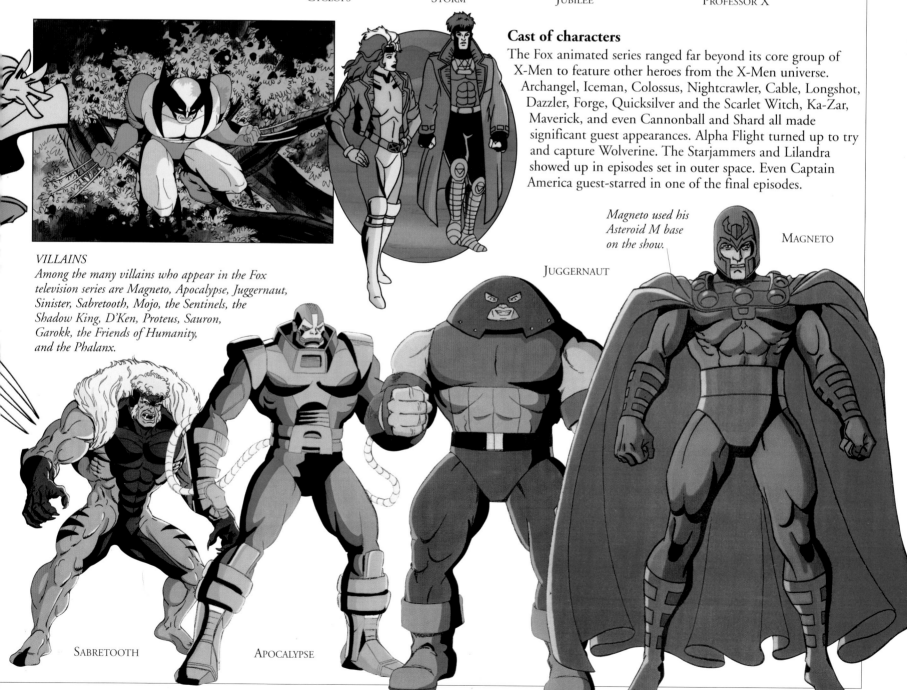

SABRETOOTH

APOCALYPSE

MAKING THE X-MEN MOVIE

STATUE OF LIBERTY
Since the film's climactic battle could not be filmed at the actual Statue of Liberty, the statue's torch and crown were recreated at Showline's Harborside Studios in Canada.

I T WAS IN 1994 that Twentieth Century Fox and producer Lauren Shuler-Donner secured the rights to make an *X-Men* movie. The following year executive producer Tom DeSanto, a longtime *X-Men* fan, began trying to convince Bryan Singer to direct the project; Singer finally agreed in 1996. Nearly $75 million was spent bringing the X-Men to the screen. Numerous writers tried their hands at the screenplay, which was finally credited to David Hayter. The X-Men's colourful costumes from the comics were replaced by sleek, black uniforms on film. Eight companies created over five hundred special effects shots. The film opened spectacularly in 2000, setting a record for ticket sales for a three-day weekend in July.

Bryan Singer
Bryan Singer directed *X-Men* and collaborated on its story with Tom DeSanto. Singer's previous films include the Oscar-winning *The Usual Suspects* in 1995 and *Apt Pupil* in 1998.

XAVIER'S MANSION
The filmmakers used the exteriors of buildings at the Parkwood Estate in Oshawa, Ontario to represent Xavier's School for Gifted Youngsters. Casa Loma, a Toronto landmark and tourist attraction, was used for interior shots of the school.

Famke Janssen
Famke Janssen took on the role of telepath Jean Grey. Born in the Netherlands, she has played roles in the films *GoldenEye*, *Celebrity*, *Rounders*, *The Faculty*, and *House on Haunted Hill*.

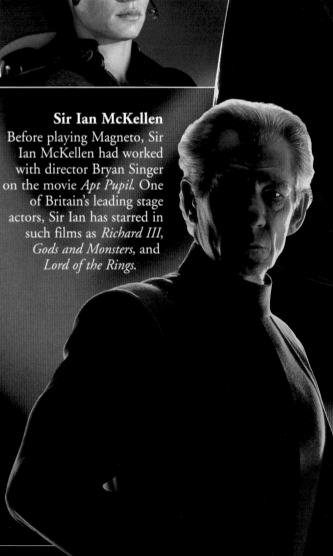

Sir Ian McKellen
Before playing Magneto, Sir Ian McKellen had worked with director Bryan Singer on the movie *Apt Pupil*. One of Britain's leading stage actors, Sir Ian has starred in such films as *Richard III*, *Gods and Monsters*, and *Lord of the Rings*.

UNDERGROUND BASE
The production team designed and constructed sets for rooms in the X-Men's secret base beneath the mansion. This included a three-storey set for the Cerebro computer room.

Rebecca Romijn-Stamos
Supermodel Rebecca Romijn-Stamos played the shapeshifting Mystique. It took eight to 15 hours to apply the body paint and 110 silicone prosthetics that gave her Mystique's scaly blue skin. And it also took hours to remove it at the end of each day!

Halle Berry
Golden Globe Award winner Halle Berry plays the regal and beautiful Storm. Her past credits include roles in the films *Bulworth*, *Jungle Fever*, *Boomerang*, *The Flintstones*, and *Introducing Dorothy Dandridge*.

Hugh Jackman
Wolverine is Hugh Jackman's first major American screen role. Jackman has acted in films in his native Australia and won fame in Britain's National Theatre's production of the musical *Oklahoma*.

James Marsden
Behind Cyclops' ruby quartz glasses is actor James Marsden. Marden's other films include *Disturbing Behavior*, *Gossip*, and *Sugar and Spice*.

Patrick Stewart
Professor Charles Xavier is played by Patrick Stewart. A distinguished classical actor in the Royal Shakespeare Company, Stewart is best known for his role as Captain Jean-Luc Picard in *Star Trek: The Next Generation* and its various movie sequels.

Tyler Mane
Canadian Tyler Mane was hired to work on *X-Men* as a stuntman until Bryan Singer cast him as Sabretooth. Mane is a former professional wrestler who competed in the Universal Wrestling Federation and World Championship Wrestling.

Ray Park
Scotland's Ray Park won fame as the sinister Darth Maul in *Star Wars*: Episode I *The Phantom Menace*. The filmmakers altered the Toad character to take advantage of Park's renowned skills in acrobatics and the martial arts.

Anna Paquin
The part of Rogue is played by Anna Paquin, who won an Academy Award for Best Supporting Actress for her role in *The Piano* when she was still a child.

X-MEN – THE MOVIE

DURING THE 20th century a new race of humans – *Homo superior* – begins to evolve. One of the first of these 'mutants' is a young boy called Eric Lehnsherr. His powers first appear when he is separated from his parents in the concentration camp at Auschwitz during World War II. Over fifty years later, some time in the near future, a young girl discovers her mutant powers when she kisses her boyfriend. As their lips touch, she absorbs all of his thoughts and memories, throwing the boy into a coma. Frightened, the girl runs away. In the meantime, humanity is becoming more and more aware of the emergence of this new breed of humans among them and is concerned. Tensions are rising, as people and politicians start to call for the registration of these mutants.

Two loners

Two lone mutants – Wolverine and the runaway girl, Rogue – come to the attention of the X-Men and the Brotherhood. The X-Men rescue them from Sabretooth and bring them to Xavier's school. But Rogue runs away from the school, and Wolverine follows her to a nearby train station. Here Magneto and his Brotherhood attack and succeed in kidnapping Rogue.

SENATOR KELLY
Senator Robert Kelly advocates passing a Mutant Registration Act to force mutants into the open. As he debates with Dr. Jean Grey in Washington, DC, two former friends watch. One is Charles Xavier, the secret head of the X-Men, and the other is Eric Lehnsherr, who has become Magneto, leader of the Brotherhood of Mutants.

Magneto's Plot

Having experienced persecution under the Nazis, Magneto is determined that mutants will not become the next victims of human oppression. The Brotherhood abducts Senator Kelly and brings him back to their hidden lair. Officials from around the world will soon attend a summit meeting in New York City. Magneto plans to transform them into mutants, forcing them to help the mutant cause.

SECRET WEAPON
Magneto's magnetic powers energize the device that transforms Senator Kelly into a mutant. But the effort severely weakens Magneto. If he is to transform everyone at the summit into mutants, he must find someone else who can power his machine.

Man into mutant

Transformed into a mutant by Magneto's machine, Senator Kelly discovers that his body has become soft and malleable. He escapes from his cell by squeezing through the bars of the window! As Magneto intended, Kelly now has a new sympathy towards mutants. But after the X-Men take the Senator in, his body completely dissolves!

TRANSFER OF POWER

Senator Kelly died because his body rejected the artificial mutation caused by Magneto's machine. Having learned about Magneto's device from Kelly, the X-Men now know that it will kill everyone else that Magneto tries to mutate. Moreover, they now realize why Magneto kidnapped Rogue. Powering the machine enough to transform everyone at the summit would kill Magneto. So (as shown above) Magneto uses Rogue's absorption power to temporarily transfer his magnetic powers to her. Then he will force her to power his machine, killing her in the process.

SHOWDOWN

As the summit commences on Ellis Island in New York Harbor, Magneto has installed his device on top of the Statue of Liberty. After racing there in the X-Jet, the X-Men battle against the Brotherhood. Magneto traps his foes inside the statue's head, but first Wolverine and then the others get free. Magneto compels Rogue to activate his device, and the lethal energies slowly spread towards Ellis Island and the entire city. Wolverine confronts Magneto on top of the statue, and Cyclops blasts apart the device just in time. Rogue returns to Xavier's school while Wolverine leaves in search of his past. Mystique escapes and, ironically, impersonates Senator Kelly to withdraw the Mutant Registration Act. Magneto is imprisoned in a cell constructed entirely of plastic where Xavier visits him and pledges that he will always be there to thwart Magneto's attacks against humanity.

X2: THE MOVIE

FOLLOWING THE WORLDWIDE success of the *X-Men* movie, Twentieth Century Fox released *X2* in 2003. In this sequel, the U.S. President responds to a mutant terrorist attack by permitting General William Stryker to combat mutants, including the X-Men. Stryker was partly based on the fanatical Reverend Stryker in Chris Claremont's graphic novel *X-Men: God Loves, Man Kills.* Bryan Singer returned to direct *X2* from a screenplay by David Hayter, Michael Dougherty, and Dan Harris.

ROGUE
Rogue, portrayed by Anna Paquin, now has a potential boyfriend: her fellow student Bobby Drake, alias Iceman, played by Shawn Ashmore.

WOLVERINE
Hugh Jackman returns as Wolverine, whose quest to discover his origin leads to Stryker and the sinister Weapon X Project.

CYCLOPS
As Cyclops, James Marsden is seen in the new film driving his character's "X-Car," Mazda's RX-8 2004 sports car.

STORM
Halle Berry returns as Storm following her Oscar-winning performance in Monster's Ball *and her role in* Die Another Day.

JEAN GREY
Dr. Jean Grey is once again portrayed by Famke Janssen, while Rebecca Romijn-Stamos comes back as the villainess Mystique.

PROFESSOR X
As Charles Xavier, Patrick Stewart plays a larger role in X2, in which Stryker's commandos attack Xavier's school for mutants.

Nightcrawler

Scottish actor Alan Cumming plays Nightcrawler in *X2*, wearing elaborate makeup, including strange, ritualistic scars. Other X-Men in the movie include Kitty Pryde (played by Katie Stuart) and Colossus (Daniel Cudmore).

X-men nemesis

British actor Brian Cox, the first actor to play Dr. Hannibal Lecter (in the 1986 film *Manhunter*), now portrays General William Stryker, who has his own sinister motives for attacking the X-Men.

Lady Deathstrike

Having appeared as the sorceress in *The Scorpion King*, Kelly Hu plays Stryker's aide Yuriko Oyama, known to comics readers as Lady Deathstrike.

MAGNETO
Magneto, played by Ian McKellen, joins forces with Xavier against Stryker. The mutant Pyro, played by Aaron Stanford, must choose whether to remain Xavier's student or to join Magneto.

AFTERWORD

IT'S OFTEN BEEN SAID OF LIFE THAT IT'S FIRST DRAFT AND EXTEMPORE...

You make it up as you go along and rarely get the opportunity to try something again.

On the other hand, there's America, which is a country founded and built upon the concept of the second chance. As comedian Bill Murray once said, in the film *Stripes*, America is a nation of mongrels and rascals, folks who came to these shores because they were thrown out of someplace better. Since the days of the Vikings (who it seems really did make it here first) and Columbus, the hallmark of this land is that it holds forth the opportunity to make something better, irrespective of whatever came before. That's why my parents came here from England, after World War II, in search of a life that offered more – in the way of opportunity and also freedoms, from class and hidebound traditions – than they had known before. Here they felt was a place where opportunity was as boundless as the western horizons; where the past stood as a springboard to a brighter tomorrow. It was a land of dreams.

As is the realm of comics, and specifically that of the *X-Men*.

When I was half the age I am today, I tripped over one of those rare, defining moments in the modern life of this medium that I and so many others love. I became the writer of the *X-Men*.

At the time, it was just a gig, a means to pay the rent and subsidize my nascent career as an actor. It was also a chance to work with an artist I greatly respected on characters I thought were extremely cool. In a word, it was fun.

As for the *X-Men* title itself, this was its second chance. Never a ferocious success over the half-dozen or so years (and 70-odd issues) of its original incarnation, the concept had been redrafted and expanded somewhat for this new try. New characters, new look, a more kinetic and dynamic visual and story-telling approach – in tune with the attitudes of the times and building on the reputation Dave Cockrum had established drawing the *Legion of Super Heroes* for our uptown rival, DC. He and I had no long-term

expectations; by the same token, however, we also had nothing to lose. There were few expectations for the title. The editorial and marketing consensus was that the book would probably succeed about as well as it had before – meaning that it would stay a mid-list, bi-monthly title until its next cancellation – the focus of most folks' attention was on the 'franchise' titles: *Spider-Man*, *The Fantastic Four*, the *Incredible Hulk*, the *Avengers*, and *Thor*. As a consequence, Dave and I were left pretty much alone. Sort of by

omission, we were granted the freedom to find the book's true voice without interference, and as well to make mistakes, to learn from them and profit from them and grow as writer and penciller and story-tellers.

The rest, to call upon a much-maligned phrase, is history. The *X-Men*'s second chance proved a bonanza for Marvel – and for the comics industry as a whole – of monumental proportions. Much of the comics landscape, for good *and* ill, that readers and scholars behold today is as much the result of the last quarter-century of the *X-Men* as the previous, ground-breaking work of Stan Lee and Jack Kirby.

As for me, in 1991, after 17 years of writing the book – and many of its associated titles in a

canon that by that time (if spun off from the parent company) constituted one of the largest potential comics publishers in the country – I moved on to other opportunities.

Time passed, the wheels of life turned, some gambles paid off, others did not. Such is fate.

And then, quite unexpectedly, I found myself facing my own second chance with the book and characters that had come to define much of my professional life. *X-Men* and *Uncanny X-Men* needed a writer – preferably the same one for both titles, to give them a coherent and focused creative vision – and it was felt that the possible candidates didn't have the requisite creative or commercial clout our current marketplace demanded.

Marvel offered it to me.

At first, I was trepidatious, far too cognizant of Thomas Wolfe's classic dictum, 'you can't go home again'. Take up these titles, I not only assume responsibility for their success – and blame for their failure – I also possibly imperil the critical reputation I'd spent a lifetime building. It's easy to be God Emperor Emeritus of the *X-Men*; past glories are unassailable; you might say the writing sucks but it's hard to argue with those sales figures. Once I threw my pen back into the arena, though, all that becomes irrelevant. Instead, there's the thought: he *used* to be good. There won't be as much freedom, writing two books in an unrelated canon of more than a dozen monthly titles, plus continuity from writers other than myself. These may have materially altered readers' perceptions of various characters and situations. No hope of anonymity here, especially with the internet looming over every thought and deed, dumpster diving for every possible titbit and scrap of gossip.

And yet... these were – and remain – characters I love. To me their stories are far from told. I'm often asked why I stayed on as writer of the book for over 17 years (first time around) and now why I've come back. To me that's almost a no-brainer. Over the course of a quarter-century, I've never lost interest in these characters and the struggles they go through to live their lives with a semblance of peace and dignity, and above all hope. The X-Men, for the most part, are outcasts, cut off from society, from friends, even from families by the genetic quirk that grants them wondrous powers. In the passage of their days they face the same questions as the rest of us – who am I, what do I want, where do I go from here? They have dreams and aspirations, for a career, for a family. They have a future – even though at times it appears to be a bleak and chaotic one.

When I was 17, just about to graduate from high school, Senator Robert Kennedy was assassinated. In his eulogy, his brother Ted offered up a quote that rings with me to this day, and through me I hope to the X-Men: 'some people see things as they are and say "why?". My brother saw things that never were and said "why not?"' The X-Men have always been a quest for family – not so much the kind we're born with but the one we make, through our friends and our associations. They're people who've been dealt a rough hand – whose weaknesses match their incredible potentials – yet who are imbued with a dream of a better world, where they (as another sixties martyr, Dr Martin Luther King, said) will be judged not by the colour of their skin, or the quirk of their genetic structure, but solely by the contents of their character.

People are wrong when they behold the *X-Men* as a book solely about prejudice, although that foundation gives it a weight and moral gravitas unique to our industry. It isn't even about the battle against prejudice, although that is an element of its make-up and a source of many conflicts, between members of the team as well as the team's ongoing battles with 'super-villains'.

At bedrock, the *X-Men* is a book about hope. We are who we are, and our purpose in life is to try to make the world a better place than when we found it. Not simply for 'mutant-kind' but for the whole of humanity itself, because we are one species. We share a home, this world, and it's our obligation – in trust to each other as to succeeding generations – to care for it.

That to me is the title's enduring strength and why, after all this time, in the face of changing styles and markets, it remains the pre-eminent comic in the United States. In the face of adversity, our heroes draw strength from one another and strive onward in service of an unquenchable hope, a dream, an ideal.

You can say the same about this country. And that's where the whole notion of second chances comes into play. I have children now, which wasn't the case when I started work on the *X-Men*

in 1974 and when I left in 1991. For most of that time, the X-Men stood as a kind of surrogate for family. Now our roles have evolved and matured. The stories I write today, and the characters themselves, have a passion and a focus they didn't have before, because I have someone tangible to write them for.

This is part of my legacy – as it is Stan Lee's and Jack Kirby's and Roy Thomas' and Neal Adams' and Len Wein's and Dave Cockrum's and John Byrne's and Archie Goodwin's and Louise

Simonson's, among many, many others. We stand upon giants that came before and strive to be worthy of that trust, as we hope those who follow will feel in return. We tell stories, as our ancestors did before the walls of Troy or at the Hot Gates waiting for the next onslaught of Xerxes' army. Some flicker like spent candles and are forgotten. Some flames endure. What matters, what always has and always will, is striking that spark.

Fate allowed me to nurture one helluva flame when I was young, and now that torch has been passed to me again. Like the X-Men in this season of rebirth and renewal, in a new century that is also a new millennium, I look upon what's to come with eagerness and hope. The heroes may go through hell, but there will always be the sense

on their part that things will work out all right in the end. They are not victims of fate, save perhaps in the accidents of birth. Their future, their destiny, is their own to shape. They choose to do so with courage and with hope. As should we all.

CHRIS CLAREMONT

INDEX

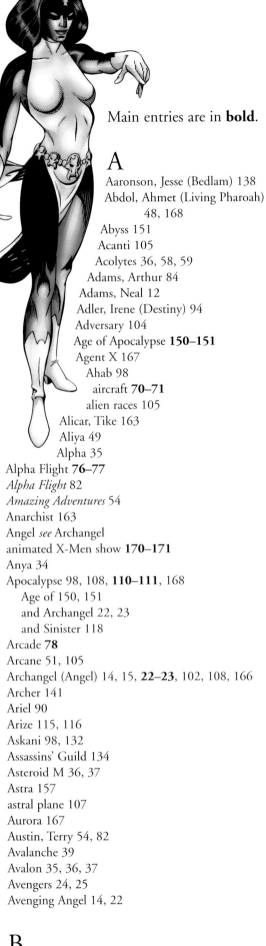

Main entries are in **bold**.